American Heart Association *A*
Guide to Heart Attack, Treatment
Recovery, Prevention
32234

C—
616.1
A

American Heart Association
Guide to Heart Attack Treatment, Recovery, and Prevention

American Heart Association
AssociationSM
Fighting Heart Disease
and Stroke

American Heart Association Guide to Heart Attack Treatment, Recovery, and Prevention

T I M E S BOOKS

RANDOM HOUSE

No book, including this one, can ever replace the services of a physician in guiding you toward recovery after a heart attack. It's a good idea to check with your doctor before using the advice found in this or any other book about health. Although we cannot guarantee any results, we hope this book will help you improve your health and work more effectively with your doctor.

Your contribution to the American Heart Association supports research that helps make publications like this possible. For more information, call 1-800-AHA-USA1 or contact us online at http://www.amhrt.org/

Library of Congress Cataloging-in-Publication Data

American Heart Association guide to heart attack treatment,
    recovery, and prevention / American Heart Association.
            p.   cm.
    Includes index.
    ISBN 0-8129-2408-8
    1. Myocardial infarction—Popular works.   2. Patient education.
I. American Heart Association.
RC685.I6A534   1996
616.1′23025—dc20   96-1175

Random House Web address: http://www.randomhouse.com/

Printed in the United States of America on acid-free paper
9 8 7 6 5 4 3 2
First Edition
Book design by Tanya M. Pérez-Rock

ACKNOWLEDGMENTS

The *AHA Guide to Heart Attack Treatment, Recovery, and Prevention* represents another way that the American Heart Association seeks to live up to its mission: to reduce death and disability from cardiovascular diseases and stroke. We hope that the information presented in this book will provide the kind of practical understanding that will help not only those who have been diagnosed with cardiovascular disease but also their families.

Many dedicated people contributed their time, energy, and knowledge to make this book a reality. Two of the key AHA staff people involved in this project were Rodman D. Starke, M.D., Senior Vice President, Office of Science and Medicine, and Mary Winston, Ed.D., Senior Science Consultant. They provided the scientific guidance for the project and paid close attention to the accuracy of the content. AHA Senior Editor Jane Anneken Ruehl managed the process of making this book a reality. She brought together the writing, editing, and production facets of this project masterfully. As the writer, Sarah Trotta listened to the experts and transformed their words and ideas into the text that follows. Pierce Goetz, our medical illustrator, created the drawings used in this book. Special thanks go to Gerre Gilford and Debra Bond for skillful word processing.

Three AHA volunteers gave generously of their time and authority in matters of cardiovascular disease treatment, recovery, and prevention. Their expertise created the foundation on which the book was fashioned. They spent many hours on the project and reviewed its contents carefully for accuracy and clarity.

Joseph Stephen Alpert, M.D., is head of the Department of Medicine, College of Medicine, at the University of Arizona. He is a well-known expert in the field of cardiovascular medicine and is editor of the journal *Cardiology*.

John C. LaRosa, M.D., is chancellor of the Tulane University Medical Center in New Orleans, as well as professor in the department of medicine. Dr. LaRosa has been an active researcher in the area of blood lipids for most of his academic career.

Gerald F. Fletcher, M.D., is widely recognized as an authority in the area of rehabilitation medicine, particularly as it relates to cardiovascular disease in exercise testing and training. Dr. Fletcher is senior associate consultant, cardiovascular diseases, at the Mayo Clinic, Jacksonville, Florida. He is also professor of medicine at the Mayo Medical School.

We are proud of this book and hope it will offer practical help to all of you who are coping with cardiovascular disease or who are helping someone who is.

CONTENTS

INTRODUCTION

Taking Stock, Taking Charge

Anyone who has had a heart attack, or knows someone who has, is naturally full of questions and fears. *What happened? Why did I have a heart attack? How can I prevent it from happening again?* Heart attack survivors commonly feel frightened and alone—overwhelmed by what they don't know about their illness. They want information and reassurance.

This book can help. The *American Heart Association Guide to Heart Attack Treatment, Recovery, and Prevention* is intended to help heart attack survivors and their families. First, it will show you how to recognize the warning signs of heart attack. It will help you understand the causes and health consequences of the event. Most important, it will help you learn what steps to take to help prevent another attack.

Unfortunately, until it happens to them or someone they love, most people don't think much about whether they might be vulnerable to coronary heart disease and heart attack. Women in particular seem to be at risk for the "not me" syndrome. Many believe heart disease is a "man's illness." The statistics indicate otherwise. Each year about 480,000 women die of heart- and blood vessel-related diseases—many more than die of cancer. What's more, women who are diagnosed with heart attack tend to have more severe outcomes than men do. The connection between women and heart attack is discussed further in Chapter Seven.

Heart attack is hardly an uncommon affliction for men *or* women. Every year in the United States, more than 1.5 million people suffer heart attacks. Almost half a million die. Heart attack is the single leading cause of death in this country.

But that's only part of the story.

In our country, more than 11 million people are alive today who have *survived* a heart attack or who have chest pains from heart disease.

The death rate from heart attack has actually declined in the United States. Between 1982 and 1992 alone, the death rate from heart attack dropped by about 31 percent—a dramatic decrease from previous decades. But why are people surviving heart attacks in greater numbers now than before? The reasons are becoming clearer. They are especially significant for any person who has had a heart attack recently or who is at particular risk for one.

Important News

The latest medical research confirms that often it's our lifestyle choices that count most where heart disease is concerned. To help prevent or minimize the risk of developing heart disease, everyone can and should do the following things:

- Get regular medical checkups. That way, if interventions are necessary, they can be made as soon as problems appear. (This is especially important if you have a family history of heart disease.)
- Follow a healthful lifestyle. That means not smoking, eating a healthful low-fat diet, keeping high blood pressure under control, and staying physically active. Fortunately, more and more people have heeded this message in the past few decades, which may account for much of the recent increase in heart attack survival rates.

Medical Gains in Heart Attack Recovery

Every year seems to bring more improvements in medical technologies and treatments for heart disease. Some of these improvements involve fast-working medications that can help stop heart attacks in progress by dissolving blockages in arteries feeding the heart. New diagnostic tools, such as noninvasive echocardiograph machines, help doctors assess heart attack damage more precisely. With these tools, doctors can tailor treatments to individual patients for maximum effectiveness. Interventions such as angioplasty clear clogged arteries of atherosclerotic plaque. Arterial bypass surgery creates new pathways through which blood reaches the heart muscle. These interventions and others are being used with success for many patients after heart attack.

Taking Responsibility

The public is becoming more educated about heart attack, and that's helped, too. More and more people are aware of the warning signs of heart attack. But even more important, *they are prepared to act quickly when the warning signs appear.* The sooner heart attack victims are taken to the emergency room, the sooner they can be treated and the better their odds for survival.

A heart attack is no longer a "watch and wait" situation. Much can be done for heart attack victims at the hospital, *but timing is everything.* To do any good, the latest medications must be administered very soon after a heart attack begins. Too many heart attack victims still wait too long after their symptoms appear before heading for the hospital. (The average delay is an hour.)

Learn to recognize all the warning signs of heart attack. The warning signs can vary. Even if you have had a heart attack already, you may not experience exactly the same symptoms another time. Not all warning signs must be present to indicate a heart attack is in progress. Ask loved ones, friends, neighbors, and coworkers to learn to recognize the warning signs, too. And when any of these signs appears, be prepared to act quickly! Although more and more people are getting this message, *everyone* needs to take it to heart.

The Warning Signs of Heart Attack

- Uncomfortable pressure, fullness, squeezing, or pain in the center of the chest that lasts more than a few minutes, or goes away and comes back
- Pain that spreads to the shoulder, neck, or arms
- Chest discomfort with lightheadedness, fainting, sweating, nausea, or shortness of breath

You Make the Difference

Like it or not, your heart attack represents a turning point in your life. Up to now, you may have been able to avoid thinking about what your daily habits meant to your overall health. But from this day forward, you *know*. And you know you'll probably have to change the way you do some things. But you're lucky: You have a second chance to do it better this time around. And you will.

Now is the perfect time to reassess your lifestyle and, with a doctor's help, begin to make changes that can help reduce your risk of another heart attack. Medical knowledge about the connection between heart health and lifestyle is evolving. Much of what we know today was only suspected forty years ago. We now know that everyday habits affect long-term health. Fortunately, more and more people seem to be getting the message.

Today, much of the public is captivated by matters of nutrition and physical conditioning. Most are aware of the dangers of smoking and the importance of controlling high blood pressure. As a result, many have adopted better eating habits, live a more active lifestyle, and do not smoke. Many people know their blood cholesterol levels and blood pressure. Many of them have taken steps with their doctor to control these levels. Thousands of people have gotten the message and are making moderate, healthful lifestyle choices that pay off in lower risk of heart disease.

You can too! You can't control everything that puts you at risk for heart attack. You can't change your gender or your age. But you do have control over other risk factors. Concentrate on those while following your doctor's total treatment plan to the letter. Make changes in your life in areas such as diet, exercise, blood pressure control, and smoking. These efforts will have the positive effect of reducing your risk for heart attack and improving your quality of life. You'll also regain a sense of control over your health. That will feel good at a time when your heart attack may have left you feeling seriously *out* of control.

Little Changes That Mean a Lot

Best of all, the lifestyle changes you make to improve your cardiovascular health don't have to be extreme to be effective. Let "moderation" be your watchword. Even small changes mean a lot in the long run. This should be reassuring news. Many of those who are asked to alter some personal habits after a heart attack fear changing or giving up all the parts of themselves that they love best. They feel so overwhelmed that they never try at all. People who love to eat, for example, fear that a low-fat diet will doom them to nothing but salads for the rest of their lives. People who hate to exercise are afraid that they will be forced to run laps and do push-ups, just like when they were in high school. People who have smoked for years and may even have tried to stop in the past are leery of giving up a comfortable routine. People who have high blood pressure may feel that it will be difficult to control. Others have tried to change their habits before and have failed. They are afraid they might fail again, despite their best efforts.

But things are different now. As a heart attack survivor, you have perhaps the best motivation you've ever had for modifying your behavior. You may have gotten a "head start" this time around because of the time you spent in the hospital. You probably learned better ways to change those behaviors, get support for your effort, and put some of those ideas into practice right away. You may feel that you now have a goal that you didn't acknowledge before—the goal of saving your life. This book can help you put those healthier habits into practice and make them a permanent, comfortable part of your life.

Let's review the lifestyle changes that can make a great difference in your recovery and for the future health of your heart. We'll discuss each in depth in the chapters to follow.

Be a Quitter

There's no doubt that it's hard to quit smoking. But it isn't impossible by any means. People who have had recent heart attacks are among the most motivated to quit. Their success rates are *higher* than those of the general public. Small wonder: Most of them learn in the hospital that smoking is directly related to heart disease and the development of atherosclerosis, the buildup of certain deposits on the inner wall of arteries. Smoking also increases the likelihood that you will have additional heart attacks. *Quitting smoking is a very important action you can take to prevent another heart attack.* If you smoke, you must quit immediately.

By quitting smoking, you will change your risk profile dramatically. Three years after you quit a pack-a-day smoking habit, your risk of death from heart disease and stroke will have dropped until it is almost the same as for people who never smoked. We discuss how to quit smoking successfully in Chapter Eight. But don't be afraid to discuss the matter with your doctor as well, even if he or she hasn't made a point of discussing how to quit with you before. Your doctor can be a strong source of support for you in your efforts.

Eat to Live

Diet is another area in which many people fear making changes and sticking to them. But learning to eat more healthfully needn't mean abandoning all the foods you love. In fact, most people rely on a fairly stable diet of familiar dishes. Simply substitute a lower-fat version of some ingredients or choose the lower-fat version of a favorite meal. That's a great way to start making dietary changes. You can do much to reduce your average daily fat consumption. You can bring it in line with the goals your physician has set for you. It really boils down to a matter of making wise choices.

For example, say you typically consume a bowl of granola with whole milk for breakfast every morning. Then you have a mid-morning snack consisting of a sweet roll and coffee. Many granola cereals are high in fat. Read the labels at the grocery store. Try switching to a lower-fat cereal. Eat it with skim or 1% milk. Then substitute a piece of fruit for a sweet roll at snack time. Those small changes can help you reduce your daily fat intake substantially. You will still feel satisfied.

Although a small amount of fat is necessary to maintain health, most Americans eat far too much fat. Currently, the American Heart Association recommends eating less than 30 percent of daily calories as fat. (Some researchers believe that the lower that percentage, the better for health.) Americans consume a diet that is 34 percent fat on average.

Saturated fats contribute to high blood cholesterol levels and formation of low-density lipoproteins (LDLs). LDL is the "bad" cholesterol believed to accelerate the formation of atherosclerotic plaques, the building blocks of heart disease. A low-fat diet helps keep cholesterol in check. Diet is discussed more fully in Chapter Nine. There we'll discuss how to read nutrition labels on food products accurately and how to make wise nutritional choices that may help keep atherosclerosis under control. The American Heart Association diet is naturally low in fat and sodium (salt), while incorporating a wide variety of the foods you should eat every day.

If you need more help finding acceptable ways to change your diet and bring down your cholesterol levels, ask your doctor for help. He or she may refer you to a registered dietitian. This professional will work with you personally to assess your current diet and show you how to make it more healthful. You can still keep it as appealing and flavorful as ever.

For many people with coronary heart disease, dietary changes alone have little or no effect. Their cholesterol levels remain dangerously high. For these people, medications may be prescribed to bring cholesterol levels into normal ranges. Cholesterol-lowering medications must be taken faithfully for them to work. Following a healthful diet is still important for people who take such medicines, of course.

Twenty Minutes a Day

The notion of starting an exercise program tends to make many confirmed couch potatoes hunker down into their pillows. Other heart attack survivors worry that exercise will make them vulnerable to another heart attack.

But a regular exercise program doesn't have to be extreme to bring results. Nor does a doctor-approved exercise program put heart attack survivors or angina sufferers at greater risk.

Your exercise program needs to be tailored to your particular condition. Your doctor will check you first and then tell you what exercise is right for you. In fact, some kind of exercise therapy will be prescribed for you shortly after your heart attack. You may find that strange, since you may still feel somewhat weak. But regular exercise is too important to your recovery to put off.

The goal of regular exercise is to strengthen the heart and lungs so they can do a better job of supplying the body with oxygen. This is called cardiovascular conditioning. Several practical benefits are associated with regular exercise. A conditioned heart is better able to survive heart attack. People with angina will find they can work longer before feeling chest pain if they are in good cardiovascular condition. Very energetic exercise, such as jogging, can do even more for those whose doctors permit them to participate in such activities. Some exercise programs may help lower blood pressure, LDL cholesterol levels, and feelings of stress.

Although every survivor's case is a little different, most can enjoy some form of regular exercise within weeks of the heart attack. Your doctor will advise you on what is best for you. He or she may tell you that as little as 20 minutes of exercise each day can keep your body in good working order and enhance cardiovascular function. Recently, researchers have determined that exercise for this purpose needn't be done all at once to be useful. Ten minutes spent energetically at some task at one time of the day and another 10 minutes spent at another time both count toward 20 minutes total. Just be sure each time that you have reached the heart rates targeted by your doctor.

Best of all, your activity does not have to be exhausting or elaborate to be beneficial. Walking for 20 minutes or more a day is fine exercise. It's also very good for the heart. All you need to pursue that activity is a good pair of walking shoes and clothing suitable for the weather. If you don't want to brave the elements, take your walk in an indoor shopping mall. Other everyday activities count too. Many forms of housework , from vacuuming to washing windows, can qualify. So can yard work, such as raking leaves or planting a garden. As long as the activities increase the heart rate a certain amount for a certain period of time and are done regularly, they count as "exercise."

Some people resist exercising because they equate it with a boring routine. Do you hate the thought of devoting yourself to just one activity, be it swimming, walking, or riding a bike? If so, this new manner of "exercise accountability" provides maximum flexibility for maximum enjoyment. And exercise *should* be an opportunity for fun. Exercise is discussed more fully in Chapter Ten.

Controlling High Blood Pressure

If you have high blood pressure, you should work with your doctor to control it. High blood pressure is a risk factor for stroke and heart disease. When it coexists with obesity, smoking, high blood cholesterol levels, or diabetes, the risk of heart attack or stroke increases several times.

To keep your high blood pressure under control, your doctor may have told you to eat a proper diet, lose weight, exercise regularly, restrict your intake of salt, and follow a program of medication. More information about high blood pressure as a risk factor can be found in Chapter Seven. More information on treating it with diet appears in Chapter Nine. If your doctor has prescribed medication to help lower your blood pressure, you may want to read Chapter Three on medications. You and your doctor can work together to help lower your blood pressure and keep it within healthy limits.

Dealing with Emotions After a Heart Attack

Depression is not uncommon after a heart attack. It can interfere with recovery if it goes on too long. Although most people who are depressed following a heart attack recover on their own within a short time, others experience deeper emotional problems and may need additional help to overcome them. Signs of depression should never be ignored. We discuss depression and what to do if it becomes a problem in Chapter Twelve.

Reason for Hope

Having a heart attack is a life-altering experience—or should be. But by no means is it the end of life as you know it! You have the help and guidance of your doctor, the medicines and treatments he or she recommends, and your own resolve to make reasonable, consistent changes in your daily living habits. With those you can be sure that you're doing all you can to minimize the possibility of having another heart attack. Six months or a year from now, you may even find yourself thinking, "I've never felt better in my life!"

Let's get started.

American Heart Association
Guide to Heart Attack Treatment,
Recovery, and Prevention

CHAPTER ONE

What Happens During a Heart Attack—and Why

❦ *Claudia and her husband were out with friends at a movie early one evening when she began to experience a tight feeling in her chest. At first she thought it had to be indigestion since they had just finished dinner. Still, it wasn't quite like any indigestion she had ever had. She was perspiring heavily and she felt anxious. But Claudia did not want to complain.*

At the back of her mind, Claudia was aware that something serious was happening to her. As apprehensive as that made her feel, however, she was actually more embarrassed at the thought of inconveniencing her friends than she was fearful. She certainly didn't want the evening to end on her account! Feeling worse and worse, Claudia sat through the movie, moving about in her seat. The couples even went out for coffee afterwards. Her husband shot her sidelong glances and asked several times whether she felt OK. Her friends commented that she didn't seem to be quite as jolly as usual. Even then, Claudia waved off their questions and concerns. "Nothing a good night's sleep won't cure," she said.

After the group broke up, Claudia went home and for a short while really did try to sleep, despite ongoing discomfort. After several hours, she couldn't stand it anymore. She asked her husband to drive her to the hospital. Claudia was immediately admitted to the emergency room, where tests confirmed that she

*had suffered a major heart attack. A large area of heart mus-
cle tissue had died. Because so much time had passed between
Claudia's first symptoms and her treatment, doctors couldn't do
a lot for her heart. They admitted Claudia to the hospital and
continued to monitor her. But the heart tissue affected by Claudia's heart attack was lost for good. Her heart was permanently
weakened.* 🍎

*🍎 Like Claudia, Jack was an outgoing person who enjoyed
getting together with friends and family. He particularly loved
the annual family reunion that attracted relatives from all
over the country to his hometown. He spent hours during the
year helping to plan it, collecting park permits, making motel
reservations for visitors, and organizing events especially for
the young people. The highlight was the afternoon's big softball
game, followed by a barbecue in the county park.*

*When the day finally came that year, Jack was ready. He
was up at dawn, and he had made two batches of potato salad by
the time he was to pick up the first arrivals from the airport.
Everything went along fine until just after noon. That's when
Jack began to feel a deep, spreading pain in his chest, accompanied by the most unsettling dizziness. Jack sat down heavily on
a bench and was soon surrounded by concerned relatives.*

*"It can't be," Jack thought to himself, "not today!" But he
didn't doubt what was happening. After all, his mother had
had a heart attack; so had his Uncle Tony and his cousin
Roberta. Remembering their experiences, Jack knew he had to
act quickly.*

*"I'm having a heart attack, I think," he said softly. "I need
someone to drive me to the hospital, please." Immediately, the
family responded. Two cousins helped Jack into the car. His
brother drove him to the closest hospital. Jack's wife and kids
followed in a second vehicle.*

*Jack had quickly identified his symptoms and did not hesitate
to go to the hospital to check out his suspicions. His family's response was immediate and supportive. All of these things combined to make it possible for Jack to receive emergency room*

treatment for his heart attack within an hour of onset. The emergency room staff was able to administer medicines that restored blood flow to the ischemic, or dying, tissue in Jack's heart. They were able to act in time to save much of his affected heart tissue and to stabilize Jack's other vital signs. 🍎

If you are reading this book, you may have already suffered a heart attack. You know it is one of life's more frightening experiences. You aren't alone. An estimated 1.5 million Americans suffer a first or recurrent heart attack every year. Of this number, almost half a million people die each year. A heart attack may have been your first indication of advanced coronary heart disease, the number one single cause of death in this country. Undoubtedly you have many questions about your condition. You may wonder exactly what happened to you when you had a heart attack. You may wonder why it happened—and why at this particular time in your life. You are probably worried about the effect your heart attack will have on your future and your family. And you may wonder what to do next—especially what to do to prevent another heart attack. This book can help you answer these questions. It can be a useful reference throughout your recovery. Your personal physician and the other health-care professionals working with you toward new health goals can help, too.

Or perhaps you haven't had a heart attack. You are reading this book because you were diagnosed with coronary heart disease or felt episodes of chest pain that coronary heart disease often causes. Such chest pain, called **angina** or **angina pectoris** (an'jeh-nah or an-JI'nah PEK'tor-is), afflicts over five million Americans. It is a condition in which the heart muscle doesn't receive enough blood. It can be a warning sign that you are at risk for heart attack.

You may have been told you have one or several **risk factors** for a heart attack. Risk factors are characteristics that increase the probability of having a heart attack. Now you want to learn how to minimize your personal risk and maximize healthful habits and behaviors. This book can help you begin to make positive changes in your life—changes that will help protect you from more heart attacks.

No matter what your experience with heart attack or heart disease has been, it is very important for you to learn the warning signs of a heart attack. It's also vitally important to know what to do if you or someone close to you is experiencing what may be a heart attack.

The Warning Signs of Heart Attack

A heart attack is almost always accompanied by symptoms (see the box below). They may not be recognized as such, or the people who experience them may deny their significance. Either situation is common. Unfortunately, failure to recognize or denial of these signs can also cause serious delays in obtaining life-saving treatment.

Each year more than 250,000 people die of a heart attack within one hour of onset of symptoms and before reaching the hospital. Unfortunately, research indicates that many heart attack victims do not seek help right away. Many people are still unaware of how important quick action is where heart attack is concerned.

Much can be done today to help most heart attack victims—but for maximum benefit, treatment must be started very soon after the symptoms appear. People have very different personal reactions to their heart attack symptoms, and they have very different outcomes as a result of those reactions. What should your response to heart attack be? Let's look at that right now.

The Warning Signs of Heart Attack

Not all of these signs appear with every heart attack. Sometimes they go away and then return. If you experience any of these sensations, *don't delay: get help immediately.* Call the emergency rescue service, or if you can get to the hospital faster by car, have someone drive you to the nearest facility with a 24-hour emergency cardiac care unit (select this in advance if you have had a heart attack previously or are at risk for one).

- Uncomfortable pressure, fullness, squeezing, or pain in the center of the chest that lasts more than a few minutes, or goes away and comes back
- Pain that spreads to the shoulders, neck, or arms
- Chest discomfort with lightheadedness, fainting, sweating, nausea, or shortness of breath

---

Learn the Warning Signs

If you have already had a heart attack, your risk of another is higher than other people's risk of an initial event. You are also at a greater than average risk if you haven't had a heart attack but have risk factors that predispose you to one. Risk factors include conditions such as high blood cholesterol levels, high blood pressure, family history of heart disease, and physical inactivity, as well as smoking. Everyone should know how to respond to a heart attack—his or her own or someone else's. But it's even more important for those whose risk is especially high. Family members and close friends of those at risk should know how to identify the warning signs of heart attack. Delaying treatment has very serious consequences.

A heart attack may occur anywhere, at any time—at rest or during activity, at night or early in the morning. Because everyone is different, warning signs vary substantially from person to person. Occasionally, a heart attack kills outright, with no "warning" signs at all. Sometimes symptoms disappear for a short while and then return. Many heart attack victims experience some warning signs, and a few experience all of them. Any combination is possible. A person having a heart attack may or may not lose consciousness.

Pain, discomfort, or a feeling of pressure associated with a heart attack usually comes on suddenly, and it lasts more than half an hour. The length of discomfort involved distinguishes heart attack from angina or a panic attack. (See the box on page 8 for a discussion of panic attacks versus heart attacks.) Nitroglycerin, a medication for angina, doesn't get rid of heart attack pain as it does angina pain.

Many people report that they did not feel conventional chest pain during their heart attacks. Instead, they describe "discomfort," "pressure in the chest," "a feeling of weakness," or even "a feeling of indigestion." (In some cases, no pain or discomfort is felt at all.) Because a heart attack may affect circulation, breathing, and the lungs, victims may become lightheaded or find breathing difficult after onset. Finally, a person having a heart attack may feel apprehensive and may move about a lot in an effort to become more comfortable.

Learn the warning signs of a heart attack by heart. As a reminder, copy them and post them in an easily accessible, uncluttered place. Put the list by your telephone, on the refrigerator door, or on a kitchen or

Panic Attacks Versus Heart Attacks

Many people delay going to a hospital when they have a heart attack because they are afraid that their discomfort may not be an emergency at all. They fear that their "heart attack" will prove to be a false alarm. They worry that they might bother people and they don't want to be embarrassed. How can *you* be sure that what you feel really is a heart attack?

The short but important answer is: You probably won't know. That is the job of health-care providers, and you should leave it to them to make that diagnosis. Your only job is to recognize that you have a problem and to get yourself to the hospital immediately. It is very important for a medical team to evaluate you in a timely fashion.

That said, people often wonder how to differentiate between panic attack and heart attack symptoms. Panic attacks and heart attacks are very different problems. They do share certain characteristics, however, that may confuse those who experience either one of them. Panic attacks may cause a person to feel short of breath and agitated. They don't last long and are harmless. Heart attacks also may make a person feel short of breath and agitated. With a heart attack, there is usually (although not always) a feeling of pain or pressure in the chest or arms. Perhaps the most important distinguishing characteristic of heart attack symptoms is their persistence. They don't usually go away—they last longer than a few minutes.

Telling the difference between a panic attack and a heart attack isn't always easy. If you are having an attack of some kind, stay calm. If you are with someone having an attack, try to calm that person.

Above all, *if symptoms persist or you aren't sure what is happening, go to the emergency room and have the person suffering the attack checked out!* The doctors should be able to tell whether a heart attack is occurring. They will know what to do. In a few cases, the symptoms may be confusing. People with such symptoms may be admitted to the hospital overnight for observation, just for safety's sake. Their doctors want to be sure that a heart attack hasn't occurred.

bathroom cabinet. Know the steps to take if you or someone with you has a heart attack.

Deal with Denial

In a way, it is unfortunate that the warning signs of heart attack are so diverse. That gives people plenty of opportunity to make excuses for their symptoms. Many think, "It's just indigestion," or "a touch of the 24-hour flu going around, I'm sure." Understandably, it's frightening for people to think that they may be having a life-threatening heart attack. The impulse to deny that possibility is very common, even in the face of evidence to the contrary.

Women in particular tend to downplay or deny their symptoms. As a group, they take longer to get to a hospital for treatment. In addition to denying heart attack symptoms out of fear, many women still believe that they *can't* have a heart attack. They consider heart disease and heart attack a "man's problem." Most of the publicity about heart attack in the past 40 years or so has emphasized how men are affected. Actually, heart disease is an "equal opportunity" killer. As we'll see, almost half of the people who die each year from coronary heart disease are women. Women do tend to have heart attacks somewhat later in life than men. For now, it's enough to note that women should remain as alert as men to their own heart attack symptoms, should they appear. We'll look more closely at women's heart attack risk in Chapter Seven.

People near the person having the heart attack may deny it, too. They often take their cue from the victim and contribute to an atmosphere of denial. Sometimes friends are too concerned with "minding their own business" and being polite. This is done at the expense of asking—clearly and directly—what is wrong. Or sometimes people are preoccupied with fear themselves. They may be afraid that they will not be able to do the right thing to help a heart attack victim.

Embarrassment is often coupled with fear. Most of us feel embarrassed at even the thought of inconveniencing others. We don't want to make a fuss that turns out to be "unnecessary." The risk of a false alarm makes many heart attack victims hesitate to ask for help they truly need. They don't want to bother anyone—friends, family, or even personnel in an emergency room. Yet indecision of this sort can extract an unfairly high price on their health. Doctors will tell you that they would much rather examine a dozen "false alarms" than miss one actual heart attack in progress. You would probably urge a loved one or friend to go to an emergency room if he or she seemed to be having symptoms of a heart attack. So be your own best friend, and do it for yourself as well!

With a little foresight, heart attack victims and the people around them can avoid dangerous denial and indecision. The first rule is to be prepared to recognize a heart attack—your own or someone else's—for what it is and to anticipate what you should do next. If you should find yourself in the presence of someone having a heart attack, expect denial but don't accept it!

Be familiar with the warning signs of heart attack. Have confidence in what they indicate. Then you can break through that wall of denial and act with assurance.

Plan Ahead

Start now to plan what to do after recognizing the signs of heart attack. Once you have devised your plan, memorize it. Remember, acting quickly may save your life. It pays to be prepared.

Know who to call and how to get to the nearest hospital emergency room. Find out now which hospitals in your area have 24-hour emergency cardiac care. Make family and friends aware of which of these hospitals are closest to your home and office. Tell them that you would like to be able to call on them for help getting to a hospital in an emergency. (You'd do the same for them.) Keep the name of that hospital (or hospitals) on a card near your telephones at home and at work and in your wallet or purse. (See the sample card shown in the box below.) On the same card, write the telephone number of an emergency rescue service. You might want to add a bold mark or identifying color to

---

Plan Ahead

Name of hospital nearest home with 24-hour emergency cardiac care:

_____

Name of hospital nearest work with 24-hour emergency cardiac care:

_____

Names of people to call on for help getting to a hospital in an emergency:

_____

Telephone number of emergency rescue service: _____

---

the card. That way you can always find it easily. Taking this simple step may save you valuable time later. This is lifesaving information. Why not do it right now?

What to Do if a Heart Attack Occurs

Have you ever thought of acting quickly as "first aid"? In the event of a heart attack, this is perhaps the most important first aid you can give yourself or someone else. With the medicines and technology available to doctors today, much can be done for a heart attack victim even while the heart attack is in progress, as we'll see. If you or someone with you shows signs of having a heart attack, act quickly to get help. Don't wait! Acting quickly can limit heart tissue damage. (See the box on page 12 for a quick summary of what to do if a heart attack occurs.)

Be prepared to call on family, friends, or coworkers for help—whoever is nearby. Don't hesitate! If possible, one of these people can drive you to the hospital. If no one nearby can drive, someone can telephone an emergency rescue service for you and stay with you until help arrives. (Helpers can also direct emergency rescue workers to you as they arrive.) If you are alone, *don't try to drive to the hospital yourself.* If you can't easily call on someone close by, go directly to a telephone and dial 911 or an emergency rescue service for help.

Once you know how you'll get to the hospital, there is something else you can do. Take two aspirins immediately. It's best to crush them and dissolve them in a glass of water. (Pulverizing the aspirins and drinking them in a glass of water helps your body absorb them faster.) You may also chew the aspirins and then drink a glass of water. If a glass of water is not available, chew and swallow the aspirins without water.

Aspirin is a blood thinner. Consuming two crushed tablets may help restore blood flow through some clogged arteries by dissolving small blood clots that block the way. If that happens, heart muscle damage may be delayed, buying you time to get to the hospital to start other heart-saving measures. Chewing a couple of aspirins is *not* a substitute for getting the other treatment you need. However, research has proven that taking aspirin during a heart attack helps a little bit. It cer-

---

In an Emergency

- Act quickly! Do not hesitate!
- Call for help—ask whoever is nearby to help you.
- If possible, ask someone nearby to drive you to the hospital.
  Or
- Ask someone nearby to call the emergency rescue service.
- Ask someone nearby to stay with you until help arrives.
- Ask someone to direct emergency rescue workers to you as they arrive.
- Chew two aspirins thoroughly and swallow them. Follow with a drink of water if possible.

---

tainly won't make a heart attack worse. Taking this simple precaution also puts you back in some control of an admittedly frightening situation: It may help calm you.

Coronary Heart Disease: Many Names, One Problem

Your doctor may have described your **heart attack** as a **myocardial infarction.** That is the medical term for heart attack. The term is quite literal: **myocardial infarction** (*myocardial* = heart tissue; *infarction* = tissue death due to a lack of blood). In a heart attack, heart tissue dies for lack of blood.

If you asked your doctor what condition caused your heart attack, the answer may have been atherosclerosis; arteriosclerosis; cardiovascular, or CV, disease (also known as CVD); coronary artery disease (CAD); or coronary heart disease (CHD). Many people find these terms confusing, because they are often used interchangeably or nearly interchangeably. ("Cardiovascular disease" is used more broadly; it encompasses stroke as well as coronary heart disease.) (For individual definitions, refer to the box on page 13.) Where heart attack diagnosis, prevention, and treatment are concerned, however, these terms all refer to problems with blood vessels. For the purposes of our discussion, they refer specifically to problems in coronary arteries that carry blood

Vessel Disease Terms

Arteriosclerosis. Arteriosclerosis is a general term for thickening and hardening of the arteries. Some hardening of the arteries normally occurs as people age.

Atherosclerosis. A type of **arteriosclerosis,** atherosclerosis describes the buildup of certain deposits on the inner wall of the artery. These include fatty deposits (cholesterol), calcium, and the clotting material fibrin. They also include other products carried in the bloodstream. Atherosclerosis comes from the Greek words *athero-* (meaning gruel or paste) and *-sclerosis* (meaning hardening). The buildup in the arteries is called **plaque.** Atherosclerosis affects large- and medium-size arteries. Exactly which arteries varies from person to person.

Atherosclerosis is a slow, progressive disease that may start in childhood. It may not cause overt medical problems until the person who has it is 50 or 60 years old, although some people develop atherosclerosis much earlier—in their 20s or 30s.

Cardiovascular disease. Cardiovascular disease is an umbrella term that refers to any of a number of diseases affecting the heart and blood vessels. High blood pressure, coronary heart disease, stroke, and rheumatic fever are all examples of cardiovascular diseases. In 1992 an estimated 58.9 million Americans had some form of cardiovascular disease.

Coronary artery disease. Conditions that cause narrowing of the coronary arteries so that blood flow to the heart muscle is reduced are known as coronary artery disease.

Coronary heart disease. Coronary heart disease is a general term that describes diseases of the heart caused by atherosclerotic deposits, or plaque, that result in a narrowing of the coronary arteries. This narrowing may cause angina pectoris or subsequently a heart attack.

and nutrients to the heart muscle. In this book we use the term **coronary heart disease** (or **CHD**).

Where Heart Attacks Begin

Many people assume that, as they get older, their hearts "wear out" naturally. They think that a heart attack is just more evidence that time is passing. They believe that they can do nothing about it. Actually, nothing could be further from the truth. No matter what your age, you can probably benefit from preventive care.

Bottom line: Most hearts don't wear out—they "rust out."

What does that mean? What is the connection between coronary heart disease and heart attack?

Heart disease in general has many sources. Some heart problems are **congenital,** which means they are present at birth. Congenital problems are almost always identified in childhood. Most heart disease, by far, is **acquired**—it develops after birth. Acquired heart disease often takes years to establish itself in the body, and it usually appears in adults. People develop it in a number of ways. Sometimes a type of bacteria causes heart disease, infecting the heart valves. The valves may narrow or become leaky.

Disease in the coronary arteries, the arteries that supply the heart muscle with the nutrients it needs to survive, affects the heart profoundly. In this case, heart disease may be partially "self-inflicted," the result of a lifestyle developed over many years. Thus, coronary heart disease in many people is a preventable condition that is directly related to heart attack risk.

Coronary heart disease is the most common cause of cardiovascular death in the United States. Yet until the twentieth century, it was uncommon. The death rate from CHD in this country increased steadily after World War II. Rapid changes in our national lifestyle—such as lower activity levels and richer eating habits—played a major part in this unhappy change. Fortunately, the trend began to reverse itself in 1963. Since then, our national habits changed again, this time for the better. Today, more people exercise and eat more healthfully than at midcentury, although there is still a long way to go. We also have a better medical understanding of coronary heart disease. Coronary heart disease death rates *decreased* more than 55 percent between 1963 and 1992. That's great news. It reemphasizes the important role that good personal habits play in good health.

It can't be said too often: Atherosclerosis and coronary heart disease are *not* natural consequences of aging. They develop over time from injury to the arteries. This injury is caused by a variety of predisposing factors. These factors are risk factors for coronary heart disease and atherosclerosis. The connections between individual risk factors to CHD and atherosclerosis are discussed in Chapter Seven.

To understand heart attack and coronary heart disease better, let's take a minute to look at how the heart is constructed and how it does its job.

The Heart and Circulatory System

A muscular organ about the size of a fist, the heart lies near the center of the chest, slightly to the left, nestled between the lungs. The heart is the all-important pump of the body's circulatory system. The **circulatory system** is composed of the body's heart, lungs, and blood vessels (see figure, below). Through the blood vessels, the blood transports from the lungs oxygen and other vital nutrients to every

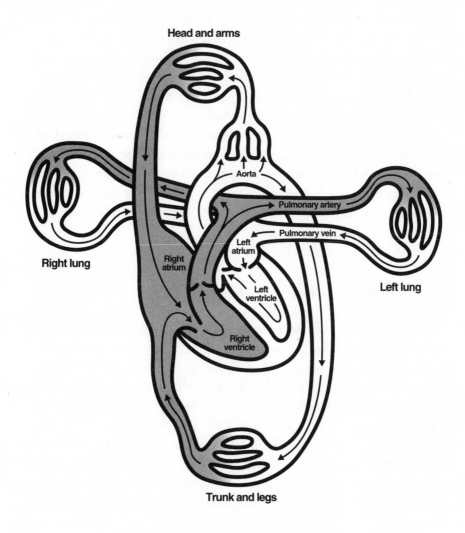

The circulatory system is made up of the body's heart, lungs, and blood vessels.

part of the body. After making its delivery, the blood picks up waste gases from the cells and returns them to the lungs, where they are expelled from the body. The pumping action of the heart circulates blood within this closed system.

Blood vessels associated with these critical jobs have different names. **Arteries** deliver oxygen-rich blood from the heart to every part of the body. Traveling through **veins,** blood returns to the heart carrying waste gases (carbon dioxide) discarded from the body's tissues. **Capillaries** are very tiny blood vessels that connect arteries to veins and keep the circulatory system closed. It takes only about 12 seconds for a drop of blood to make the trip from lungs to tissue and back again!

The heart keeps this nonstop activity humming along. The strong pumping action of the heart is heard as a heartbeat. With that heartbeat, the heart provides the push that moves blood from the heart to the lungs and to all the tissues of the body. Literally thousands of miles of blood vessels are required to deliver blood wherever your body needs it. Your heart has a very big job to do in moving blood through this vast network. Fortunately, the heart is a very strong organ; it can take a lot of abuse and keep on ticking. In fact, unlike any other muscle tissue, and despite its constant activity, healthy heart muscle never fatigues.

The Right Heart and the Left Heart

So, the circulatory system has two major functions. The first is to deliver newly oxygenated blood to all body tissues from the lungs. The second is to carry waste gases back from the tissues to the lungs, to be expelled when breath is exhaled. Similarly, the heart, the engine of the circulatory system, has two parallel functions: to move blood from the lungs to the cells and to move blood from the cells back to the lungs. These functions are performed by what your doctor may call the **"right heart"** and the **"left heart."** These terms really mean the right side of the heart and the left side of the heart. The right and left sides are completely separated by a thick muscle wall that bisects the heart's interior.

Despite its reputation as a tough, muscular organ, the heart is not solid. Much of it is hollow (see figure below). In fact, you might imagine the heart as a snug, thick-walled house, a duplex, really. It is composed of four rooms, or **chambers,** that share an interior wall. Each chamber also has a one-way door, or **valve,** leading out of it.

Each side of the duplex that is the heart is made up of two rooms: an **atrium** and a **ventricle.** (The plural form of atrium is **atria.** The two atria of the heart are smaller than the two ventricles.) Each side of the

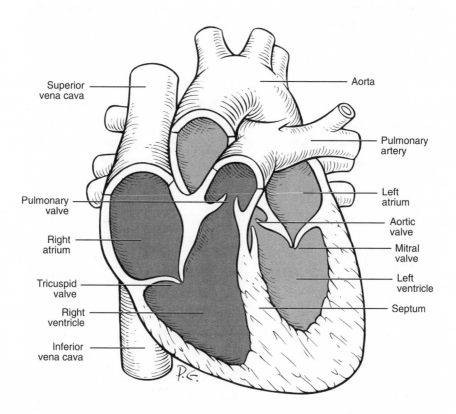

The structure of the heart.

heart has a slightly different function. By following the path blood takes as it flows through the heart, we can see how each side of the heart does its job.

Like a magnificent system of rivers heading for the ocean, the veins through which blood returns to the heart merge repeatedly as they approach their destination, getting bigger at every junction. Eventually, all blood on its way back to the lungs passes through one of two enormous veins, the **superior vena cava** or the **inferior vena cava,** before it enters the heart. The superior vena cava collects blood from the upper part of the body; the inferior vena cava receives blood from the lower part. ("Superior" and "inferior" aren't value judgments in this case, of course. *Superior,* used here, simply means "upper," and *inferior* means "lower." Think of Lake Superior, the northernmost of the five Great Lakes.)

Oxygen-depleted blood enters the right heart first. It flows into the **right atrium,** a holding chamber. It takes just a moment for blood to collect in the atrium and fill it completely. Then, with a rhythmic contraction, the heart muscle forces the blood out of the atrium through the tricuspid valve into the **right ventricle.** When the right atrium has emptied, pressure in that chamber drops, and the tricuspid valve closes. The blood now collected in the right ventricle faces increased pressure in that chamber. The pressure there forces open a different "one-way door," the pulmonary valve, and blood flows out of the heart. It is pumped into the **pulmonary artery** to the lungs. *(Pulmonary* means "related to the lungs.")

In the lungs, blood picks up oxygen as it circulates through a delicate web of very specialized vessels. (If this network of vessels were laid out on the ground, its surface area would equal that of a tennis court!) These vessels, called **arterioles,** have even tinier, round attachments called **alveoli.** Alveoli are small sacs through which oxygen enters the bloodstream and through which waste gases are expelled back into the atmosphere. Oxygen bonds to an agent in the blood called **hemoglobin.** It is hemoglobin that actually delivers oxygen to body tissues.

After waste gas is exchanged for oxygen in the lungs, blood turns from a dark, dull color to a bright red. But all that blood is now spread over quite a large surface area; it can create no movement or energy of its own to send it into the body to every cell. The blood has to be collected again and given a considerable push to accomplish that job. That force is again supplied by the pumping action of the heart.

In the closed circulatory system, there is enough force in each heartbeat to push oxygen-depleted blood from the right heart into the lungs, displace freshly oxygenated blood, and send it the short distance back to the heart. There it is once more collected and consolidated in the left heart, to be pumped into the body through the arteries. In its short trip from the lungs to the heart, blood travels through the **pulmonary veins.** (Incidentally, this is the only place in the body in which oxygen-rich blood travels through veins instead of arteries.) This time, the blood enters the left heart, collecting in the **left atrium.** After the blood fills the atrium, a contraction of the heart muscle pushes the blood through an opened valve to the **left ventricle.** The left ventricle then pumps the blood through the aortic valve and out through the arteries to all the tissues of the body.

The right heart is responsible for pumping the blood into the lungs, across that huge surface area of vessels, and back to the left heart. The left heart is responsible for pumping the blood literally everywhere else in the body. Not surprisingly, the left heart is slightly bigger than the right heart. The left ventricle is considerably larger, and its walls are thicker than those of the right ventricle. Heart attacks involving the left side of the heart are more common than those involving the right side.

Valves and Walls

The right heart and the left heart each consist of one atrium and one ventricle, as we've seen. The associated chambers are connected by valves that open and close. Valves perform an important function in the heart: They ensure that blood always flows in the same direction. Valves open and close with special flaps. Closed, they form a seal; no blood leaks from one part of the heart into another. The seal also helps maintain pressure in the chambers, so that when the heart contracts, the valves associated with their respective chambers are forced open. Blood flows out of the chamber and continues on its way. After the chambers empty, pressure falls, the valves close, and the whole process starts over.

Each valve has a different name. On the right side of the heart, the **tricuspid valve** connects the right atrium to the right ventricle. In the left heart, the left atrium is connected to the left ventricle by the **mitral valve.** Blood also passes through valves upon leaving the heart. From the right heart, blood goes through the **pulmonary valve** to get to the lungs. On the left side, blood starts its trip back to the body tissues by exiting the heart through the **aortic valve.** (The **aorta** is the body's largest artery.) Valves are usually not directly involved in a heart attack. If they are diseased or abnormally formed, however, they can create further problems for a heart already weakened by a heart attack.

The right side and the left side of the heart do different jobs. The right side collects oxygen-depleted blood from the body for delivery to the lungs. The left side pumps oxygen-rich blood to the body. Because these jobs are so different, it is important for the two sides of the heart to remain completely separated. No blood must mingle between them. To maintain the integrity of each half, a thick muscular wall, called the **septum,** separates the right and left sides of the heart. (Your nostrils are also divided by a septum.)

The layers of the heart wall are made up of the pericardium, the epicardium, the myocardium, and the endocardium.

- The **pericardium** is a closed sac surrounding the heart. It helps hold the heart in place within the chest.
- The **epicardium** is the outer layer of the heart wall.
- The **myocardium** is the muscular wall of the heart. This muscle tissue is unique in the body. It lies between the outer layer (epicardium) and the inner layer (endocardium). It is about an inch thick. It is thickest around the ventricles and slightly thinner around the atria.
- The **endocardium** is the thin smooth membrane forming the interior surface of the heart.

The Heart's Blood Supply

Anyone who has had a heart attack should understand how the heart itself is supplied with blood. A problem in this area caused your heart attack.

The heart is an extremely hard-working muscle. As we've seen, it pumps blood to every part of the body. To do such a mammoth job, the heart itself requires a constant, extraordinary amount of oxygenated blood for nourishment. You might say that the heart "feeds itself first" to keep the whole system going. The first arteries to branch away from the aorta are the coronary arteries that supply the heart itself with oxygenated blood. If you have ever flown on a commercial airplane, you may have noticed that adult passengers traveling with small children are instructed to put on their own oxygen masks first, and then their children's, in case of an emergency. It is understood that the adult can't help a child breathe if the adult can't breathe himself. Similarly, by receiving oxygenated blood first, the heart is more likely to be able to continue its job and supply the rest of the body with oxygenated blood, too.

Simply put, a **heart attack** occurs when oxygen can't be delivered to some part of the heart because of a blockage in one or more of the **coronary arteries.** In Latin, *coronary* means "like a crown." The coronary arteries "crown" the top of the heart (see figure, page 22). They twine around the heart and even reach into it—a little like ivy growing along a wall. The coronary arteries branch repeatedly until every part of the heart is supplied with blood. Some arteries penetrate the heart to feed the septum as well.

Coronary arteries have many unique features. Unlike most arteries, each coronary artery usually supplies a particular portion of the heart, and that's all. Should an artery have trouble delivering blood to a certain area of the heart, no backup supply is available from other arteries. If coronary arteries are blocked or injured, the part of the heart they "feed" starves. If the blood supply isn't restored very promptly, that muscle tissue dies. This is what is popularly called a **heart attack,** which means "death of or damage to heart muscle." In medical terms, a **heart attack** is a **myocardial infarction.**

But no two hearts are exactly alike. Sometimes a person has coronary arteries that overlap slightly, giving that person **collateral circulation.** A few people are born with collateral circulation. Some people develop it in response to ischemia that results from chronic narrowing of blood vessels. With collateral circulation, a portion of the heart is actually fed by two arteries. These two arteries work in a way similar to the way two water sprinklers on your lawn would if they were placed

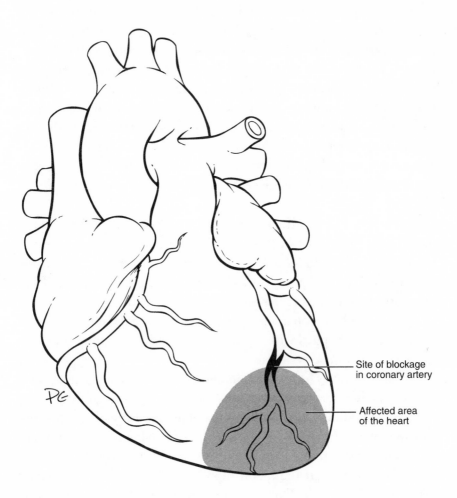

Site of blockage
in coronary artery

Affected area
of the heart

Coronary arteries supply the heart with oxygenated blood. The shaded area (lower right) shows a heart attack or myocardial infarction. A blockage in a coronary artery kept oxygenated blood from flowing to that area of the heart. The heart tissue died as a result of being deprived of oxygen for a prolonged time.

close together. The lawn between the two sprinklers is actually watered by both. The heart tissue between the overlapping arteries is actually fed by both. People with arteries like these are a bit luckier than the rest of us. They have a slightly better chance of surviving a heart attack and living with coronary heart disease. Their ischemic heart tissue may be in an area with two sources of blood. If so, that area may receive just enough blood from nearby unclogged arteries to keep the heart tissue alive for a short time. That may be enough time for the person to reach a hospital and receive treatment.

If health professionals can intervene early enough during a heart attack, they can sometimes restore blood flow. It's a brief window of opportunity, however, and they must work very quickly. During this sensitive period, the heart tissue is dying but not yet dead. This condition is called **ischemia** (is-KE′mia).

The Electrical System

Blood moves through the circulatory system because of the heart's pumping action, which we hear as the heartbeat. With each beat, the heart muscle contracts rhythmically and then relaxes. It goes through this short cycle about 60 times every minute. Each contraction forces blood from the atria to the ventricles or out of the ventricles and into the lungs or the rest of the circulatory system. In the relaxed moment between contractions, chambers of the heart refill with blood.

Actually, the heart doesn't contract and relax everywhere at the same time. In a coordinated action, the atria of the heart relax and fill while the ventricles contract and push blood into the system. Then the situation reverses. The ventricles relax, while blood from the atria empties into them. Most of the pumping work is done by the ventricles; triggered by ventricular activity, the atria empty and fill.

A rhythmic contraction moves across the heart muscle progressively, from top to bottom. Think for a moment of the popular "wave" that sports fans in a stadium sometimes attempt during a dull moment in a game. From one side of the stadium to the other, groups of people throw up their arms, rise briefly from their seats, and sit down again. This motion creates a spike or "wave" pulse that seems to move across the stands. To spectators, it looks like a giant ripple moving across a sea of people. The rhythmic contraction of the heart is a mechanical wave that is stimulated by a preceding electrical wave passing from the top of the heart to the bottom. That electrical wave activates and then quiets the muscle it passes over. The **electrocardiogram,** or **EKG,** is a diagnostic test that tracks this electrical activity and turns it into graph form for physicians to analyze. From the EKG, doctors can determine whether or not a problem exists in the electrical activity of the heart.

What starts this pulse? The electrical pulse originates from the **sinoatrial node** (the **SA node**). The SA node is one of several nodes scattered throughout the heart. Electrical nodes comprise a very special part of the heart. They resemble nerve cells more than regular muscle cells. Nodes are unique. They can start an electrical impulse that causes muscle reaction. The SA node normally acts as the heart's **pacemaker.** It starts a chain reaction of electrical impulses that travel down the heart from atria to ventricles. However, if the SA node becomes damaged for some reason, any of the other nodes may conceivably become the pacemaker node instead. This wonderful ability is one of the ways the heart protects itself and keeps functioning if it is damaged.

The SA node builds up an electrical charge, and then it discharges. The electrical discharge causes a localized twitch or contraction of heart muscle. When the SA node discharges, an electrical pulse wave starts, and the atria contract.

As the electrical pulse moves down the heart toward the ventricles, it passes through the **atrioventricular node** (the **AV node**). As its name implies, the AV node straddles the area where the atria and the ventricles meet, at roughly the midpoint of the heart. Its function is to slow down the electrical pulse as it sweeps across the heart, so that the atria have time to contract fully before the ventricles start. After pausing at the AV node, the electrical pulse continues to the ventricles. The ventricles are larger than the atria. Therefore, the bigger job of making them contract is distributed across a specialized heart muscle network that extends in three directions. The network is called the **bundle branches.** After the ventricles contract, the process starts again—"from the top," as a bandleader might say. Occasionally the damage from a heart attack damages the specialized electrical cells that conduct the electrical pulse through the bundle branch system. Doctors refer to the problem this interruption creates as **bundle branch block.**

How frequently this cycle (the **heart rate**) is played out depends on signals sent from the brain to the nervelike AV node. Thus, brain activity plays an important part in slowing down or speeding up the heart rate. Other conditions, such as ambient temperature, physical activity, pain, and psychological stress can affect the heart rate, too.

❧ *While resting in the cardiac care unit a day after his heart attack, Tran felt a strange sensation in his chest. Unlike the day before, this sensation didn't hurt. But his heart was racing.*

Tran rang for a nurse, who seemed to appear at once. With some apprehension, he told her what he felt.

Tran sat up slowly with the nurse's help. She explained that he was still recovering from the heart attack and that irregular heart rhythms were sometimes part of that process. Tran's heart had been beating too fast, a condition called tachycardia. The nurse had seen the episode begin because Tran's electrocardiogram had picked it up. The monitor at the nurses' station indicated that Tran's heartbeat had quickened.

"I'll tell the doctor that you've experienced a rapid heartbeat," the nurse told Tran. "I'm glad it didn't cause you any pain, because it sometimes can. We'll keep watching you carefully. If changing your position doesn't help stabilize your heartbeat next time, the doctor may prescribe a drug to help bring your heartbeat back into a normal range." ❧

Blood Pressure

Blood pressure plays a significant role in the proper function of the circulatory system. It ensures that blood flows through the vessels to all parts of the body.

Blood pressure is affected by several organs in the body. The heart—specifically, the left ventricle—dictates the forcefulness with which blood enters the arteries. Blood vessels, by their shape and size, also affect blood pressure. Kidneys affect blood pressure by influencing the total fluid volume operating within the circulatory system. Kidneys control the balance of sodium and water in the fluids of the body, and that also affects blood pressure. Normally the kidneys control this balance easily by excreting extra sodium or water from the body in the urine. Sodium is an essential element for health (table salt is a sodium compound). When the ratio of sodium to water in the body falls out of balance because of either too much sodium or too much water, problems occur.

A beating heart both contracts and relaxes, so blood pressure is measured as two values, not one. Both values record the pressure of blood against artery walls. The **systolic value** reflects pressure that is exerted on artery walls by the heart's contraction. It represents the higher pressure required to force blood from the heart into the arteries and throughout the circulatory system. The **diastolic value** of a blood pressure reading represents the lower pressure in the arteries when the heart is at rest between beats. Medical personnel record this information as the systolic value over the diastolic value. (Blood pressure is measured in millimeters of mercury [**mm Hg**]. For more information, see the box on page 27). The two values can vary a bit from person to person and still fall within normal ranges. To get an accurate sense of a person's blood pressure, health professionals take several readings over a period of time. A single measurement that shows elevated blood pressure levels is not considered troublesome. Consistently high blood pressure readings, however, are taken very seriously. Generally, a blood pressure reading of 140/90 mm Hg and above needs looking into.

The Unhealthy Heart: When Things Go Wrong

Now you understand how the heart is constructed and how it works. But what happens when things go wrong? What happens when a heart attack disrupts that work?

How Blood Pressure Is Measured

High blood pressure is closely associated with a number of very serious health problems. Yet because the condition itself is painless, it often goes undiagnosed. Of the estimated 50 million Americans with high blood pressure, it is estimated that more than a third don't know they have the condition.

The only way to find out whether or not you have high blood pressure is to have your blood pressure checked. For greatest accuracy, two measurements should be taken at least 30 seconds apart. Your blood pressure will be recorded as an average of those two measurements. Additionally, the test should be repeated on at least three occasions to confirm a high blood pressure diagnosis. The test itself is quick and painless. A medical instrument called a **sphygmomanometer** (SFIG'mo-mah-NOM'et-ter) is used to measure blood pressure. Here's how it works.

A rubber cuff is wrapped around the upper arm. When the cuff is inflated, it compresses a large artery in the arm. That compression momentarily stops blood flow through the artery.

At that point, air in the cuff is released, and the health-care professional measuring the blood pressure listens with a **stethoscope.** (A stethoscope is an instrument for listening to sounds within the body.) When the blood starts to pulse through the artery again, it makes a sound. The sounds continue to be heard through the stethoscope until pressure in the artery exceeds the pressure in the cuff.

While listening and watching the gauge, the health-care professional records two measurements. The **systolic** (sis-TOL'ik) **pressure** is the pressure of the blood flow when the heart beats (the pressure when the first sound is heard). The **diastolic** (di'as-TOL'ik) **pressure** is the pressure between heartbeats (the pressure when the last sound is heard). Blood pressure is measured in millimeters of mercury, which is abbreviated as mm Hg.

Differences in either or both pressure readings can help determine what may be causing your high blood pressure and how to treat it. For example, a high systolic measurement may be coupled with a normal diastolic measurement. Such a reading may indicate that the arteries are somewhat rigid and unable to expand and contract normally as a response to changes in blood volume. A high diastolic measurement may mean that the arteries are unnaturally constricted. This constriction leaves less room in which blood may circulate, raising total blood pressure values as a result.

Normal blood pressure readings vary among individuals, depending on age and other factors. High blood pressure exists when blood pressure is equal to or greater than 140 over 90. The first, larger number represents systolic pressure, and the second represents diastolic pressure.

There is one very important thing to remember about blood pressure numbers. The harder it is for blood to flow through the vessels, the higher the numbers will be.

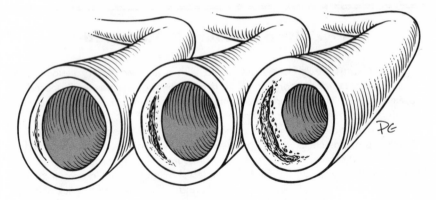

Artery being occluded by atherosclerotic plaque.

What Actually Happens?

Prolonged starvation of heart muscle causes a heart attack. It usually happens because of a blockage in a **coronary artery,** or heart blood vessel. A heart attack might be thought of as a one-two punch to the heart. At first, a coronary artery is blocked, typically by an atherosclerotic plaque and blood clot. This deprives a portion of the heart muscle of oxygenated blood. Part of the heart tissue fed by that artery begins to die. The extent of damage depends on whether the involved artery is large and at which point along the artery the blockage occurs. Significantly, the tissue doesn't die immediately. Rather, it starves for lack of oxygen and other nutrients—and starvation takes time. Not much time, but some. At this point, the involved heart tissue is considered **ischemic.** The medical term for this intermediate condition is **myocardial ischemia.** That literally means "withholding blood from heart tissue" *(myocardia* = heart tissue; *ischemia* = withholding blood).

❧ *The snow was coming down faster now. Randa hated the stuff, but she especially hated shoveling it out of her driveway, as she was doing that moment. Bending to take another scoop, the 58-year-old woman was stopped short by a hot, squeezing pain in her chest that made her gasp. She shifted her feet. Maybe it was another angina attack, she thought doubtfully. She checked her watch. Randa had taken a nitroglycerin tablet just 15 minutes ago, before starting the shoveling. Usually that was enough for jobs like this. Now she was feeling a little woozy. That wasn't typical, either.*

Randa went inside, took another angina tablet, and checked her watch again. The pain wasn't going away. It was getting worse, spreading up her neck and into her jaw. Moving restlessly around the kitchen, Randa concluded that what she was feeling was not an episode of angina at all, but a heart attack. Knowing that she had to act quickly, Randa picked up the phone and dialed 911 for an ambulance. When she arrived at the emergency room, treatment began almost immediately. ❦

Given the opportunity, doctors have a chance to limit the amount of permanent tissue damage that the heart suffers during a heart attack. They can do this by interrupting the ischemic process and restoring blood delivery to the affected heart tissue. Taking quick action can reduce the aftereffects of heart attack. Measures that might be taken while tissue is ischemic can't work once the tissue has died.

The second part of the heart attack occurs when heart tissue actually dies for lack of blood. At this time, the heart attack itself is "complete." Medical complications associated with the heart attack, however, such as heart failure, may begin or continue.

A heart attack, then, is the product of *prolonged* myocardial ischemia that eventually infarcts tissue. A blockage in the artery prevents blood from being delivered to heart tissue. That tissue starves. Usually the arterial blockage is caused by **atherosclerosis.**

Atherosclerosis is the form of artery disease that is the result of a buildup of fatty deposits along inner artery walls. The artery walls become thick and irregular due to these deposits. Doctors diagnose coronary heart disease if atherosclerosis is observed in the coronary arteries. The deposits gradually develop into plaques that narrow blood vessels. That process takes many years and eventually interrupts blood flow.

However, conditions other than atherosclerosis can sometimes trigger a heart attack. An episode of **vasospasm,** or sudden constriction of a coronary artery, can cause a heart attack in rare instances. (Vasospasm is discussed more fully in the box on page 30.) An episode of extremely severe **hypertension** (high blood pressure) can also cause a heart at-

About Vasospasm

Also called **coronary artery spasm,** or **Prinzmetal's angina,** vasospasm refers to the sudden constriction of an artery in the heart. When a vasospasm occurs, the smooth muscle of the blood vessel constricts very tightly, causing an ischemic condition. If the vasospasm is severe enough, a heart attack occurs, but that is rare.

Doctors aren't always sure what causes vasospasm. Its appearance is unpredictable. Although vasospasm occurs most frequently in arteries damaged by atherosclerosis, it can also occur in relatively clear, or "normal," arteries. In some people, vasospasm develops spontaneously. In others, it develops in response to excessive cold, severe emotional stress, or certain medications. Cocaine use can also induce vasospasm-related heart attack.

Usually coronary artery spasm strikes a person at rest. This helps to distinguish it from angina pectoris, which usually strikes when a person is engaged in activity.

Vasospasm is usually, but not always, accompanied by chest pain. Sometimes vasospasm is "silent," meaning without symptoms. Doctors can confirm that vasospasm has occurred by studying changes on an electrocardiogram.

tack but, again, rarely. Cocaine use stimulates blood vessels, causing them to expand and contract suddenly. This may also trigger severe vasospasms that cause infarctions.

Some Complications

Obviously, an event as catastrophic to the body as a heart attack creates a number of associated problems that your doctors must resolve quickly. When you had a heart attack, for example, your heart rate may have been racing, a condition called **tachycardia.** Or your heart rate may have been much slower than normal, a condition called **bradycardia.** Your blood pressure may also have been affected. Perhaps it was extremely high, which is common for people who are already **hypertensive.** Or it may have been very low, **hypotensive,** if your body went into shock in response to the heart attack. You may develop a fever that lasts for a day or two.

Some people can't breathe easily during a heart attack. This is usually a sign of **heart failure,** a condition in which the heart is unable to pump blood at an adequate rate or in adequate volume. The electrical impulses that regulate the heartbeat may have been compromised. The source of those impulses is the electrical nodes of the heart (see page 24). Sometimes these nodes are damaged when the heart tissue becomes ischemic. The heart cannot maintain a strong, steady beat. Instead, it beats shallowly and incompletely, making it impossible to pump blood back into the body properly. Yet the blood has to go somewhere—and it backs up into the lungs. Too much blood in the lungs overwhelms the delicate web of tiny blood vessels there and makes oxygen exchange nearly impossible. The person to whom this happens feels short of breath and gulps for air.

Mild or Severe?

A heart attack may be mild or severe. By definition, a mild heart attack involves only a small area of infarction. Overall heart function usually remains normal. A severe heart attack involves a larger area of infarction. It permanently damages the heart tissue. It often sets the stage for complications such as heart failure or **hypotension** (dangerously low blood pressure). Such complications make the patient's recovery more difficult.

Whether in the end a heart attack is severe or mild depends on a few factors. The location of the arterial blockage in the heart is important. So is the number of these blockages, or **occlusions.** Another important indicator is the nature of the individual's circulatory system, which varies slightly from person to person. Some people have more **collateral circulation** than others (see discussion on page 21). With collateral circulation, more than one blood vessel delivers blood to the same area. These people can usually survive a heart attack better, with less permanent damage, than those who do not have extensive collateral circulation.

Where heart muscle is concerned, collateral circulation is often a matter of luck—you either have it or you don't (and most of us don't). Other factors affect heart health, too. Some, like collateral circulation, are "givens" in our lives, and there's nothing we can do to change them. But others can be manipulated to improve an overall health profile. Let's look at the risk factors for coronary heart disease next.

Risk Factors

As we mentioned earlier, **risk factors** are characteristics that increase an individual's chances of developing a certain disease or other health problem. Risk factors may be personal habits or health problems. They can also be genetic susceptibilities. Extensive studies have identified several factors that increase the risk of heart attack and stroke. Some risk factors for coronary heart disease (CHD) are preventable; some cannot be changed. Some that cannot be changed entirely can be partially neutralized by changes in personal habits or through proper medical care. Understanding your personal risk factors can help you learn how to minimize your personal risk and maximize healthful habits and behaviors. We'll look at individual risk factors more closely later in this book.

Risk factors for CHD and atherosclerosis can be divided into two categories: major and contributing risk factors. **Major risk factors** are those that medical research has shown to be definitely associated with a significant increase in the risk of cardiovascular disease. Some of these can be changed; others cannot. The major risk factors for heart attack that cannot be changed are a family history of atherosclerosis, being male, and increasing age. The major risk factors that can be changed are exposure to tobacco smoke, having high blood cholesterol or high blood pressure, and being physically inactive. If you have any of the nonmodifiable risk factors for CHD, it's even more important to address the risk factors that you can control.

🐛 *Ranjit was a 62-year-old police officer who had worked the desk of his local precinct for more than 15 years. As a beat cop before that, Ranjit had been in top physical shape, walking much of every day. In those days, he ate what he wanted to, when he wanted to—without gaining any weight. Since moving to the desk job, however, the officer had continued to eat whatever he wanted while giving up most of the physical activity. He had to admit he wasn't looking quite as trim in his uniform as he used to. Okay, he was fat. He had definitely picked up a junk-food habit. But he was surrounded by the stuff! There seemed to be a candy machine on every floor of the precinct. And then there was Eileen, who came by every morning with the doughnut cart.*

The change to the desk job had provoked other changes as well. Ranjit had picked up a smoking habit. His doctor was always after him to quit, but Ranjit never seemed to find the right time to do it. He did feel guilty about not sticking with his medicines, though—the ones that were supposed to help him bring down his high blood pressure. Since his father had died of a heart attack, Ranjit knew that controlling his blood pressure was important. But having to take medicine every day made him feel less independent and strong than he liked to feel. In Ranjit's mind, only really sick people took medicine. And he felt fine.

This police officer unknowingly started down a very dangerous path 10 years earlier. He has several risk factors for heart attack. He can't change his age or his family history of heart attack, but he can reduce his own personal risk. He can begin by looking at the risk factors he can change. These include his lack of physical activity, poor eating habits, addiction to cigarettes, and uncontrolled high blood pressure. All of these things have combined to put him on a collision course with heart attack or stroke.

Ranjit doesn't realize how much better he will feel and how much more energy he will have if he would only eliminate or control his risk factors for heart attack or stroke. Eliminating or controlling even one or two of them to begin with could have a powerful effect on his total risk for these diseases. ❧

Contributing risk factors are those associated with increased risk of cardiovascular disease. For heart attack, these include diabetes and obesity. Stress may also be a contributing factor.

The more risk factors you have, the greater your chance of developing heart disease. For these reasons, it is important to eliminate or mitigate as many risk factors as possible.

What Does It All Mean?

At the moment that a heart attack begins, of course, you haven't time to consider the science of what is happening to your body or what your risk factors may have been. Your overriding concern is to get help—quickly! You go directly to the hospital. In the next chapter we'll take a look at what happens in the emergency room and beyond.

CHAPTER TWO

The Hospital Experience

❦ *Less than one hour ago Carsten had been working at his desk when he was seized by a fierce pain in the center of his chest. Carsten was used to being in charge of things—"ordering everyone around," his wife said. But this time was different. He felt helpless and could hardly breathe.*

It was a good thing his assistant Jeremy had been nearby and knew what to do. Jeremy told Carsten to take it easy and leave everything to him. Carsten had tried to deny that anything was wrong, but Jeremy just took over.

Jeremy told somebody that Carsten might be having a heart attack. He then asked someone to call ahead to the hospital emergency room and tell them that Carsten would be coming in. Jeremy and a coworker put Carsten in Jeremy's car and headed for the hospital a few blocks away.

In the automobile, Carsten became restless, moving about in his seat. "Stay cool, boss," Jeremy said. Carsten nodded but continued to move around a lot, trying to get more comfortable.

When they arrived at the emergency room entrance, Carsten stayed in the car while Jeremy went to get help. When Carsten saw the orderly approach the car with a wheelchair, he didn't object. By now he was ready to admit that he felt pretty bad, and he was scared. He had never felt anything like this before in his life.

After that Carsten was moved, prodded, poked, and pushed.

Somebody gave him oxygen, and someone else started an IV. One doctor told him that his friend was right. He had had a heart attack—and survived. "So far, so good," Carsten thought. Another doctor told him that he was lucky to get to the hospital so quickly after the pain began. "So, Jeremy was right about that, too," he thought. Somebody gave him medicine through his IV tube. He was beginning to feel better.

There was so much going on, it was hard to follow—so much equipment and so many people. "What is it all for?" he wondered. He wanted to ask questions, but he didn't know what to ask. Someone had said, "Don't worry, we're going to take care of you." That was comforting. He decided just to rest for a few minutes. ❦

Arriving in a hospital after a heart attack is a disorienting experience: You suddenly find yourself at the center of a great deal of activity, and you don't know what will happen next.

Treatment and Recovery

Emergency room personnel begin to provide immediate, lifesaving care as soon as the patient arrives. This short-term, or **acute,** care has many phases and continues during the patient's stay in the hospital. In this chapter, we'll discuss acute care and give you an idea of what happens in the hospital to help you get well. Later chapters will tackle issues related to long-term recovery.

In the emergency room, doctors work quickly to:

- determine whether a heart attack has occurred and
- stabilize the patient's condition.

When the patient's condition is stable, he or she is transferred to a **cardiac care unit,** or CCU. (The CCU is also sometimes called a coronary care unit.) There the medical staff tries to:

- minimize the extent of heart damage caused by heart tissue death or infarction and prevent (or resolve) any complications that are a consequence of the coronary event;
- determine how much permanent damage was done; and
- evaluate the cause of the heart attack. This is necessary in order for the doctors to recommend future medical therapy and risk factor modification.

When a patient leaves the CCU, he or she is often transferred to a **step-down unit,** which we'll discuss later.

Let's take a closer look at the first step along the way. Let's see what happens when someone having a heart attack arrives at the hospital.

The Emergency Room

A heart attack victim arriving at the hospital **emergency room (ER)** is admitted immediately. An ER generally has a cardiac room for treating heart patients. This room is often smaller than other examining rooms. It is well equipped with monitoring devices, oxygen, **intravenous drips (IVs),** and other pertinent tools, all within easy reach. Physicians, nurses, and other medical personnel are in charge of the various activities needed to stabilize the heart attack victim.

Tests and treatment begin when the heart attack patient arrives. An **electrocardiogram (EKG)** is taken immediately. The results usually show doctors whether the patient is having a heart attack. Electrocardiography provides a graphic record of the electrical activity of the heart. Twelve "leads" (small, electrical sensors) are placed on the patient's chest at specific points. Each lead sends information to a system that integrates the input from all the leads and presents the findings as a graph. Looking at the graph, doctors can also recognize abnormalities that indicate where changes are occurring in the heart.

While an EKG is run, other activities are taking place. An IV drip is started. The patient can receive medicines, nourishment—whatever is needed—through the IV. Drugs are usually administered in the ER to ease the heart's workload. Depending on the patient's condition, doctors may choose from a variety of drugs. These include aspirin, nitrates, beta-blockers, and, especially, thrombolytic agents to dissolve blood clots. Blood is drawn and sent to the laboratory for evaluation. The attending physician may call in a **cardiologist,** a doctor who specializes in heart care. The cardiologist may provide a consultation or take over the case.

Doctors also look for arrhythmias, problems in the way the heart beats. If the patient's heartbeat is unsteady or ineffective, a defibrillator may be used to restore steady action. A **defibrillator** is a portable machine that is capable of delivering a strong electric current to the heart to "shock" the heart's electrical system. This emergency procedure restores a regular rhythm. The doctor places the two broad paddles of the defibrillator on the patient's chest, over the heart, and applies electricity in short, strong bursts. Defibrillation is meant to interrupt cardiac arrest—the complete shutdown of the heart.

To learn certain information about the heart, the doctor may have the patient undergo catheterization. (For more information about cardiac catheterization, see pages 44–45.)

The flurry of activity in the ER begins to slow down as soon as the heart attack victim is stabilized. By then, the doctors have administered several tests to establish that the patient was having a heart attack. They have given painkillers intravenously, administered oxygen to ease the load on the patient's heart, and started drug therapy to limit damage to heart tissue. These steps help the patient through the crisis and keep him or her alive.

The Cardiac Care Unit

After the patient is stabilized in the ER, he or she is transferred to the CCU. Family members usually accompany the patient to this area. However, they may be asked to wait outside the patient's room until the patient is settled and any remaining tests are completed. They may also be asked to wait outside if complications develop. Once the patient is in the CCU, care passes from the attending ER physician to a cardiologist or the patient's own doctor.

The first CCU was developed in the 1960s to monitor patients with cardiac arrhythmias. Today the CCU is a highly specialized, protective environment. It is designed to treat heart attack victims and prevent complications. It is filled with specialists, from highly trained nurses to cardiologists.

❦ *Sumi was resting quietly in the cardiac care unit only hours after the trauma of suffering a heart attack. Her husband sat quietly in a chair not far away, watching his wife carefully. He was exhausted, too. He had been the one to persuade Sumi that something really was wrong, and he had driven her here under protest. To think that she had tried to refuse! Harold shook his head. It had been a close call.*

It was hard for Harold to see Sumi hooked up to so many machines in the CCU. She had one tube for oxygen and several wires for monitoring her heart in different ways. Her doctors had even had to run a catheter into her heart to see what was happening there. She had an IV drip for medications and nutrients, too. But Harold was relieved that the tubes and things seemed to bother Sumi less than they did him.

After the scare they had had, Sumi looked much better. She was still quite weak, of course. Harold had been told she would probably sleep a lot for the first 24 hours. It was certainly quiet enough for that on this floor, he noticed.

Quiet and kind of dark. But it felt good for the moment— soothing. ❦

The CCU Atmosphere

Visitors are allowed in the CCU, but only one or two at a time, and visits are kept short. The CCU has a quiet, subdued atmosphere. People speak softly, and lights remain low. Patients receive a great deal of personal care in the CCU. A heart attack patient may have his or her own nurse or may share a nurse with one other patient. Two nurses may be assigned to care for a very sick patient. A portable defibrillator is kept nearby, too, in case a patient's heart rate becomes erratic.

Patient Monitoring

The CCU is notable not only for providing patients with a great deal of personal care but also for its highly complex monitoring equipment. The doctors and nurses monitor the heart attack patient's blood pressure and heart rate, as well as the electrical activity of the heart. The EKG leads attached to the patient's chest are also attached to an electrocardiograph monitor. This monitor is placed near the patient's bed. Information from the EKG is also relayed to the nurses' station, which has a similar monitor for each patient. Members of the medical staff can glance at a monitor screen to see exactly how a patient is faring from moment to moment. The screen alerts them to any sudden changes in the patient's condition.

❦ *Edgar did not feel good. It had been almost three hours since he had been admitted to the hospital emergency room. Now he was upstairs, settled into the cardiac care unit. Well, maybe "settled" was the wrong word, Edgar thought. He wasn't too comfortable with all the medical equipment surrounding him; it just seemed to emphasize how sick he really was. And one way or another, it looked like he was attached to all of it. What could it be for? Was he more ill than he thought? Did all this equipment mean that he might not make it? Although part of him wanted to ask these questions, part of him didn't want to know. He'd never felt so helpless. The oxygen machine—he was attached to that, too—hissed quietly. At least the pain was gone, more or less. A nurse passed by in the hall. "Maybe I'll just try to rest a while," he thought.* ❦

Rest and Recovery

In the CCU, patients rest and begin to recover. Drug therapies begun in the ER continue in the CCU. While in the CCU, patients often receive oxygen to ease this part of the heart's job a little. Patients in the CCU take it easy. Bed rest is required for at least the first 24 hours. Most patients are encouraged to sit up in bed for some portion of the day as soon after their heart attack as possible. During this critical period, patients are limited to a clear liquid diet. That's because digestion diverts blood from other parts of the body to the digestive tract, which is more work for the heart. A liquid diet is easier on the system. Toileting may be possible for patients who are fairly stable medically. If indicated, patients may be encouraged to start walking around the hospital floor two to four days after their heart attack.

Do Your "Sit-ups"

In the old days, bed rest meant just that: rest. Today, doctors know that too much bed rest can actually cause problems instead of resolving them. Lying down for long periods of time without changing position gives blood the chance to pool in places it shouldn't. It also encourages muscles to cramp and "freeze" in uncomfortable positions, called **contractures.** Finally, just lying in bed all day can be gloomy and depressing for a heart patient—or any patient. These complications are easily avoided with a little exercise. Even in the CCU patients are soon expected to participate in very light exercise.

At first, you will be encouraged only to sit up in bed for short periods twice a day. After that, you'll graduate to sitting up in a chair twice daily. Some people notice that they become faint when they sit up after lying in bed or when they move from bed to chair. It's probably nothing to worry about. A change in blood pressure is triggered when you move into a new, upright position after lying for a long time on your back or side. That is probably what is causing the faintness that you feel. It should subside fairly rapidly. If it doesn't, discuss it with your CCU nurse or doctor.

To keep your limbs flexible, you may start an easy program of **passive range-of-motion exercises** that a nurse or occupational therapist will help you perform in your bed or in your chair. (Family members who have been trained to provide range-of-motion exercise therapy often make wonderful exercise partners and cheerleaders.) In passive range-of-motion exercise, the therapist, family member, or nurse gently moves an arm or leg through its full range of motion, stimulating circulation and joint movement. After you become stronger, you will be able to make the same movements yourself, without help. Range-of-motion exercise is very important for preventing limb contractures and skin sores and should be performed several times each day until you're back on your feet. Ultimately, of course, the degree of activity you attempt will depend on the severity of your heart attack.

The Emotional Side

Lying in a hospital bed after your heart attack, you may have felt helpless. After all, you were subjected to circumstances over which you had no control and surrounded by strange, somewhat threatening equipment. As a survivor, you probably felt a number of changing, even conflicting, emotions related to your heart attack: fear, anxiety about the future, concerns about mortality, and depression. Or perhaps you or a loved one had difficulty acknowledging just how serious the heart attack was or were in denial that it happened at all.

Many heart attack patients have these feelings. Such feelings are understandable, and they usually pass with time. Patients' mental and emotional health are evaluated informally in the CCU. Patients who seem to be having an especially difficult time coping with what has happened can be helped right away. (For more information about the psychological impact of heart attack, see pages 56–59.)

A Great Resource—Right at Hand

It's worth noting that the nursing staff in the CCU can be a wonderful source of information for patients and their families. Anyone who has had a heart attack, or who has a family member who has had one, has many questions. Even in the CCU, issues of rehabilitation and modifying or eliminating risk factors for heart disease will be on your mind. Don't hesitate to discuss them with the cardiac care nurse. He or she is highly trained and interested in these issues and will have important information to share with you. As a resource, these fine professionals can't be beat. Take advantage of their knowledge and use it!

Tests, Tests, and More Tests

Diagnostic procedures, and the machines that make them possible, are another important component of the CCU. Tests help doctors confirm that a heart attack did occur, and it helps them assess the damage it did. The tests may be **invasive,** meaning they penetrate the body. Or, they may be **noninvasive,** performed without breaking the skin. Many patients are mystified by the number of tests they undergo and the questions they or family members are asked to answer. Understanding why these tests are so important and how they contribute to a better outcome can help make enduring them a little more tolerable.

Initial Tests

Five tests are usually routine: electrocardiography, monitoring (to check for arrhythmias), blood tests, X-ray, and echocardiography. For a smaller percentage of heart attack patients, catheterization may also be recommended. In addition, imaging tests are available in many hospitals. Some of these tests, including electrocardiography and blood tests, start as soon as the patient is admitted to the ER. Others are done in the CCU.

Electrocardiography

Electrocardiography is probably the first test a doctor will use to determine whether a heart attack has occurred. In the ER, an electrocardiogram is useful for establishing that a heart attack is developing or has already occurred (see page 37). In the CCU, electrocardiography is used to monitor patients. Changes in EKG readings can identify the onset of another heart attack.

Monitoring Devices

Heart attack patients are most vulnerable to second heart attacks and other complications soon after the initial event. For this reason, observation in a CCU is an important element of recovery. Patients are carefully monitored for changes in their heart rhythms.

Blood Tests

In response to injury, the heart releases certain **enzymes** into the bloodstream. (Enzymes are proteinlike substances in the cells that trigger certain chemical reactions.) These enzymes are intended to start certain healing chemical reactions in the cells. Taking blood samples and analyzing them for enzyme content helps doctors determine how large—and therefore how damaging—a heart attack was for the patient.

X-ray

Doctors use a chest X-ray (a noninvasive test) to find out whether the heart is enlarged or fluid is accumulating in the patient's lungs as a result of the heart attack. X-rays can also be performed within the heart itself, using a catheter. (In such cases, the test is invasive.)

Echocardiography

Also referred to as **ultrasound,** this noninvasive test is extremely useful to doctors. It gives a clear picture on film of the heart chambers and valves at work, as well as their size and overall condition. An echocardiogram provides further evidence of the extent of damage to the patient's heart, as well as remaining heart function. Echocardiograms are less useful for showing the condition of the coronary arteries.

Cardiac Catheterization (Angiography)

Catheterization is not appropriate for every heart attack patient. Only about one tenth to one third of all heart attack patients need catheterization. But catheterization can provide information that doctors cannot get any other way.

In catheterization, the doctor inserts a flexible wire into one of the patient's major arteries, generally in an arm or the groin. The doctor carefully threads the wire through arteries leading back to the heart and into the heart itself. The **catheter,** a flexible, wirelike tube follows the wire. After the catheter reaches the heart, the doctor pulls out the wire, leaving the catheter in place. There it acts as the eyes and ears of the doctor, sending information back to a machine for the doctor's interpretation. This test can measure blood and how much oxygen is in the blood of the heart chambers. It can provide other information as well. It may also allow X-ray still photos or movies to be taken of the chambers. In some cases, the doctor performs an angiogram. A special fluid called a contrast medium or dye is injected into the bloodstream through the catheter. An X-ray screen picks up the dye and shows how blood flows through the blood vessels and chambers of the heart. In this way, doctors can easily detect blockages in the vessels.

Catheters are left in the body for as short a time as possible, because they can cause complications. Infection, artery punctures, and catheter breaks are possible, although not common. Blood may clot around catheters, too, making arterial infarction more likely. Catheterization is the basis for angioplasty, a procedure to widen coronary arteries (see discussion on pages 88–93).

Magnetic Resonance Imaging (MRI)

This noninvasive test is occasionally used to evaluate heart tissue. It provides clear pictures of the heart muscle and the vessels that supply it with blood. These pictures can tell doctors such things as the size of the heart chambers, the thickness of the heart walls, and whether there are any congenital (birth) defects. If MRI pictures are taken in quick succession, they also can show doctors how well the left ventricle pumps blood.

Computed Tomography (CT)

Computed tomography is a noninvasive test occasionally used to provide doctors with pictures of the heart in cross section, or "slices." An advantage of CT is that the pictures it provides are clear, not blurry—something to consider since the heart is in constant motion. Doctors can analyze these pictures and learn important information about the anatomy and function of the heart. Doctors use computed tomography to examine narrowed arteries, blood flow, and the condition of the left ventricle.

Positron Emission Tomography (PET)

This noninvasive, painless imaging test is occasionally used to evaluate the condition of the heart tissue itself. Although not widely available, PET can help doctors identify areas of coronary artery disease. In the ER, doctors can also use PET to locate areas of heart tissue that may be suffering (ischemic) because of the heart attack but that are not yet dead (infarcted). That information helps them decide on the best treatment for the patient.

Follow-up Tests and Evaluations

Many follow-up tests and evaluations help your doctor determine why your heart attack occurred. They also help give the doctor an immediate snapshot of your overall health and indications of early complications. Follow-up tests usually include at least blood pressure measurement and blood tests. A thorough heart attack risk factor assessment is another important follow-up evaluation. It involves evaluating your family health history and your personal history of cardiovascular disease. These tests and evaluations point the way to an accurate long-term prognosis. They also provide useful information that can help you take advantage of treatments that are best for you. From them, you may learn to modify personal behavior with a doctor's help. All of these are positive steps that can go a long way toward preventing additional heart attacks.

Blood Pressure Tests

Did you know that high blood pressure is one of the most significant preventable causes of cardiovascular disease? If left untreated, high blood pressure, or **hypertension,** is dangerous. It enormously increases a person's chances of developing many other problems. Chief among these is stroke, caused by hemorrhage or blockage of an artery. High blood pressure also increases the risk of angina pectoris, heart attack, heart failure, and kidney failure. It is an extremely dangerous disorder that appears in most cases without an identifiable cause.

Your blood pressure is important to those who treat your heart disease. It will be checked many times while you are in the hospital. Fortunately, doctors and other health-care professionals take blood pressure measurements quickly and painlessly (refer to the box on page 27 for a discussion of how they do it).

Blood Tests

Blood drawn and analyzed when you were first admitted to the hospital told doctors something about how much damage your heart attack caused. As mentioned earlier, blood tests can measure enzymes released into the bloodstream by damaged heart tissue and estimate the severity of the heart attack.

Blood tests right after a heart attack are good for measuring blood cholesterol levels, as we've seen, and for other reasons, too. Blood analysis can also reveal previously undiagnosed conditions, such as diabetes mellitus. Diabetes, a known risk factor for heart attack, is a condition in which the body is unable to process sugar (glucose) adequately. People with diabetes mellitus lack a critical amount of the hormone **insulin** and/or cannot utilize insulin properly. Insulin makes the absorption of sugar by cells possible. Without it, glucose remains in the bloodstream and cells suffer; they are deprived of the energy glucose provides for cell maintenance and growth. People with diabetes are more prone to developing coronary heart disease and having heart attacks than others. They are also more likely to have heart attacks at a younger age.

There isn't a cure for diabetes, but there are ways to keep it under control. By identifying diabetes through a blood test, people who have it can adopt treatments and learn ways to modify their behavior for the maximum health benefit.

Cholesterol, a fatty substance circulating in the blood, has been called the "building block of heart disease." Yet a certain amount of cholesterol is important to health. Cholesterol is an important source of energy for cells. It is manufactured by our bodies. In fact, we make all the cholesterol our bodies need. But we also get cholesterol when we eat foods that come from animals. Too much cholesterol in the blood contributes to the development of atherosclerosis, and high blood cholesterol levels are known to be predictive of coronary heart disease. And, as we saw in Chapter One, coronary heart disease is a primary cause of heart attack (see pages 12–14).

When you are admitted to the hospital, your blood will be drawn and your serum cholesterol levels tested. You'll find out whether your levels are "too high" or "within an acceptable range." (No unacceptable low range for total blood cholesterol levels has been determined.) The medical term for high blood cholesterol levels is **hypercholesterolemia.** Many people develop this condition because they eat a diet rich in fats, especially animal fats, such as red meat, chicken with skin, whole-milk products, and the like. A much smaller number of people—about 5 percent of those with high cholesterol levels—have an inherited tendency toward high cholesterol levels. For these people, the problem is not only related to diet but also body chemistry. Generally this group is successfully treated with medicine. Drug therapy for hypercholesterolemia is discussed in Chapter Three.

Not all cholesterol is thought to be harmful. Two components of cholesterol circulate in the blood: **low-density lipoproteins (LDLs)** and **high-density lipoproteins (HDLs).** They serve different functions. LDLs, the "bad" cholesterol, transport cholesterol to the cells from the liver. HDLs, the "good" cholesterol, pick up excess cholesterol circulating in the blood and carry it back to the liver to be expelled from the body. It's important for doctors to know how much of each kind of cholesterol you carry in your bloodstream, as well as your total cholesterol level. That's why a blood cholesterol test reflects not one but three measurements: a total cholesterol score and the breakdown of that score into HDL and LDL components. These measurements are recorded as **mg/dl,** or milligrams of cholesterol per deciliters of blood.

The levels of LDL and HDL cholesterol in the bloodstream are more important indicators of atherosclerosis risk than total blood cholesterol level alone. Sometimes a high total blood cholesterol level, upon closer look, is revealed to be the result of an elevated HDL component. Because HDL cholesterol is considered protective against atherosclerosis, a person whose cholesterol levels fall in this configuration is not at high risk of developing coronary heart disease from this source. A high total blood cholesterol level with a high LDL component or a suppressed HDL component, on the other hand, paints a very different picture.

For more information on high blood cholesterol levels, see pages 133–140.

Family History

Has anyone else in your family tree had heart trouble, diabetes, or stroke? Your answer here contributes to your total risk profile, so your doctor is certain to ask you or a member of your family for information of this sort. If you don't know but can find out, try to do so. A family history of high blood pressure or high blood cholesterol levels is also of interest.

Speaking of family, bear in mind that family history has a past and a future. Statistically, because you had a heart attack, your children are more likely to have one. Be sure that your children take the matter of your heart attack personally! Whatever you learn about adopting healthful living habits and avoiding heart attack, your children must also "take to heart"—literally. Try to be a good example for them.

Your Personal Health Profile

Doctors don't rely completely on tests or family history to make an accurate diagnosis or prognosis. They also need to ask some questions about who you are and what your day-to-day life is like. This helps them determine how best to help you avoid another heart attack. They will want to know whether you smoke cigarettes, whether you exercise regularly, what your diet is, how old you are, and so forth. From the answers you give, a treatment strategy can be developed. This plan modifies or eliminates some risk factors. It also takes into account risk factors, such as age, that can't be changed. We'll look in greater depth at risk factors and their contribution to coronary heart disease and heart attack in Chapter Seven.

Complications

Complications can happen. If they do, the best place to be is in a CCU; after all, that's why these specialized hospital wards were developed in the first place. A heart attack challenges the body in a very punishing way; it isn't surprising that, in such a weakened condition, the body becomes susceptible to additional problems.

A heart attack is considered complicated if the patient develops any of a number of conditions. These include **arrhythmias** (erratic heart beats that are too fast or too slow), cardiac arrest, angina pectoris, heart failure, and cardiac emboli. A heart attack is also considered complicated when there is an inflammation of the membrane surrounding the heart (pericarditis) or if muscle in the heart ruptures. Another complication is the presence of other illnesses, such as high fever or pneumonia, that develop as a result of the initial heart attack. A patient who is considered at extremely high risk for another heart attack, perhaps because of his or her coronary history, may automatically be considered a "complicated" case. Some complications are more common than others, and some are more serious than others.

Complications usually mean a longer stay in the CCU; how much longer depends on the patient and the complication(s). Listed below are some of the most common complications, with a brief discussion of what is usually done to try to resolve them.

Abnormal Heart Rhythms

Heart attacks often compromise the heart's electrical system, creating disturbances in the way the heart beats, among other problems. In some cases, the heart beats erratically and too fast, a condition called **tachycardia.** A person with tachycardia may feel a pounding in the chest or other chest discomfort and shortness of breath. Sometimes the electrical "pathway" along the heart that paces its contraction is "obstructed" by a patch of infarcted tissue. The electrical impulse, which normally would make the heart tissue contract ("beat") at that point and then continue, is interrupted. In that case, the heartbeat becomes erratic and very slow, a condition called **bradycardia.**

To correct abnormal heart rhythms, doctors usually prescribe medicines that are administered intravenously or by mouth. If medication doesn't give the desired effect, or if the arrhythmia becomes life-threatening, doctors may turn to electric shock to correct the condition. (See page 101 for a more complete discussion of defibrillation.)

If the arrhythmia doesn't respond to medications but isn't life-threatening, doctors may decide to use **cardioversion** to nudge the heart back into a regular rhythm. Cardioversion, which involves the use of a machine called a **cardioverter,** supplies electric shocks to the heart at regular intervals. These electric shocks are milder than those used in defibrillation. Usually cardioversion is planned in advance by doctor and patient.

Sometimes a **pacemaker** is implanted below the patient's skin. A pacemaker acts something like a spark plug for the heart: it provides an electrical impulse at regular intervals to maintain a regular, steady heartbeat. Pacemakers are often temporary; they may be removed after the heart reestablishes its own rhythm. Sometimes they are permanent. We will look more closely at pacemakers in Chapter Four. Pacemakers are most often implanted to correct **bradycardia,** or very slow heartbeats.

Sometimes a heart develops a condition in which disordered electrical activity causes the ventricles of the heart to "lose control." The heart contracts in a rapid, unsynchronized way. When that happens, only a small amount of blood is pumped out of the heart, triggering cardiac arrest. **Ventricular fibrillation,** as it is known, is an extremely serious complication that requires immediate medical attention to prevent collapse and sudden death. Electric shock is applied to restore normal rhythm, which may be maintained with medicines thereafter. Monitoring devices, exercise tests, medicines, and pacemakers can prevent or treat this dangerous condition. Ventricular fibrillation is most likely—but not exclusively—to occur within four hours of the initial heart attack.

Heart Failure

Obviously, heart attack is tough on the heart. Tissue has been destroyed that can never be replaced. The heart not only must repair itself, replacing the dead tissue with scar tissue, but it must also learn to use less muscle mass to do the same pumping job. In most cases, the heart adapts in about eight weeks. Until then, however, it is susceptible to heart failure, a condition in which the weakened heart pumps less efficiently. Blood backs up into the lungs, making it hard for the person with heart failure to breathe.

Sometimes it's hard to tell whether a person has heart failure or not. In those cases, doctors are likely to diagnose the condition after measuring pressure in the heart chambers themselves. Using cardiac catheterization, they can take pressure readings and establish the presence or absence of heart failure. If heart failure is diagnosed, doctors can sometimes correct the problem adequately with drug therapy.

Blood Clots

As we discussed earlier, atherosclerosis plays a large part in most heart attacks. Heart attacks are usually caused when an embolism—a floating bit of atherosclerotic debris in the bloodstream—travels from a distant place in the circulatory system to block a coronary artery. If a heart attack victim gets to the hospital very soon after the event, doctors can administer special so-called clot-busting medications to help dissolve the clot and restore blood flow. After the initial crisis has passed, blood-thinning drugs (**antiplatelet** and **anticoagulant agents**) may be given to help prevent more clots from forming. That's because if a person has one embolism, he or she is very likely to generate more. It's a smart precaution. Once the patient is released from the hospital, that person probably will continue to take aspirin on a regular basis under a doctor's supervision. These and other medicines used to treat heart attacks are discussed more fully in Chapter Three.

Respiratory Complications

Some patients develop respiratory (breathing) complications, such as **pleurisy,** after a heart attack. Pleurisy affects the membrane sac holding the lungs in the chest. Its appearance is associated with the normal healing process following heart attack. In other instances, it is caused by blood clots in the lungs. Patients with pleurisy notice a sharp pain at the back of the chest or side that worsens each time they take a deep breath. Fortunately, pleurisy is not common, nor is it a serious complication in the majority of cases.

The heart sits in the **pericardium,** a membrane sac of its own. The pericardium can become inflamed after a heart attack, making every breath the patient takes painful. This condition, **pericarditis,** may appear months after a heart attack. It is treated successfully with drug therapy.

Moving On

How long a patient stays in the CCU varies from person to person. Someone who has not experienced complications from the heart attack may be transferred to a less restrictive ward, called a **step-down unit,** after two or three days in the CCU. Those with complications often stay in the CCU until the complications can be resolved.

The Step-Down Unit

Moving to the step-down unit is good news for everybody. For the heart attack survivor, it means a little more freedom and activity. For friends and family, it means expanded visiting hours and beginning preparations to bring the patient home. This floor tends to be brighter and less subdued than the CCU. The ratio of patients to nurses is higher. (There are more patients and fewer nurses than in the CCU.) Many patients "graduate" from a 12-lead EKG monitor to telemetric monitoring: EKG monitoring by radio signal. In telemetry the 12 leads on the chest are not needed, and the patient has more freedom of movement.

Typically, patients remain in this area of the hospital for five to nine days. By the fifth day in the hospital, heart attack patients are usually allowed to move around in their room. By the seventh day, they can take walks around the hospital floor (often pushing a mobile IV drip).

In the step-down unit, stabilized patients and their families have the chance to think more clearly about the implications of their experience. They begin to learn more about heart attack and its prevention. Patients also increase their exercise levels, while in general continuing to be monitored for potential setbacks.

Commonly, patients at this point have fears and doubts about, as well as hope for, their future as heart attack survivors. Patients in step-down units often find that talking with nurses and their fellow patients is both comforting and informative. They contemplate going home and making changes that will help them avoid another heart attack. Some of the material covered in this section occurs during rehabilitation—often in the step-down unit and even after the patient is released from the hospital. Let's take a closer look at this critical phase of the recovery process.

Charlie chuckled to himself. It was almost as if he were back in school again. Here he was, walking laps around the third floor of the hospital as if he were in some kind of rehab gym class! And later, he would meet with one of the nurses to go over exercise and diet plans he would follow after leaving the hospital. He liked to tease the nurses and ask whether he would be tested on it. They would laugh together, but Charlie knew it was serious. He planned to do everything he was taught to do. He was so happy to be feeling better again after that heart attack.

The step-down unit, he was surprised to find, was rather upbeat, all in all. There was a lot more freedom. But also, it was nice to have a place to catch your breath before going home and think about what had happened. Charlie thought a lot about his heart attack. His doctor and all the nurses had explained very clearly to him why they thought he had had one. He had learned a lot. Before the heart attack, he had never really thought regular medical checkups were necessary, for example. But he had learned that doctors might have caught his high blood pressure condition much earlier and put it under control if he had.

Same thing with eating. Charlie loved eating, but he wasn't accustomed to thinking about what he ate—he just did it. He always associated watching what you eat with slimming diets, and he wasn't interested in that. Now a dietitian was teaching him about low-fat, low-cholesterol foods. He was learning how to put them together into a healthful eating plan. It was interesting. And here in the step-down unit, he actually had time to absorb it. He knew he would take that new interest in nutrition home with him. Charlie liked the sense of control that gave him. His wife did, too. She visited every day and often sat with Charlie while the nurses talked with him about setting reasonable exercise and nutrition goals after he was discharged. They would work on it together. Charlie liked that, too. 🍎

A Learning Experience

In the step-down unit, cardiac rehabilitation begins. The first step is often education. Patients and family members learn to modify or eliminate personal risk factors for heart attack. They learn how to stop smoking and begin a sensible exercise program. They learn ways to reduce the amount of fat and sodium in their diet, lose weight, and control their blood pressure. If you will be following a long-term course of drug therapy, you will learn how to take the medicines and what side effects they might cause. As in the CCU, a very knowledgeable nursing staff works on this floor. Rely on your nurses for practical, proven information about heart attack recovery and risk factor modification. Ask questions! Helping patients learn about what happened to them when they had a heart attack, why, and how to deal with the aftereffects is an important part of the nurse's job.

Making Lifestyle Changes

If you smoke cigarettes, now is the time to quit and plan how you will overcome the temptations that are sure to present themselves in the days ahead. Now is the time to establish a new exercise routine based on your doctor's recommendations. You may be able to include your spouse, your children, or your friends in your exercise routine. Now is the time to learn how to eat more healthfully and enjoyably for the rest of your life. Now is the time to work with your doctor to bring high blood pressure, diabetes, and cholesterol levels under control, and to learn how to keep them that way.

Now is also the time to reflect on how you spent your time in the past and how you might spend it in the future. Were you a couch potato who thought heavy exercise meant rushing into the kitchen for a bag of chips and a soft drink during television commercials? Were your stress levels often out of control? Now you have an opportunity to make plans to change behaviors that need to be changed when you leave the hospital. If you're like most heart attack survivors, you really have a lot to think about before you go home.

Your rehabilitation team will meet with you and members of your family before you are discharged from the hospital. They will give you a customized plan for your rehabilitation that covers the areas we've just mentioned. This book can help you, too.

Taking an Exercise Test

Before being released from the hospital, you may undergo a supervised exercise test. Usually, an exercise test is performed on a treadmill. You'll be connected to an EKG monitor, then asked to step on the treadmill and walk at a leisurely pace. Slowly, the treadmill speeds up, forcing you—and your heart—to work a little harder to keep up. Once symptoms develop, such as changes on the EKG monitor or chest pains, the test is stopped. This test gives doctors a good idea of how well your heart is recovering from its ordeal and how much work it can tolerate. Six to eight weeks after discharge, you may be asked to take another exercise test under your doctor's supervision. This will establish your heart's maximum or near-maximum heart rate. It will also determine how much activity you should expect to engage in.

An exercise test is not appropriate for patients who have heart failure, persistent arrhythmias, or postinfarction angina. For most others, however, it is a perfectly safe and useful prognostic tool in the hospital setting.

Coping with Difficult Emotions

During that first week in the hospital, most heart attack survivors swing through an exhausting range of emotions. A life-threatening heart attack understandably knocks loose all sorts of questions and fears. You may feel disbelief, even denial, at the severity of your illness ("Why am I still in the hospital? I'm just fine!"). You may feel anger ("Why did this happen to me?"). Usually, you'll feel a good deal of anxiety, uncertainty, and vulnerability, too ("Am I going to be all right?"). Family members may share some or all of these emotions, though not necessarily at the same time as the heart attack survivor.

Emotions after heart attack vary in range and depth. While some survivors may seem crippled by their feelings following heart attack, others may want to race back to their usual routine, not looking back—even when their doctor recommends taking it easy for a while. Survivors who report feelings of depression, on the other hand, may be unable to stir themselves for any sort of activity, even when their doctor recommends it.

Fear

For some time after a heart attack, a nagging fear of death or pain is common. People who have had a heart attack may be very sensitive to the smallest twinges in their bodies for a while. They may complain that they feel very tired. (They may indeed be tired when they return home. They'll need time to readjust to normal activity after the inactivity of the hospital.) Some heart attack survivors develop an unnecessarily strong dependence on their spouse or another family member because they are afraid to exert themselves or be left alone. Every day that goes by uneventfully, however, helps restore survivors' confidence in their ability to "get back to normal" and lessens the sense of fear and anxiety.

Anger

Most heart attack survivors pass through a phase in which they are very angry about what happened to them. (Incidentally, close family members may pass through this phase also, feeling angry at their loved one for having had a heart attack and at least temporarily "rearranging" their lives.) The person who has survived a heart attack may lose patience with others easily—even those who are trying to help. A sense of injustice may prevail. Friends and family may notice remarks that seem bitter or resentful of others' good health. If a loved one makes angry comments, take them in stride as much as you can. Try to understand the feelings of the heart attack survivor. You might also gently remind him or her to avoid taking out those feelings on others.

Depression

Perhaps the most crippling emotion that heart attack survivors commonly experience is depression. They have the deep conviction that "life is over" or that "nothing will ever get better." Heart attack survivors suffering depression may be gripped by fears that they are "damaged" or no longer "like everyone else." While depression after a heart attack is quite common, in most cases it resolves itself within four months.

However, if signs of depression do not go away within that time or seem severe, find help. A family doctor, cardiologist, psychiatrist, nurse, psychologist, clergy member, favorite relative, or a support group can help you sort through your feelings and take action to dispel feelings of despair. If talking alone isn't enough, a psychiatrist or other physician may recommend a course of antidepressant drug therapy to help you through the crisis. For more information on depression, see Chapter Twelve.

Depression needs prompt treatment. Someone who is depressed will not be motivated to care for himself or herself. Nor is that person likely to work at rehabilitation, which is so important to recovery and prevention of further heart attacks. Signs of depression can be subtle. Often, the person who is depressed does not fully recognize that he or she is depressed. Do not ignore the signs of depression if you see them (see the box on page 265). Depression is a crippling disorder, but it can be treated with great success.

Finding Ways to Cope

If you or someone close to you has had a heart attack, expect mood swings. They will pass. Concentrate instead on resting and gathering your strength. It's likely that you won't feel good for the first two or three weeks after your heart attack. It's best to accept it, and try to keep in mind that you will start to feel better soon.

A positive attitude may be your best weapon against depression and other distressing emotions after a heart attack. It's natural, and even desirable, to think about your mortality in the wake of a life-threatening experience like heart attack. Self-reflection promotes positive lifestyle changes that can mean a healthier, longer life for you and your loved ones.

Some people cope by deciding that they were granted a "second chance at life." They vow to make the most of it! Knowing that their heart attack can't be "cured," they resolve to consider themselves "enhanced" by the experience and to learn all they can from it. The fact is, most people who survive a heart attack do lead lives that are very much like the lives they had before (with some positive lifestyle changes). Even those who are restricted from some activities because of a complicated heart attack may still focus on a number of others that remain possible.

Time resolves most feelings of fear, anxiety, anger, or depression. But if you have trouble coping with the way you feel, don't keep your worries to yourself. Talk them over with someone you trust. For many people, putting troubles "on the table" substantially reduces their power and makes them seem much less important or scary.

While the heart attack survivor faces certain doubts and fears, family members may face a few of their own. They too have found their lives challenged in a fundamental way, and it is important for them to address their feelings. Teenagers especially can feel guilty about the heart attack of a parent; they may believe that they are somehow responsible. Spouses may feel annoyed or angry that the heart attack "came at a particularly bad time." Then they feel guilty for having those thoughts. Complicated worries and emotions like these need to be aired. Keep the lines of communication open and discuss your fears with other family members. If the feelings don't resolve themselves in a reasonable amount of time, or become worse, counseling may help. Ask your doctor for a referral.

When caring for the heart attack survivor, family members may react in unexpected ways. Some may become depressed and be unable to help themselves or their loved one. Some may become overly protective, to the irritation of the heart attack survivor. Still others who would like to help the heart attack survivor during the recovery period may have hurt feelings if their well-meaning efforts are rebuffed.

How can misunderstandings such as these be avoided? It helps if everyone involved resolves to communicate openly and honestly with one another. Too often, "going it alone" backfires emotionally and creates misunderstandings that everyone regrets. Work on expressing how you feel and what you need or want from others, without accusations. Sometimes counselors can help facilitate this kind of dialogue among family members. Your doctor can provide you with a referral.

Taking Action

Perhaps the best way to dispel depression or anxiety is to do something positive for yourself or someone else. For heart attack survivors, time spent in the hospital and rehabilitation environment is perfect for planning recovery strategies. Having a heart attack and brushing against one's own mortality is frightening, of course, but it can also be a great motivator. Now is the time to "get real" about what happened when you had a heart attack—and why. Learn from your experience to treat your body better. Listen to its rhythms more carefully, too. Take small steps first, and give yourself a pat on the back frequently.

Preparing to Go Home

Much of what began in the step-down unit continues after you are discharged from the hospital. While in the hospital, you began to learn about your risk factors and ways to change some of them. You also learned ways to cope with your condition. This learning doesn't end when you leave the hospital. It continues during your rehabilitation and for a long time after.

CHAPTER THREE

Medications

Heart patients are reminded frequently during the course of their recovery to "follow doctor's directions." Very often the directions include taking certain medications in a certain way. Drug therapy can help you avoid future heart attacks and hospitalizations. Given in the right quantity and taken exactly as prescribed, medications can do wonders. They can help prevent complications and slow the progression of coronary heart disease. When taken haphazardly, however, medicines can be ineffective at least and life-threatening at worst.

In this chapter we'll look at the different kinds of medications prescribed for heart attack patients. We begin with medicines given during the acute stage of heart attack—in the hospital. We then look at drugs used to help prevent another heart attack. Finally we'll consider systems you can use to make following your own therapy schedule an easier, more natural part of your daily life.

We have listed generic names for many of the drugs used to treat heart attack patients. We've also listed some of the trade names under which these drugs are sold. We cannot list every drug that may be prescribed for you. Nor can we list all the trade names for these drugs. Remember that your doctor is your best source of information about your medications. Don't hesitate to ask him or her questions you have about your medications or any other aspect of your health care.

Most of us feel somewhat reluctant to take medicine. Sometimes in the short term the drug doesn't make us feel good. Doctors are concerned about drug therapy *adherence*. By that we mean taking medicine exactly when and as prescribed. When people understand how the drugs they take work and why taking them as prescribed is important, they're more likely to adhere to drug therapy. Your doctor (or nurse) will explain why you should take the medicines that have been prescribed for you. In this chapter we review some common side effects of and contraindications for many of these drugs. Your own doctor, however, will always have the last word on this subject. You must discuss possible side effects and cautions together.

Your doctor and nurses should also help you devise a system you can use to follow your program easily (see pages 82–85 for some ideas that may help you). In addition, you'll want to make a follow-up appointment or two with your doctor once you start a drug therapy program. At that time you'll have an opportunity to talk about any problems you may be having with the therapy and, if necessary, adjust it so that it will work better for you.

If you are under the care of more than one doctor, be sure that all of your doctors know about all of the medications you're taking. It's a good idea to make a list of all the prescription and over-the-counter drugs you take. Then give that list to each of your doctors. That way they can plan your complete medication therapy. They can also be on the lookout for drug interactions.

In the Hospital

As soon as a heart attack patient is admitted to the emergency room, medical personnel begin a number of very specialized activities. Medications are an important part of proper treatment. Medications help stabilize the patient's condition, but that's not all. Some drugs can help limit the damage done to the heart muscle, but only if they're administered within a very few hours of the onset of the heart attack. Many drugs are used to treat heart attack patients. The doctors decide in each case which medications are best for the patient. Let's take a brief look at several medications that are commonly used in the hospital.

Oxygen

Oxygen is a gas. It is necessary for life. As we've seen, the heart muscle plays a critical role in maintaining the circulation of oxygen throughout the body. It also makes it possible to expel waste gases from the tissues of the body. Many heart attack patients receive oxygen as soon as possible after heart attack symptoms appear. Oxygen is administered through a tube from an oxygen tank. The tube is inserted through the nostrils or attached to a mask placed over the mouth. In therapy, additional oxygen delivered under pressure eases the heart's workload somewhat. The heart doesn't have to pump quite as hard to distribute oxygen through the circulatory system to the tissues. Oxygen therapy may also help limit damage done to the heart muscle if it's administered soon (within hours) after infarction.

For some people, breathing becomes much more difficult after a severe heart attack. (Fortunately, this is not a common complication.) When this happens, oxygen is administered from a respirator through a mask or a tube placed in the windpipe. The respirator pumps oxygen into the lungs and maintains the circulation of oxygen throughout the body. It also promotes the exchange of gases in the lungs. The heart still pumps, too, of course, but its job is made easier by the respirator. That affords the heart a much-needed "rest" and a better chance to heal properly. The respirator may remain in place for several days or until the patient has regained enough strength to breathe on his own.

Complications of oxygen therapy can include problems with overinflation or underinflation of the lungs and oxygen mixtures that are too rich. These problems can be addressed quickly. Doctors do this by stopping the therapy or changing the oxygen mixture or the placement of the tube in the windpipe. Your doctor will carefully monitor the oxygen mixture you receive by taking blood samples at regular intervals during treatment.

Aspirin

For most people, aspirin is a pain reliever. However, doctors are learning that this common chemical compound has properties that make it an effective medication for heart patients, too. Even a small amount of aspirin—from less than one-half of a tablet to one tablet taken daily—

produces an important effect. When taken after thrombolytic (blood-clot-dissolving) therapy has been started, aspirin helps prevent newly dissolved clots from re-forming in the blood vessels.

Aspirin affects blood platelets. Platelets are blood components that circulate in the bloodstream. When damage to a vessel is detected, platelets collect protectively at the site so the vessel can begin to repair itself. In some people, this clotting activity works too well, and clots form when they're not needed. Aspirin interrupts the clotting mechanism and helps maintain the free flow of blood throughout the circulatory system.

Taken immediately after a heart attack for a number of days, aspirin is not likely to generate noticeable side effects. Patients may become slightly more susceptible to bleeding, but this susceptibility stops when the drug is stopped. For most heart attack patients, however, aspirin may be considered a long-term therapy. Long-term aspirin therapy to prevent additional heart attacks is discussed on pages 71–72.

Nitrates

Administered just after a heart attack, vasodilators (nitrates) are used to help improve the delivery of blood to heart tissue and to ease symptoms of heart failure. Doctors can help ease the heart's workload when it is in a vulnerable state by administering nitrates. Vasodilators work by relaxing the blood vessels so that the inside opening (the "lumen") gets bigger. More blood can pass through the vessel with less activity by the heart. In the process blood pressure is lowered. Erythrityl tetranitrate (Cardilate), isosorbide dinitrate (Isordil, Sorbitrate), and nitroglycerin (Nitrostat) are some vasodilators of the nitrate variety. Nitrates may be administered intravenously, orally, as an oral spray, in patches placed on the skin, or as an ointment rubbed into the skin. (If you use a patch, be sure to take it off for several hours every day so that you don't develop a tolerance to the drug.) Nitrates are not taken with food. If you're told to discontinue nitrates, you will be advised to do so gradually.

Aside from delivering more blood to the heart muscle and relieving angina, nitroglycerin and the other nitrates may not improve a person's chances of survival after a heart attack. People who suffer from anemia (low iron) should not take nitrates. Women who are pregnant or nursing or anyone with glaucoma should be supervised by a doctor and take special caution when taking this drug. Side effects that may occur include rapid heartbeat (tachycardia), headache, or very low blood pressure, causing dizziness.

Nitroglycerin may be prescribed for long-term therapy after a heart attack and is discussed later in this chapter (see page 78).

Painkillers

A heart attack is frequently painful. To relieve chest pain, a nitroglycerin tablet may be taken under the tongue. If the pain persists, your doctor may prescribe small doses of morphine sulfate, a narcotic derived from the opium poppy and given intravenously. These small doses may be repeated every 15 minutes until the pain subsides. Tranquilizers, such as those discussed on page 70, are also effective as painkillers in some situations.

Side effects associated with morphine are dose related. Too much morphine has serious physical and behavioral consequences, such as depressed breathing. The drug is habit-forming when taken for too long. However, in the controlled atmosphere of the hospital, dosages are kept well below such levels.

Thrombolytic Agents

Thrombolytic agents break up blood clots. Blood clots lodged in the coronary arteries cause most heart attacks. When the clots have been dissolved, oxygenated blood flow through the affected artery can be restored, and heart muscle below the blockage may yet be saved. However, these drugs must be administered in the first few hours after a heart attack. They are most effective when given during the first hour. After that first hour the critical advantage of these drugs diminishes. A little bit of heart muscle dies with every 15-minute period that passes after the first hour. The medications still work somewhat when given within the first six hours after a heart attack, but some heart muscle will have been irreversibly damaged. The effectiveness of these drugs after the first six hours is vastly diminished. That's why it's so important to go to a hospital as quickly as possible. If these drugs are administered soon after symptoms start, some heart muscle that might otherwise die without oxygenated blood can still be saved. *Bottom line:* The earlier that treatment with a thrombolytic drug is started after a heart attack, the more effective it is. That means that there is likely to be *less permanent damage* to the heart than there might have been if treatment were delayed.

Anisoylated plasminogen streptokinase activator complex, also called APSAC or anistreplase (Eminase); recombinant tissue-type plasminogen activator (rt-PA) (Activase); and streptokinase (Streptase, Kabikinase) are all thrombolytic agents. These drugs are injected intravenously.

The most serious complication associated with thrombolytic agents is excessive bleeding. A small number of patients who receive a thrombolytic drug for heart attack will experience some spontaneous bleeding. Such bleeding is most serious in the brain (brain hemorrhage). People who tend to bleed easily or who have a history of cerebrovascular disease, uncontrolled high blood pressure, recent head or spine injury, or recent surgery are usually not candidates for thrombolytic therapy. Patients who are more than 70 years old may not be candidates either, depending on the judgment of their doctor. Statistics show that older people tend to have more complications as a result of thrombolytic therapy than younger patients do.

Unlike the other thrombolytic agents, streptokinase is usually given to a patient just once. That's because many people develop an allergic reaction to it that includes chills, rash, and a fever. Sometimes with a second injection a very severe and potentially fatal allergic reaction, anaphylaxis, can occur. In anaphylaxis the body goes into shock. All of these allergic complications are reversed when the medication is stopped.

Anticoagulant Drugs

Anticoagulants work by inhibiting the ability of blood to clot, or coagulate. Anticoagulants are not designed to dissolve existing blood clots. Rather, they are given to prevent new clots from forming or to prevent existing clots from getting larger. That helps prevent additional heart attacks. Anticoagulants are frequently prescribed for people who have received artificial heart valves. They are also prescribed after a heart attack for patients in whom blood tends to pool in the heart chambers or leg veins, creating emboli. (Emboli are loose blood clots that travel throughout the body until they lodge in an artery that is too small to allow them to go further. This may be in the lungs, the brain, or the heart.)

The most common anticoagulant drugs are heparin and warfarin. Heparin is a faster acting preparation. It is only administered intravenously to patients in the hospital and only for the first several days after a heart attack. When heparin is stopped, some doctors give their patients warfarin, which is taken orally for weeks, months, or indefinitely thereafter. (One trade name for warfarin is Coumadin.)

Not all doctors routinely prescribe anticoagulant therapy after a heart attack, however. Some are not sure that the side effects are worth the potential protection the drug can provide. Headaches, joint pain, abdominal pain, and paralysis are some reported side effects. The most serious side effect of anticoagulant therapy is an increased risk of bleeding, so the drug is always prescribed very carefully. Patients on anticoagulant therapy need to be extra careful not to bruise or otherwise injure themselves. If bleeding does not stop when pressure is applied to the wound, patients should go directly to the emergency room for help. If you take warfarin, regular blood tests are a must, so that your doctor can be sure that the prescribed dosage of warfarin continues to be appropriate for you.

People with uncontrolled high blood pressure and kidney or liver disease should not be placed on warfarin therapy. Women who are pregnant or nursing and people who have heart failure must be monitored very carefully if they are on warfarin therapy. Aspirin (another anticlotting drug) and penicillin should be avoided when taking warfarin unless your doctor indicates otherwise.

Drugs for Arrhythmias

People who have had a heart attack sometimes develop problems associated with the heart's electrical system, which regulates the heartbeat. The heart doesn't pump effectively. *Tachycardia* is the medical term for a heartbeat that's too fast. *Bradycardia* is the term for a heartbeat that's too slow. *Ventricular fibrillation*, which can be life threatening, is an example of a severe cardiac arrhythmia. Ventricular fibrillation is the rapid, uncontrolled contraction of the left ventricle. It is most likely to occur in the first few days after a heart attack.

Hospital staff members are always alert for signs of cardiac arrhythmia in heart attack patients. They are prepared to take action if one occurs. Drug therapy is one of the methods used to treat cardiac arrhythmias and steady the heartbeat. (The other two methods are defibrillation, or electric shock therapy, and implantation of a cardiac pacemaker).

Drugs used to treat cardiac arrhythmias include amiodarone (Cordarone), atropine, bretylium, disopyramide (Norpace), lidocaine (Xylocaine), procainamide (Procan), propafenone (Rythmol), propranolol (Inderal), quinidine (many trade names), and sotalol (Betapace). They may be taken orally on an empty stomach, and they may be administered alone or in some combination to correct an erratic heartbeat.

Side effects vary, depending on the individual drug taken. Some people experience stomach distress (nausea, vomiting, or diarrhea), drowsiness, confusion, fever, rash, aching joints, insomnia, and sometimes dizziness. Heart failure can be a side effect. If you have swollen feet and ankles or trouble breathing, see your doctor immediately. Women who are pregnant or nursing should not take these drugs.

Beta-blockers

Beta-blockers are frequently given intravenously right after a heart attack. Beta-blockers slow down the heart rate. That decreases the work of pumping blood through the circulatory system ("cardiac output"). By helping the heart to "take it easy," beta-blockers afford the heart a better opportunity to heal itself. Administration of beta-blockers can also help prevent ventricular fibrillation, a potentially serious complication.

Beta-blockers are also frequently administered as part of long-term therapy for high blood pressure. Long-term therapy involving beta-blockers is discussed later in this chapter (see page 74). Beta-blockers include atenolol (Tenormin), metoprolol (Lopressor), nadolol, pindolol (Visken), propranolol (Inderal), and timolol (Blocadren).

Beta-blockers can cause side effects in some people. They can lead to higher triglyceride levels and lower levels of HDL cholesterol, the "good" cholesterol. Bradycardia, an abnormally slow heart rate, may develop. Asthma may develop in those who are predisposed to it. Electrical conduction problems in the heart can also appear. Emotional upsets, including nightmares and feelings of confusion or excitement, are rare side effects. Fatigue and impotence have also been documented. Rarely, patients on beta-blocker therapy, especially women, exhibit Raynaud's phenomenon, in which the fingertips become very white and cold. People who may not be good candidates for beta-blocker therapy include those with severe congestion in the lungs and some persons with insulin-dependent diabetes or asthma. Pregnant or nursing women should not take beta-blockers.

ACE Inhibitors

Angiotensin-converting enzyme (ACE) inhibitors are a new class of drugs used to manage and prevent heart failure and in some cases to control high blood pressure. ACE inhibitors reduce the resistance against which the heart beats. That makes them ideal for treating certain forms of heart failure. They are specifically designed to relieve a condition called left ventricular systolic dysfunction. In this condition the main pumping chamber of the heart fails to pump properly. This can result in heart failure. ACE inhibitors are indicated for stable heart attack patients with diminished pumping function or symptoms of heart failure. Use of ACE inhibitors may extend the lives of these patients. The medication may be continued indefinitely.

ACE inhibitors are taken one to three times a day (depending on the drug) on an empty stomach. Side effects are relatively uncommon and mild when they do appear but include cough, rash, swelling of the feet or stomach area, loss of taste, and headache. Women who are pregnant or nursing shouldn't take ACE inhibitors. Occasionally, taking ACE inhibitors causes very low blood pressure. This effect is remedied by discontinuing the drug. Trade names for ACE inhibitors include Altace, Capoten, Lotensin, Monopril, Prinivil, Vasotec, and Zestril.

Diuretics

Heart failure sometimes develops in the days or weeks following a heart attack. The heart pumps blood with difficulty and less effectively. Fluids collect in the lungs and elsewhere in the body. The person who has this condition has a difficult time breathing. The legs and ankles may swell also.

Diuretics can help rid the body of those excess fluids through urination. These drugs are also used to help control hypertension. Commonly prescribed diuretics include bumetanide (Bumex), chlorthalidone (Hygroton), chlorothiazide (Diuril), furosemide (Lasix), hydrochlorothiazide (HydroDIRUIL, Esidrix), spironolactone (Aldactone), and triamterene (Dyrenium). These medications are usually administered as tablets. In an emergency they may be given intravenously.

Unfortunately, when diuretics rid the body of excess fluids, potassium, an element needed for good health, is also removed. This can produce a side effect called **hypokalemia.** This is sometimes remedied by eating foods high in potassium. Potassium is found in oranges, grapefruit, melons, dried fruit, cabbage, bananas, apricots, raisins, potatoes, tomatoes, meats, poultry, and fish.

If potassium deficiency persists, your doctor may prescribe a potassium supplement. Trade names for some of these supplements are K-Lor, K-Lyte, and Slow-K. They are usually available in liquid or powder form and may be mixed with water or juice.

Other side effects associated with diuretics include muscle cramps and weakness, poor appetite, and sometimes swelling in the joints. Potassium supplements can also produce side effects, including nausea, vomiting, heartburn, and poor appetite.

If you are taking diuretics, do not drink alcoholic beverages unless your doctor gives you permission. Diuretic drugs may be taken with food or milk to lessen the probability of stomach irritation. Women who are pregnant should not take some types of diuretics. Check with your doctor if you may be pregnant. Women who are nursing should not ordinarily receive diuretic therapy at all.

Tranquilizers

Tranquilizers can be appropriate for patients who have just undergone the trauma of a heart attack. As prescribed, mild sedatives can help relieve anxiety and pain. Diazepam (Valium) and lorazepam (Xanax) are typical choices.

Tranquilizers are generally safe when taken as directed. Side effects from these drugs are related to dosage. If they are abused through overuse, they are highly habit-forming and can have bad effects on behavior. However, tranquilizers prescribed after a heart attack are used only for very short, specific periods in the hospital. Problems of abuse in this situation are less likely.

After the Hospital: Medicines to Prevent Another Heart Attack

After they leave the hospital, heart attack survivors frequently take a number of medications. You may continue to take some medications that you took in the hospital. You may also start new medications. In this section we review some of the more common drug therapies that help heart patients after they leave the hospital. Some of these are taken for a few weeks or months. Others are taken indefinitely. The combination of drugs prescribed for you may need some adjustment in the coming months. It may take some time to make sure that dosages are right and cause the fewest side effects possible.

It's important to treat your medications with care and respect. Store them in an appropriate place where you won't forget to take them. Take your medications with you if you are traveling. Be sure you know the names and dosages of all the medications you've been asked to take. If you can't remember this information, write it down on a sheet of paper that you can fold and carry in your purse or wallet. Never suppose that if one pill is good, then two pills must be better—it's not true. Never try someone else's medications. Taking drugs that haven't been prescribed for you is dangerous. Take medications only as prescribed. If you have questions, call your doctor or talk with your pharmacist.

If you have a hard time following your doctor's directions for any reason, talk it over with him or her. There may be a way to help you improve your adherence to the program. If you're having trouble with side effects, your doctor may be able to substitute another drug of the same type that you can tolerate better. After all, everyone is different. Don't be discouraged if it takes you some time to become comfortable with the regimen. But don't make any changes on your own—work them out *only* under the supervision of your doctor. Let's take a closer look at some of the medications your doctor may prescribe for you.

Antiplatelet Agents

As mentioned earlier, aspirin helps prevent excessive blood platelet clumping. Doctors often start their patients on aspirin therapy while they are still in the hospital (see pages 62–63). In fact, most people who have had a heart attack continue to take a small daily dose of aspirin as an antiplatelet agent after they go home. Some drug trials are showing that antiplatelet therapy can help prevent heart attacks from recurring. When they do recur, patients on antiplatelet therapy have lower mortality rates. Other trials have shown that taking aspirin can help prevent new atherosclerotic lesions from forming in the arteries. These lesions might have led to more heart attacks. Aspirin may be prescribed for people with unstable angina pectoris.

Aspirin is not a miracle drug, however. It's easy to fall into the trap of thinking that "an aspirin a day will take my heart attack away." Unfortunately, life isn't that easy. Better health is really something you earn—it takes time and effort. Taking an aspirin every day does not cure the basic problem of coronary heart disease. You also need to address underlying risk factors. These include smoking, high blood cholesterol, high blood pressure, and physical inactivity. It is the combination of these things that will make it possible for you to take back some control over CHD.

That said, aspirin is considered extremely beneficial for those who can take it. It is inexpensive and has relatively few side effects. The most important side effect is bleeding and a slightly increased risk of hemorrhagic stroke. Aspirin should be taken with food and water. Do not take ibuprofen (Advil or Nuprin) without your doctor's permission while you're on aspirin therapy. If you drink alcoholic beverages, check with your doctor about whether you can continue to do so with this medication. He or she may suggest you limit your alcohol intake while you're taking aspirin. Women who are pregnant should take aspirin only under the direct supervision of their doctor.

So far, doctors are not in complete agreement as to what the proper daily dose of aspirin should be. However, they do agree that the proper dose should be the least possible amount to achieve the desired effect. This is *usually* in the range of 80 to 325 milligrams per day. One problem with determining the correct dosage is that the trials completed to date have all involved men only. However, a large trial now under way will observe the effect of aspirin therapy on women's health. The results of that trial are still a few years away. Your doctor will decide what the proper dosage of aspirin for you might be, based on your risk profile for heart attack and stroke.

Blood Pressure-Lowering Drugs

Controlling high blood pressure helps protect against heart attack, stroke, and heart failure. Antihypertensive drugs can help control blood pressure when diet and exercise alone have not succeeded. Most people on antihypertensive therapy start with either diuretics or beta-blockers. These proven medications can reduce mortality rates associated with heart disease. Usually a doctor will prescribe one or the other initially. However, if high blood pressure readings persist, a combination of antihypertensive drugs may be prescribed along with a diet and exercise program. Be patient. It may take several months to find the therapy program that both controls high blood pressure and avoids as many side effects as possible.

Diuretics
We discussed diuretics on page 69 in association with treatment for heart failure, including side effects and dosages. Diuretics lower blood pressure by causing the body to rid itself of excess fluids and sodium through urination. In treatment of high blood pressure, diuretics are versatile. If the desired effects are not achieved with diuretics alone, in combination they may enhance the effect of other blood pressure medications. Common trade names for diuretics include Aldactone, Bumex, Diuril, Lasix, Lozol, and Midamor.

Beta-blockers

Beta-blockers were discussed earlier in this chapter in association with therapy for cardiac arrhythmias (see pages 67–68). They are sometimes used to treat angina pectoris (see page 68). They are prescribed for people with high blood pressure because they decrease the heart rate and cardiac output, which lowers blood pressure. There are minor variations in the way that beta-blockers work, but they all have the same kinds of side effects, which were described in the earlier section. People with heart failure should take a different type of drug to lower blood pressure, if necessary.

ACE Inhibitors

ACE inhibitors, a newer class of drugs, were discussed earlier (see page 68). These drugs are also used to treat high blood pressure, but they have not been tested in long-term controlled clinical trials. Doctors tend to prescribe ACE inhibitors to treat high blood pressure only when diuretics and beta-blockers don't work or are not tolerated by the patient. ACE inhibitors work to lower blood pressure by decreasing the resistance of the blood vessels. ACE inhibitors are sometimes combined with a diuretic.

Calcium Channel Blockers

Calcium channel blockers, also known as "calcium antagonists," work by interrupting the movement of calcium into heart and vessel tissue. Doctors are evaluating the use of these drugs in patients with heart disease. For more information, check with your health-care provider.

Lipid- and Cholesterol-Lowering Drugs

High blood cholesterol is a major modifiable risk factor for heart disease. By lowering your blood cholesterol level, you can help your arteries and yourself. A healthful, low-fat diet is an important way to control your cholesterol levels. The American Heart Association recommends that *less than* 30 percent of your total calories should come from fat. For people with evidence of cardiovascular disease, we recommend that less than 7 percent of your total daily calories should come from saturated fat. Remember that saturated fat can raise your blood cholesterol more than anything else you eat. We also recommend that if you have evidence of cardiovascular disease, you limit your consumption of cholesterol to less than 200 milligrams per day (see Chapter Nine on nutrition).

However, for most people with coronary heart disease, diet is not enough. Medications are available that can help bring down stubbornly high blood cholesterol levels and get triglycerides (blood fats) under control. Anyone who takes medications to lower cholesterol levels must follow a proper diet as well. Drugs alone are not the answer. Better eating habits and a reasonable exercise program will help maximize the effects of these drugs.

A variety of medications that can help lower blood cholesterol levels are available. They may be prescribed individually or in combination with other drugs. They work in a number of ways.

Statins
Statins are a relatively new class of drugs for treating high blood cholesterol levels. They work by interrupting the formation of cholesterol in the liver. When that happens, the liver has to collect cholesterol from the circulating blood. It produces more LDL receptors for that purpose. LDL receptors take LDL cholesterol out of the bloodstream and into the liver to be broken into other components and eventually eliminated.

This class of drugs causes a major drop in LDL cholesterol levels: from 25 to 45 percent (and a 5 to 10 percent rise in HDL cholesterol levels). Relatively small dosages are needed for this effect, which is another advantage. The drug is taken in tablet form. At first it is taken once a day, usually in the evening. If necessary, dosing may increase to twice a day over a period of months.

So far, reports of side effects with these drugs have been minimal. However, this is still a relatively new class of drugs (they have been available for six to eight years). Doctors are still measuring the long-term effects of statins. A few people have reported gastrointestinal discomfort. Some people have developed liver problems that can be reversed if the drug is stopped. Slight muscle damage in some people may cause enzymes to get into the bloodstream. Sore muscles are a tip-off to this side effect. If you take these drugs and develop sore muscles, contact your doctor immediately. If you don't stop taking the medication, you could damage your muscles and kidneys.

Statins appear to have a very impressive success rate. Some studies have shown a lower number of heart attacks and deaths from heart attack among patients who took statins. They are often the drug of first choice for patients with high cholesterol who have had a heart attack.

Resins

Resins are also called bile acid-binding drugs. This type of drug works in the intestines, where it binds with bile acids, which carry cholesterol. This promotes increased disposal of cholesterol. That in turn reduces the liver cholesterol content. The liver then makes more LDL receptors, which are responsible for removing LDL cholesterol from the bloodstream. Your cholesterol level falls.

There are two kinds of medications in this class: colestipol (Colestid) and cholestyramine (Questran). These drugs lower cholesterol levels from 15 to 30 percent in most people who take them. They do not lower triglyceride levels. In fact, they may raise those levels, so they're not indicated for people who have very high triglyceride levels already. The drugs are usually taken in powder form at least twice a day, usually mixed with water, juice, or applesauce. Side effects may include stomach distress, constipation, nausea, gas, and a feeling of fullness. Constipation may be a problem because bile acids are a natural laxative. To combat this side effect, your doctor may recommend you eat more dietary fiber or take a fiber supplement such as psyllium. However, don't use regular laxatives because they may have side effects if used for any length of time.

Nicotinic Acid

This drug works in the liver by affecting the production of blood fats. Nicotinic acid is used to lower triglycerides, lower LDL cholesterol, and raise HDL (the "good" cholesterol). LDL cholesterol levels drop 15 to 30 percent on average among those who take nicotinic acid. HDL levels rise 10 to 15 percent.

Nicotinic acid is taken in tablet form after meals (not on an empty stomach). One problem with this medication is the uncomfortable side effects it may produce, including flushing of the skin, itching, and skin rash. For that reason, doctors typically prescribe it in low doses at first. Patients gradually increase the amount taken daily as their tolerance increases. (Flushing of the skin can sometimes be relieved if aspirin is taken half an hour before nicotinic acid is taken. The effect may also disappear by itself after you have taken the drug for a few weeks.) Gastrointestinal pain or discomfort can also be a problem. The drug adversely affects the liver in some people, in which case it must be discontinued. People who have gout or are diabetic should not take nicotinic acid. Because of possible side effects, people who are on this type of therapy are monitored regularly with blood tests. Nicotinic acid is available in long-acting and short-acting preparations. The long-acting ones are often better tolerated but may not be as effective as the shorter acting ones. Trade names for nicotinic acid are Niacinol, Niacin-Time, and Nicolar. Health food stores and other retail outlets sell a product called nicotinamide over the counter. That is *not* the same as nicotinic acid and will *not* have the same effect.

Gemfibrozil

This drug lowers blood fats, but scientists are still not entirely sure how. Gemfibrozil (Lopid) also raises HDL cholesterol levels by 8 to 15 percent. LDL cholesterol is lowered only moderately. Gemfibrozil is taken in tablet form, usually before breakfast and dinner.

Side effects are relatively few. There may be some gastrointestinal discomfort or diarrhea. Gemfibrozil enhances the effects of any anticoagulant (blood-thinning) drugs you may be taking as well. In some people, this drug affects liver function. People who have gall bladder disease should not take this drug because it increases the likelihood of gallstones.

Clofibrate

Clofibrate (Atromid-S) raises the HDL cholesterol levels of those taking it, on average, 10 to 15 percent. It also lowers triglyceride levels. This medication works in a way that is similar to gemfibrozil. Side effects are few but may include nausea and vomiting. In a clinical trial in which clofibrate was carefully monitored in a large group of people, researchers found evidence of side effects that may be more troublesome. In the World Health Organization Clofibrate Trial, non–heart-related deaths seemed to be slightly higher for those treated with clofibrate than for those who were not treated with it. However, since then, the actual occurrence of serious side effects has not been proven. Still, on the basis of that trial, doctors prescribe clofibrate less often to treat high blood cholesterol levels.

Probucol

Probucol (Lorelco) is sometimes used to lower LDL cholesterol levels. A problem with this drug is that it can also lower levels of HDL cholesterol. Some researchers think that this medication may help reduce CHD risk in another way, although this is only a theory now. Probucol is an antioxidant, and antioxidants are known to interrupt the formation of foam cells in blood vessels. Foam cells are an important component of the atherosclerotic process in the arteries. This potential benefit of probucol still must be verified by clinical tests, however. Potential long-term side effects have not been identified yet, either.

Probucol is taken in tablet form twice a day, with morning and evening meals. Side effects identified with this medication are few and infrequent. They include gastrointestinal distress (nausea, diarrhea, abdominal pain, flatulence, and vomiting). Rarely, heart rhythm disturbances develop. People who have these arrhythmias or who are given other drugs that may cause them should not be given probucol. To be safe, electrocardiographic monitoring should be performed before and periodically during the course of therapy.

Antianginals

Many persons who suffer heart attacks have been previously diagnosed as having angina pectoris, chest pain triggered by exertion. In angina pectoris the heart needs more oxygenated blood in order to increase the heart rate adequately. However, it cannot get enough oxygenated blood from arteries that have been narrowed by atherosclerosis. Chest pain follows.

A number of drugs may be prescribed to prevent the pain of angina pectoris. Different drugs used for this purpose achieve the same end through different means. These medications are loosely grouped as "antianginals."

We discussed nitrates earlier in this chapter (see pages 63–64). Nitroglycerin is an example of one of the most common nitrates used to treat angina symptoms. Nitrates dilate blood vessels and reduce blood pressure. That eases the heart's workload and reduces the severity and frequency of angina symptoms. Beta-blockers, which were also discussed earlier in this chapter (see pages 67–68), slow the heart rate and decrease blood pressure. Beta-blockers may be prescribed for high blood pressure and arrhythmias, too. Calcium channel blockers, which were discussed on page 73, are also used in some patients to help control angina symptoms. Nitrates, beta-blockers, and calcium channel blockers are frequently prescribed as long-term therapy. Review the common side effects and precautions for these drugs on pages 64, 68, and 73.

Anticoagulant Drugs

Anticoagulant medications, sometimes called "blood thinners," prevent formation of clots that can lead to heart attack or stroke. We discussed these drugs earlier in the chapter (see pages 65–66).

Warfarin (Coumadin) delays blood clotting. It does this by interfering with clotting factors in the blood. It may take almost a week for warfarin to exert its full effect. The correct dosage will vary among patients. Some people take warfarin for one to three months. Sometimes, however, warfarin therapy is continued indefinitely. This is particularly true for patients who can't take aspirin.

Hemorrhage is the most serious potential side effect of warfarin therapy. Watch out for excessive bleeding from cuts, easy bruising, bleeding gums, nose bleeds, red urine, or a red or black stool. Contact your doctor if you notice any of these symptoms to a degree that is unusual for you. Your doctor will give you a blood test periodically to make sure that the dosage remains correct for you. Women who are pregnant should not take this drug. Other medications, including aspirin, sleeping pills, and antibiotics may interact with this drug, changing its effect. Discuss drinking alcoholic beverages and eating foods high in vitamin K (leafy green vegetables) with your doctor when you start this therapy.

ACE Inhibitors

This new class of drugs was discussed earlier in this chapter (see page 68). These drugs are used to treat a condition in which the main pumping chamber of the heart does not function properly. Use of ACE inhibitors may extend the lives of these patients. ACE inhibitors are also used to correct symptoms of heart failure and to lower blood pressure (see page 68). If you have any of these conditions, your doctor may decide you need to take this medication indefinitely.

Drugs for Arrhythmias

People who have had a heart attack sometimes develop problems associated with the heart's electrical system, which regulates the heartbeat. The heart's pumping action is not effective. Drugs used to treat cardiac arrhythmias in the hospital were discussed earlier in this chapter (see page 67). Digitalis compounds and beta-blockers may be used to treat or prevent arrhythmias after the patient is released from the hospital.

Digitalis Compounds

Digitalis drugs are used to treat heart failure. This kind of medication stimulates the heart's pumping action. It also helps correct fast, irregular heartbeats by slowing down the conduction of electrical impulses across the heart. Some common trade names for digitalis include Crystodigin and Lanoxin.

Digitalis is usually taken in pill form. At first it is administered in small doses, slowly, over approximately three days. During that time the concentration of the drug in the blood gradually rises. Once the desired level is reached, the medication is taken once a day in a maintenance dose, to keep the concentration of the drug in the blood at a steady level.

Digitalis has been used to treat heart failure for a long time. It remains overall a safe, effective treatment. Side effects associated with too much digitalis can be very serious, however. Digitalis can build up in the blood to dangerous levels. You will need to be very careful to take it as prescribed. Your doctor will monitor you closely. You should not use nonprescription antacids or cold remedies unless your doctor gives you permission on a case-by-case basis. Symptoms of digitalis poisoning include nausea and vomiting, headache, loss of appetite, changes in vision (halos and changes in color perceptions), and disorientation.

Digitalis can cause cardiac arrhythmias if the correct dosage isn't taken. This may be accelerated if the potassium level of the blood is low. If you are taking diuretics, you may be asked to eat foods rich in potassium (such as oranges, grapefruit, melons, dried fruit, cabbage, bananas, apricots, raisins, potatoes, tomatoes, meats, poultry, and fish.) Or you may need to take a potassium supplement. If digitalis has caused cardiac arrhythmias, your doctor may instruct you to stop taking it. That will usually stop the side effects.

Beta-blockers
Beta-blockers, which were discussed earlier in this chapter (see pages 67–68), slow the heart rate and decrease blood pressure. They may be prescribed for arrhythmias. Beta-blockers can help prevent ventricular fibrillation, a potentially serious complication. Review the common side effects and precautions for these drugs on page 68.

Estrogen Replacement Therapy

It has long been observed that women tend to develop coronary heart disease about 10 to 15 years later in life than men do. Noticeably, women's incidence of heart disease starts to climb in the sixth and seventh decades—after menopause. A link has been drawn between low incidence of heart disease and a potentially protective effect of estrogen. That link is still being investigated today. Estrogen is a naturally occurring hormone produced in the ovaries. After menopause (or after complete hysterectomy—surgical menopause), women's estrogen levels drop.

In the recent past many women and their doctors hesitated to use estrogen replacement therapy as a means of protecting against heart disease. That may have been because of the history of estrogen medications. In the 1960s, when birth control pills were first formulated, women who took them were at greater risk of heart attack and stroke. Birth control pills contained high estrogen levels at that time.

Today the amount of estrogen used in birth control pills and estrogen replacement therapy is much lower than it used to be. In addition, progestin, another hormone, has been added in small quantities to these medications. Progestin appears to help reduce the blood clotting effect of estrogen. Results of recent studies indicate that lower estrogen dosages appear to exert a powerful protective effect on risk factors for heart disease. Several studies have found that postmenopausal women taking estrogen replacement therapy have up to 50 percent less risk of developing CHD. Other studies have indicated that estrogen replacement therapy appears to have an even more powerful effect in women with CHD. Women with CHD who take estrogen replacement therapy seem to fare better than other women with CHD who do not take the medication.

Estrogen affects blood lipid levels. In animals it has been shown to help prevent lipids from attaching to blood vessel walls. Estrogen medications reduce LDL cholesterol levels in women by approximately 15 percent, and they raise HDL cholesterol levels by about the same percentage.

Unfortunately, these results are not definitive because the studies from which they were drawn did not meet exact experimental requirements. The studies did not answer some important questions about the connection between estrogen replacement therapy and women's health. For example, it may have been that many women in these studies were already more health-conscious and therefore at a lower risk of developing CHD. No one knows. For that reason, it is difficult to claim that estrogen replacement therapy is a good idea for every woman who has gone through menopause. However, it's best to take an individualized approach to the question with your own doctor. Together you can consider the possible side effects of this type of therapy. You will then be able to reach a decision that you can be comfortable with. Your age, whether you smoke, and a doctor's evaluation of your medical history may all be factors that will help determine the best course of action.

So far, the benefits of estrogen replacement therapy appear clear for many menopausal women. This form of therapy may be good for you if you suffer from symptoms of menopause or to help avoid osteoporosis, a condition in which bones become brittle and porous and are more prone to fractures. It may also help lower your cholesterol levels. However, side effects are possible, as they are with any medication. Women who take estrogens but have not had a hysterectomy have shown a higher risk of developing uterine cancer. (Researchers think that adding progestin to the medication may lower the risk of uterine cancer, but it hasn't been proven yet.) Estrogen can also cause changes in vaginal bleeding patterns, tender breasts, nausea, bloating, headaches, dizziness, and depression, among other effects. This form of therapy is not recommended if you are pregnant, if you have liver or kidney disease, or if you have a history of uterine cancer.

When Taking Any Medication

Medications for treating heart attack and underlying heart disease can do much to brighten the recovery outlook for most heart patients. But to work, these drugs often require a certain amount of commitment from you.

Discuss with your doctor all the drugs you take. Be sure you understand everything you're told about their desired effects and possible side effects, which you should be able to recognize. Also be sure you understand the medication schedule for each. Follow your doctor's instructions for taking the medications exactly as you are told. Don't play fast and loose with medications. They are doing an important, very complicated job for you, and they only work under prescribed conditions. You change those conditions if you miss a dose here and there or take less at some times and more at others, or combine them with other drugs in an unsupervised way. If you do any of these things, you run the risk of ruining their effectiveness or worse.

Bring a notepad when you visit your doctor for a checkup. Write down questions you have about your medications or other concerns. Then write down the answers you receive. If you forget to ask a question while you're with your doctor, don't give up. Ask to speak with him or her for a moment before you leave.

❦ *The alarm clock rang. Charles got out of bed and padded into the bathroom. A note was taped to the mirror: "Order medicines today!" On the first of the month Charles regularly ordered refills on his medication. Tomorrow he would pick up the supplies he needed from the pharmacist.*

Charles, a 70-year-old African-American, had been diagnosed with high blood cholesterol and high blood pressure. He was taking two medications. At first, that was hard. He hadn't taken medicine regularly his whole life. But now things had fallen into place. He had devised a system that worked well for him.

He took cholesterol-lowering medicine twice a day, just before lunch and supper. He took a diuretic for his high blood pressure just once a day. That was great, Charles noted. His doctor had told Charles that by following a low-sodium diet and a regular walking program, he was doing a lot to help keep this prescription to a minimal dosage. Charles took this pill at lunchtime.

He kept a one-week supply of the medicines on the lazy Susan on the kitchen table, where he always ate. That way he would see them readily. Because there were no children in the house, this was a safe place. He put one diuretic pill in each compartment of his pill box. That way he would know he took it. He put fourteen packets of cholesterol-lowering medicine on the lazy Susan. He also put some of each medicine in the glove box of his car for when he ate lunch and dinner away from home. He phoned the pharmacy and ordered refills.

"Doc was right," Charles thought, "I really did get used to taking my medicine regularly. My system works." ❦

At home, organize your medicines. You might find that using a pill organizer helps you remember to take drugs at certain times of the day or on certain days of the week. You may want to use a labeled container for medications to help you remember to take your medication on time. Some containers have compartments for each day of the week. Others have three or four compartments for different times of each day. No matter how many compartments a container has, the principle

Daily medication dispenser.

is the same for all. At the beginning of the week, carefully place your medicines for the entire week in the appropriate compartments. During the week, take out the medications you are to take at that time. At the end of each day, you'll know you took all your medicine for that day. At the end of the week, you'll know you didn't miss a single dose.

If possible, put the medications in a place where you won't forget about taking them: You don't have to keep them in the bathroom medicine chest. Some people put a clearly labeled pill bottle in their sock drawer so that they'll be sure to see it every morning. Others choose to keep their medications in the kitchen. You may have your own favorite place. Just remember that some drugs have certain restrictions for storage. Nitroglycerin tablets, for example, should be kept in a cool, dry, dark place. Be sure to keep all medications out of the reach of children.

When you travel, take two supplies of your medications. Keep one with you at all times and keep the other set in your luggage. That way you'll be less likely to lose all your medications on the trip.

Know when your medicines were purchased. If you have any with an expiration date that has passed, flush them down the toilet. You may find it easier to keep track of the purchase date on the bottle if you use a heavy, waterproof marker to write it on the cap or side of the bottle.

Sometimes it may seem that having to take your medications at precisely the same time and in the same amount each day complicates your life or ruins your day. Instead, try to view your medicines as strong allies in your recovery campaign. Give them the attention and respect they deserve.

CHAPTER FOUR

Considering Surgery
or Other Interventions

Heart disease is treated in several ways. With a doctor's help, it's possible to reduce or eliminate some problems associated with heart disease. We can do this by changing our habits (what we eat and drink, how much we weigh, how we exercise, and whether we smoke). We can also take prescribed medications faithfully and control preexisting conditions such as diabetes, high blood pressure, and high levels of blood cholesterol. Often these two approaches are enough to reduce the chance of a first or additional heart attack occurring. For some heart patients, however, these measures are not enough. Sometimes an additional intervention is required.

The purpose of most surgery or other interventions is to restore blood flow through severely blocked coronary arteries. Restoring blood flow relieves symptoms of angina, which allows patients to become more active again.

In rare cases, surgery or another intervention is performed to resolve problems with a torn or faulty part of the heart muscle. Pacemakers may be implanted in the body temporarily or permanently to help maintain a steady heartbeat. **Shunts,** artificially created passageways that redirect coronary blood flow, are needed in exceptional cases to correct abnormalities or tears in the heart structure. If a heart attack is severe and damages a great deal of heart tissue, it may be necessary to repair a defect in the heart muscle wall or replace a heart valve with an artificial one.

This kind of intervention is not meant for every heart patient. Surgery—or any invasive procedure—carries its own risks. These risks must be balanced against the patient's risk factors, including complications that may have resulted from the heart attack or other unrelated medical conditions. Many factors unique to the patient are considered before a decision is made.

The timing of the procedure is also carefully weighed. Generally, doctors do not perform an invasive procedure until several weeks after the patient's heart attack so that the patient can recover some physical strength. Such delays are reserved for elective procedures. **Elective procedures** are considered desirable and beneficial for the patient but not urgent.

Who Is a Candidate for Intervention?

Revascularization—the reopening of blocked arteries—is the most common intervention performed in heart attack patients. It can be beneficial for many patients, but not all. Usually a doctor will have tried other means of reopening the blocked arteries before resorting to an invasive technique. If thrombolytic therapy—the so-called "clot-busting" medications—isn't effective and the patient continues to have coronary ischemia, interventions should be considered. Other candidates include those who perform poorly on exercise tests, have several severely diseased coronary arteries, show evidence of a malfunctioning left ventricle of the heart, or have signs of ischemia.

Many people who have had a heart attack are not candidates for this kind of intervention simply because it is not necessary for their recovery. They are doing well enough without it. Many people have had heart attacks and survived without complications. Others have no troubling symptoms of ischemia or left ventricular dysfunction. These patients have a fine prognosis without undergoing surgery.

Those who have responded well to thrombolytic therapy typically do not need invasive revascularization. People with only mild ischemia that does not limit their activities, with or without left ventricular dysfunction, probably don't need such procedures either.

Two Methods of Revascularization: Angioplasty vs. Bypass

To restore blood flow in coronary arteries manually, doctors can choose between two very different procedures. One is **percutaneous transluminal coronary angioplasty (PTCA).** The other is **coronary artery bypass surgery.** In angioplasty, the physician widens the interior space, or **lumen,** of a blocked vessel by compressing atherosclerotic plaque. The vessel is effectively "reopened," and blood flows through it again. PTCA is not a true surgery. The patient remains awake throughout the procedure, which is done in a special laboratory, not an operating room.

Coronary bypass surgery is another approach to the problem of revascularization. Instead of reopening the blocked vessel, the doctor performs a surgical bypass operation by creating a detour around the blockage. The doctor takes a similarly sized vessel from another part of the patient's body and grafts one end of it to the diseased vessel below the blockage. The other end is grafted to a small opening made in the aorta for that purpose. The new vessel takes over the job of the diseased vessel. It carries blood to the heart tissue on the far side of the blocked vessel.

Angioplasty and bypass surgery are common interventions in the United States today. Yet each revascularization method has pros and cons that make it right for some people and not for others. Or one might be right under some circumstances but not others. Let's take a closer look.

Percutaneous Transluminal Coronary Angioplasty

Originally, the basic method now used to perform angioplasty was developed as a diagnostic tool (see discussion of cardiac catheterization [angiography] on page 90). In both procedures a computer-connected device is threaded through a catheter. A catheter is a flexible, hollow tube that is passed through blood vessels from the arm, neck, or leg all the way to the heart. With angiography, information collected at the tip of the catheter can be sent back to a computer for instant analysis.

In the 1970s and 1980s, doctors began to look for other ways to make use of the access to the heart that catheterization provided. They realized that specially designed tools could be threaded directly to the most diseased parts of the coronary arteries through catheters. These tools could be used to widen and reopen blocked arteries, in much the same way that a drill bit might be used to reopen a blocked pipe far underground.

Lily had had a heart attack three months ago. Since then she had been following her doctor's orders. She was taking aspirin and watching what she ate. She was also taking nitroglycerin for chest pains. But despite these changes, she still suffered from chest pains. They seemed to be worsening. She went back to her doctor. After examining her, the doctor told Lily that she needed to have an angiogram. Depending on what that showed, he told her that she might be a good candidate for balloon angioplasty. He told her the procedure could lessen the number and intensity of ischemic episodes she had. Lily had heard of balloon angioplasty. She even knew people who had had one. When her doctor suggested it, Lily was all for it at first. Anything her doctor could do, she thought, would help her get better.

The doctor described the procedure and discussed the possible pros and cons with Lily. She realized that angioplasty was not the quick fix she thought it was. It was clear that balloon angioplasty could provide benefits. She also realized those benefits might not be permanent. The doctor told her that she must also continue to work on lifestyle changes.

Lily agreed to have the procedure. She also promised herself that she would work harder to make those lifestyle changes the doctor recommended. She resolved to eat right, get enough exercise, and take her medications as prescribed.

The first PTCA was performed in 1977 on arteries that were not coronary. In 1983 the Food and Drug Administration approved the use of angioplasty. By 1993 more than 360,000 angioplasties were being performed annually in the United States. Today more patients are treated with PTCA than with coronary artery bypass surgery.

Procedure

The purpose of PTCA is to dilate, or widen, coronary arteries blocked by atherosclerotic plaque. The procedure is performed in a hospital, in the **cardiac catheterization laboratory.** The day before the procedure is scheduled to take place, the patient begins to take anticoagulant medications, including aspirin. This helps prevent blood clots from forming around the catheter, which might cause other problems.

In the catheter laboratory a specialist administers a local anesthetic to the patient. The anesthetic will deaden feeling at the site where the catheter is inserted. The patient otherwise remains awake and alert throughout the procedure. Some patients experience angina pain during angioplasty, as well as other changes in blood and heart function. These are usually temporary and disappear after the procedure.

A skilled medical professional performs the PTCA. He or she inserts the catheter into the circulatory system through one of the larger arteries in the upper leg. A contrast dye is injected into the catheter. The operator can then follow the catheter's progress on an X-ray screen as he or she guides the catheter into place.

The catheter stops on the near side of the blocked vessel (see figure, page 91). A very thin guidewire is then passed into the catheter. It actually goes beyond the catheter to cross the blocked section of the coronary artery to the other side. Finally, a skinny, deflated balloon is threaded along this pathway. It follows the guidewire across the blocked section.

Slowly, using a syringe, the doctor inflates the balloon with contrast dye. He or she watches the inflation closely on the X-ray monitor. Pressure in the vessel is also carefully monitored. The balloon remains inflated for about one minute at a time before it is deflated. The **dilatation** cycle may be repeated up to 10 times. The inflated balloon puts direct pressure on the atherosclerotic plaque in the vessel. This pressure cracks it and compresses it. The interior space of the vessel widens. The outer wall of the vessel bulges a little to accommodate the plaque. The plaque isn't so much compressed as it is moved into another part of the vessel.

If this pattern of dilatation doesn't achieve the results the doctor hopes for, the balloon may be left inflated for slightly longer than a minute before deflation. Doctors can tell whether the procedure has worked by looking at the condition of the artery as it appears on the

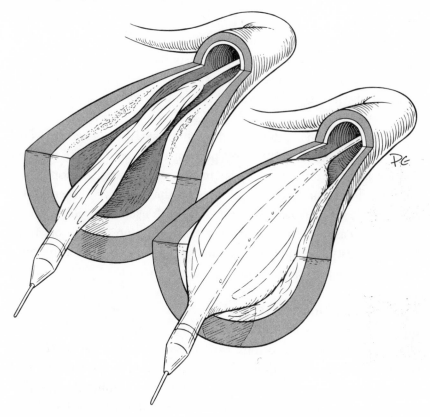

Percutaneous transluminal coronary angioplasty (PTCA).
A catheter is placed near the blocked section of the coronary artery. A guidewire is then placed in the blocked section. A deflated balloon is threaded into place and inflated.

X-ray monitor. The vessel lumen (center space), which looks pinched initially, looks wider after successful angioplasty. Pressure readings taken at the site of blockage will confirm the visual information.

When the procedure is over, the catheter is left in place for up to a day. The patient is given heparin, a powerful blood thinner. Aspirin therapy is also continued. If there is some angina discomfort, the patient may be given nitroglycerin intravenously overnight. When the catheter is removed, the patient is usually monitored for another day and then discharged from the hospital. Two weeks later the patient is given an exercise test to check for angina pain and to see how well the angioplasty relieved the ischemia.

Success Rates

Experienced operators can thread a deflated angioplasty balloon across 90 percent of blocked vessels. Angioplasty has a very good initial success rate. A successful angioplasty reduces vessel blockage by more than half of what it was before the procedure, without creating other complications.

Within six months of the procedure, however, the opened vessel becomes blocked again in 40 to 60 percent of all angioplasty patients. Vessel blockages tend to reappear in the same places. Although it is safe to perform multiple angioplasties on the same vessel section, the odds of that vessel *remaining* clear drop with each succeeding procedure. The reason for this isn't fully known. Some researchers think that angioplasty itself may disturb muscle cells in the vessel in such a way as to encourage plaque development at that site.

Who Is a Candidate for PTCA?

Angioplasty restores blood flow through a vessel narrowed by atherosclerotic plaque. The procedure works best on vessels that are severely narrowed rather than completely blocked. Heart attack patients with unstable ischemic conditions—such as angina symptoms at rest—tend to be the most common candidates. There is no evidence that PTCA has any effect on life span. There are a few other considerations.

- Before going ahead with the procedure, the doctor must evaluate whether this procedure is likely to be successful for this particular patient. He or she will consider noninvasive alternatives. If the same results can be achieved noninvasively, angioplasty should not be performed until appropriate alternatives have been attempted.
- The condition of the atherosclerotic plaques in question will be considered. Plaques that are not typical may not respond to angioplasty. Atypical plaques include very rigid, brittle plaques and very soft, fatty ones. Noncoronary vessels that will be involved in the catheterization must be considered, too.
- The patient's overall condition is also a factor. The doctor will need to balance the severity of the patient's heart attack, as well as the patient's age, strength, and other medical

problems, before deciding whether angioplasty is a good idea.

- The hospital's record of success with the procedure should be considered and compared with other treatments.

Possible Complications

Overall, angioplasty is very safe. However, as with any invasive procedure, complications are possible and must be considered. There is some chance that patients may develop an irregular heartbeat during PTCA. These can be detected by changes on the electrocardiogram. A blood clot may develop around the catheter, despite routine anticoagulant therapy. Arterial spasms, causing more ischemia or outright vessel closure, may also develop. Patients are carefully monitored for these possible problems. Complications usually arise during the procedure or within the following 24 hours, if they occur at all. They are easily taken care of.

An accidental cut or tear in the vessel itself is the most serious possible consequence of an angioplasty procedure. The catheter or guidewire may snag on the vessel it passes through. If that happens, the doctors must work very quickly. The patient is moved to the operating room. There, emergency coronary artery bypass surgery is performed to repair the vessel. It is important that the cardiac catheterization lab is near an operating room. Such a complication is relatively rare, occurring in 3 to 5 percent of all angioplasty procedures. However, it is very serious, with a high mortality rate.

Other Techniques

Thus far, we have discussed the most common form of coronary angioplasty. That is balloon angioplasty, which reopens coronary arteries by pressing aside atherosclerotic plaque in the vessels. However, other nonsurgical techniques that also involve the use of a catheter show promise.

One innovative technique is **atherectomy.** A device is tunneled through a catheter to the blocked part of the coronary artery. There it is manipulated to cut away plaque, collect it, and remove it through the catheter.

Laser treatment of atherosclerotic plaque may someday help doctors open blocked coronary arteries. Tiny laser beams, set at the tips of catheters, may be used to vaporize vessel blockages with great precision.

Stenting is a new type of intervention procedure that looks promising for some heart patients. Stents are metal devices that doctors introduce into the vessel on a catheter wire. They look like thin metal tubes at first. Once in the vessel, they expand, revealing a lattice-work structure. Pressed into the side of the vessel, the stent helps keep it open.

These alternatives to traditional balloon angioplasty are still in the experimental stages. More research is needed to identify which patients make the best candidates and to determine the long-term safety of the procedures.

Coronary Artery Bypass Surgery

Coronary artery bypass surgery creates new pathways between the aorta and major coronary arteries blocked by atherosclerotic plaque. By creating this detour or bypass, blood is again able to reach parts of the heart muscle that it had been blocked from reaching because of lesions in the related arteries. Bypass grafts are intended to relieve angina pain and sometimes to prevent heart attack and death.

Coronary artery bypass grafting is a major surgical procedure. In 1993, more than 300,000 patients were treated with coronary artery bypass surgery.

❦ *The sutures in Jeff's chest ached. He still felt groggy from the surgery the day before. His surgeon had created bypasses for three major arteries. He was told that he had undergone a triple bypass and that everything had gone well. But Jeff was a little worried. Even this surgery might not be enough to keep him well. He was only 54. What was he going to do now?*

His cardiologist appeared at his bedside. "How are you feeling, Jeff?"

"Okay, I guess," Jeff replied.

"Let's discuss what you can expect next," the doctor began.

"You underwent a major surgical procedure. We've already discussed your chances of developing another arterial blockage, despite our success yesterday. I know you're concerned about this, too. Part of what concerns me is your persistently high blood pressure. We were able to bring it down before the opera-

tion. You'll need to work with us, however, to make sure that it stays down from now on."

"But I take my medication," Jeff said.

"That may not be enough," the doctor warned. "We've talked about your diet before. You are sodium-sensitive. To get better control of your high blood pressure without increasing your medication, you may have to work harder at cutting down your salt intake."

"I know," Jeff said. "I've tried, but . . ."

"Do you still eat prepared foods that are very salty?" the doctor asked gently.

They continued to talk about diet. The doctor suggested that a dietitian come by the hospital and talk with Jeff. Jeff thought that was a good idea.

The next day the dietitian stopped by.

Jeff sat back and expected to hear a lecture. Instead, the dietitian asked him questions and made some suggestions. She left some reading materials and said she'd be back the next day.

Jeff thought the dietitian's ideas were reasonable. "She didn't even try to convince me to give up everything I like to eat," he thought. "Maybe I can stick to an eating plan that we work on together." ❧

Procedure

Before the surgical bypass procedure is begun, the patient undergoes cardiac catheterization and angiography. Angiography gives the surgeon a "map" of the heart. It tells what the heart looks like, where the blockages are, and where the best places to position the grafts might be. It prepares the surgeon for what is to come during the surgery itself. Angiography is performed in a hospital's cardiac catheterization laboratory.

Catheterization takes one or two hours, and the patient remains awake throughout the procedure. Only a local anesthetic is administered, at the place where the catheter is inserted. The catheter may be inserted in the arm, leg, or neck.

Before surgery, the patient is put on blood-thinning therapy. Heparin is the usual choice. In the operating room, an anesthesiologist carefully administers anesthesia to the patient.

The first order of business is to connect the patient to a **pump oxygenator.** That device circulates blood throughout the body and oxygenates it as well. The heart and lungs are stilled during surgery. A pump oxygenator is sometimes also called a heart-lung machine. Blood is also cooled through this machine. In fact, everything is kept very cool. That's because cold temperatures act as a kind of preservative on body tissue. The colder the temperature, the less oxygen the tissue needs—and the less opportunity there is for the tissue to deteriorate during surgery.

After the pump oxygenator has been connected and has started to take over for the heart and lungs, cardiac arrest is induced through electric shock. This stills the heart so that it may be operated on.

The vessels most commonly used for the graft are the saphenous vein and the mammary artery. These vessels and others used for the procedure are taken from a part of the body where they perform a nonessential function. They should be approximately the same diameter as the arteries they will bypass. More and more, mammary arteries are used for bypass surgeries. They seem to work better than the veins that have been traditionally used. However, nonessential mammary arteries are not always available.

The graft vessel is connected to the diseased artery just below the blockage (see figure, page 97). A small opening is made. The redirected blood will flow through this opening. The blood can now reach heart tissue that has become ischemic because of atherosclerotic plaque obstructing the diseased artery. When the saphenous vein is used, the other end of it is connected to the aorta through another small, newly created opening. When the mammary artery is used, the other end of it remains attached to an artery that branches off from the aorta. Most patients who undergo bypass surgery have significant coronary artery disease. They typically have three or more grafts of this type done at the same time.

Once the grafts have been completed, an electric shock is delivered to the heart that starts it pumping again. The patient is weaned from the heart-lung machine. Blood is allowed to return slowly to normal body temperature. The chest cavity is closed, and the many monitoring devices and intravenous tubes are removed. The patient is moved to the surgical intensive care unit for recovery. The entire operation takes from four to six hours, sometimes longer.

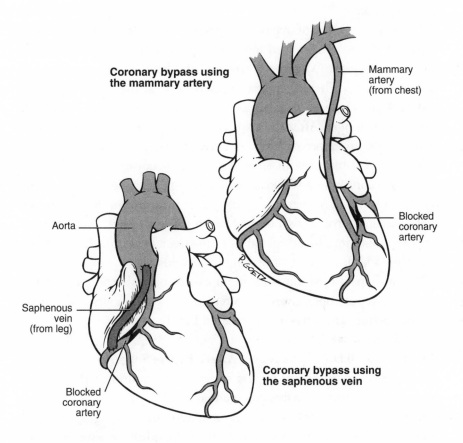

Coronary artery bypass grafts. A nonessential blood vessel is attached to the diseased coronary artery just below the blockage.

In the surgical intensive care unit, more tubes are attached to the patient, who is closely monitored. Drugs to control pain are usually given, and anticoagulant therapy is continued. For the first day or so, the patient may be fed intravenously. By the second day or so, if there are no complications, the patient will be encouraged to start to return to a normal routine. He or she will begin to eat regular food, sit up, and walk a bit. Before going home, the patient is usually moved to a nonsurgical unit for observation for a few more days. A couple of weeks after leaving the hospital, the patient often returns for an exercise test. The test will measure how effectively the bypass surgery has relieved symptoms of angina and ischemia.

Success Rates

Occlusion (blockage) of bypass grafts is common. Ten to 15 percent of bypass grafts no longer feed blood to the bypassed artery within one month of surgery. (Mammary artery grafts have a somewhat higher rate of success.) Thereafter, graft vessels close at the rate of approximately 4 percent each year. Blood-thinning drugs seem to help keep vessels clear longer. After the sixth year, graft vessel failures swing upward again, to approximately 6 percent annually. However, it is thought that failures in this later period may occur more frequently in those who continue to smoke or who have uncontrolled high levels of blood cholesterol. Surgery, of course, does not remove the conditions that caused atherosclerosis to develop in the first place. Patients who have adopted more healthful habits following a heart attack or surgery may have a better chance of beating these odds.

Repeat bypass operations or angioplasties often become necessary. However, repeat operations are often harder on patients and can be less successful. They are not considered lightly.

Who Is a Candidate for Coronary Artery Bypass Surgery?

Although coronary artery bypass surgery is common in the United States, there is still some disagreement as to when it is needed. Its purpose is to relieve symptoms of ischemia and angina. Angioplasty and drug therapy also relieve such symptoms. These less invasive remedies must be considered and ruled out before surgery is decided upon.

There is also some question as to whether or not coronary artery bypass surgery prolongs life. The answer seems to be that it does—for heart patients who have major vessel disease in at least three of the major coronary arteries, particularly those feeding the left ventricle. The arteries typically are more than half-blocked by atherosclerotic plaque. In other patients, surgery mainly relieves the most severe angina symptoms: for example, angina pain that occurs after the slightest exertion. For these patients, surgery makes more activity possible, improving their quality of life. Bypass surgery is also appropriate for those who cannot tolerate angioplasty and do not respond adequately to drug therapy.

Younger people who are in otherwise good health tend to have excellent results from bypass surgery. Older patients (more than 70 years old) and those with poor left ventricular function tend to fare less well.

People who are undergoing repeat procedures or having additional procedures done at the same time do not do as well as some others. Also, people who have some other debilitating disease tend to not do as well. Recovery in these people may be slow.

The patient should be stabilized medically before surgery, if possible. If he or she has had a heart attack, bypass surgery should not be scheduled until the patient has had a chance to recover somewhat from the event. Generally speaking, it is desirable to postpone bypass surgery for three months after a heart attack. The patient's blood pressure should be under control at that time as well.

Possible Complications

Coronary artery bypass surgery is a major surgical procedure. Any of the complications associated with major surgery are possible.

Angioplasty or Surgery?

Deciding between angioplasty and bypass surgery can be difficult. For patients with stable angina, both procedures are safe, with good results. More and more, angioplasty is used first if drug therapy isn't enough to relieve ischemic pain. Because it isn't as hard on the patient, many doctors prefer to try angioplasty, even several times if necessary, before resorting to bypass surgery. And because bypass surgeries yield progressively poorer results with every repetition, physicians often hold it in "reserve," hoping they'll need to use it only once.

PTCA is less invasive, and patients recover from it more quickly. However, bypass surgery usually has slightly better results in the first year. Life span may be improved with bypass surgery. However, there is no evidence that that is the case with PTCA. Another benefit of angioplasty is that it requires a shorter hospital stay and is less expensive than bypass surgery.

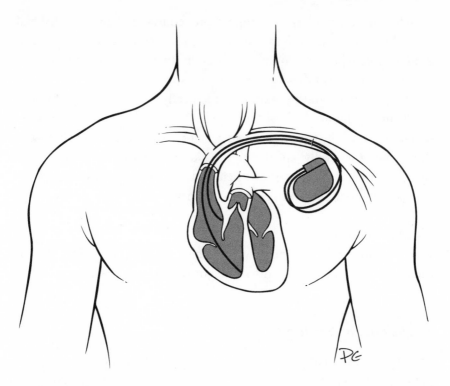

Pacemaker implant. Pacemaker leads can be placed inside or outside the heart. They make the heart beat regularly and at the right speed.

Pacemakers

A pacemaker is an electronic device that delivers electrical stimulation to the heart muscle. Pacemakers are powered by batteries. They work by connecting leads from a mechanical energy source to the surface or interior of the heart (see figure above). These leads act like the heart's own impaired electrical nodes. They take over the business of making the heart beat strongly and regularly. The generator can be set to emit electrical impulses in any pattern desired, depending on what the person with the pacemaker needs.

Several types of pacemakers are available. Some respond to what the patient's heart is doing. They provide corrective stimulation needed to help the heart maintain a regular beat. Others emit small shocks across the heart in a regular pattern. In some, leads are positioned on the left ventricle. Some rely on a single lead slipped through a catheter into the chamber of the right ventricle. Still other pacemakers work through leads positioned on both the right atrium and the right ventricle of the heart. These are known as **dual-chamber pacemakers.**

Pacemakers may be temporary or permanent, depending on the nature of the heart damage that made them necessary. A severe heart attack can damage a wide area of heart tissue. This compromises the heart's electrical system and pathways, the elements that keep the heartbeat going. If you are diagnosed with atrioventricular block, bundle branch disturbances, or sinus node problems, you may be a candidate for a permanent pacemaker.

Temporary pacemakers are generally used to restore normal heart rhythms. Patients with slow, irregular heartbeats (bradycardia) may be given a temporary pacemaker to be used until the heart recovers enough to resume its regular heartbeat after a heart attack.

Defibrillators

Also called **implantable cardioverters,** defibrillators are like pacemakers. They monitor and smooth out inconsistencies in the heartbeat. They make it easier for the heart to circulate blood throughout the body. Unlike pacemakers, defibrillators cover more of the heart with electric current. They also deliver a stronger electrical charge. If medications and surgery have been ruled out, defibrillators are recommended for certain patients. These include those with severe heart damage who are prone to bouts of ventricular tachycardia (very rapid, irregular heartbeats) or ventricular fibrillation (shallow, rapid, ineffective pumping), serious conditions that can lead to sudden death.

Pacemakers and defibrillators are easily implanted under the skin's surface. There they can be easily retrieved to change batteries. Pacemakers are generally kept under the skin near the collarbone. Defibrillators are implanted in the abdomen. A short stay in the hospital is required. Batteries for permanent pacemaker generators generally last three or four years. When pacemakers were first introduced, microwave ovens and other electrical tools could interrupt their function. Today's pacemakers are well protected from that kind of interference, and it is no longer a problem.

Shunts and Valve Replacement

Revascularization is the most common reason for a doctor to perform an invasive procedure after a heart attack. There may be other reasons, however. Sometimes the heart develops structural problems in the presence of severe heart disease or after a particularly severe heart attack. In other cases, the heart attack may lead to the first real examination of the patient's heart. Defects present at birth may be noticed for the first time, when the heart is more vulnerable to problems they might cause.

Heart attacks can sometimes so weaken the heart muscle that it tears. Blood crosses between chambers of the heart in ways that it should not, or it leaks away. Fortunately, this is rare, affecting perhaps 1 to 2 percent of all heart attack victims. A shunt is a device with which surgeons can redirect blood flow in the heart. For example, if there is a tear or hole in the septum, blood may slosh back and forth between the two atria, rather than into the ventricles, where it ought to go. Such a tear or hole makes it very hard for the heart to do its job. When this kind of leak occurs, the heart cannot move blood through the body. A shunt stops the leak and keeps blood flowing along the appropriate path.

Heart disease and massive heart attacks can also damage heart valves. The valves may not close completely. This too affects how well the heart can pump blood throughout the body. The heart must work harder to do its job. Sometimes it becomes necessary to repair a valve surgically or replace it with an artificial model. Artificial heart valves may be made of plastic. More recently, surgeons have found ways to use heart valves from pigs, cows, and other humans in transplants. Biological valves are slightly less vulnerable to forming blood clots.

Because blood tends to clot around artificial valves, people who have them are placed on anticoagulant therapy permanently. Artificial heart valves also become infected more easily. Anyone who has an artificial heart valve must inform his or her doctors and dentist of the fact. People with artificial heart valves should take antibiotics before *any* procedures—even routine teeth cleaning—to reduce that risk of infection. If you have an artificial heart valve, your doctor will talk with you about the antibiotic therapy that is best for you.

Some people may become a bit disturbed if they notice a clicking sound made by their artificial heart valve. This is perfectly normal. Most people stop noticing the sound after only a short while.

Because heart surgery is major surgery, your body will need time to heal. A period of convalescence is important to your well-being. Let's take a closer look at what you can expect after you are released from the hospital.

CHAPTER FIVE

Getting Better Day by Day

Being released from the hospital after a heart attack or heart surgery is a big event. Most patients look forward to it, and many have questions about their life activities: "How much can I do and when?" Family members have questions, too.

Although every patient is different, a rough estimate can be made for those who have experienced an uncomplicated heart attack. Your cardiac rehabilitation team, of course, will make specific decisions about you. Team members usually meet with patients at the time of discharge from the hospital and present a customized rehabilitation program, covering everything from medications to diet to exercise goals. This team follows up with cardiac patients at regular outpatient meetings held at the hospital. You may find this group of dedicated professionals a wonderful source of support as you work to modify your behaviors and improve your health after leaving the hospital.

A heart attack is a major event, and heart surgery is major surgery. Although you are likely to start feeling better sooner than you expected, full recovery takes between three and four months. In that time you will gradually resume most of the activities you enjoyed before. Of course, as in so many other areas of life, moderation is the key to a healthy recovery. Take it easy. Take your time. Listen to your body. Give it what it needs to get better.

Getting Adequate Rest and Sleep

Getting a full eight hours' rest every night is important. For a few months, you may also want to take an afternoon nap. This is completely normal; go ahead, if you feel like it. If pain from your surgery keeps you awake, take your prescribed medication. Rest is an important part of the healing process.

❦ *Harold hung up the telephone and sighed. The guys were going out for their regular golf game, and Harold had to drop out for the time being. He had gotten home from the hospital just last week. Although he was feeling stronger every day, Harold's doctor had told him not to play golf or drive just yet.*

The truth was, Harold didn't feel strong enough to golf yet, anyway. But it pained him to be told there were things he couldn't do. It was another reminder that things were different, now that he'd had a heart attack. He sat down heavily on the chair next to the phone.

His wife, Linny, looked over at him. As usual, she read his mind. "Harold, don't forget, taking it easier like this is temporary. You look so much better already than you did the day you had your heart attack! I was so worried about you—you looked ashen and sick.

"I know you've had a tough week. I know you're frustrated and worried about the future. It's natural, honey. But look how much you've improved already! You're eating well, your color is better, you're up and about. You have a lot of people on your side, including your golf pals. Why don't you call Art back and invite the guys over after the game? You can still visit with them every week. Before you know it, you'll be back on the links.

"You're getting better! Just take it one step at a time." ❦

Eating Healthfully

Before you left the hospital, you probably received counseling on how to eat healthfully and keep your blood pressure, blood cholesterol levels, or diabetes under control. You should plan to make these your new lifelong habits. Concentrate on eating fruits, vegetables, grains, and nonfat or low-fat dairy products. Reduce your daily intake of fats to less than 30 percent of your total daily caloric intake. If you drank alcoholic beverages moderately before surgery, it is acceptable to continue to do so afterward. Keep in mind, however, that alcohol can affect the absorption rates of some medications you may be taking. Discuss this possibility with your doctor. Diet is discussed in greater detail in Chapter Nine.

Caring for the Incision

If you have had heart surgery, it will take from one to two months for your incision scar to heal completely. As it heals, treat it carefully. Avoid bumping, scratching, or otherwise disturbing it. It may hurt, especially in rainy, damp weather. Don't hesitate to take the appropriate pain medication for that purpose.

Usually incision pain is sharper and more localized than angina pain. Occasionally, it may be hard to tell the difference between the two. If you have pain you can't identify and you have nitroglycerin tablets, you may want to try them to relieve the pain. If the pain is unchanged, it may be an ache left from surgery. If it is severe, call your doctor. If the pain gets a little better after you take nitroglycerin and then comes back again, it may be angina pain. If the pain persists and it feels strongly like angina pain, call your doctor immediately.

If you had a coronary bypass operation, the graft vessel may have been taken from your lower leg. Sometimes the leg swells around the ankle and becomes uncomfortable after that. It can help to elevate the leg and wrap it in an elastic stocking.

Light Exercise

Often a nurse, physical therapist, or other health-care professional will help develop an exercise program for you before you leave the hospital. This program is tailored specifically to your own condition. Your doctor will probably encourage you to enroll in a cardiac rehabilitation program. Such a program may be offered in the hospital where you were treated. In a cardiac rehabilitation program, you will continue the program created for you in the step-down unit. Your exercise will be supervised by a medical team trained in cardiac rehabilitation. A modest usage fee is usually charged, but the facilities and personnel can't be beat! Many people who have had heart attacks get hooked on treadmills, stair-steppers, stationary bicycles, and similar exercise equipment. Others enjoy working out around people who have shared similar experiences, or sometimes their own doctors, who may show up in the exercise room to pursue their own exercise regime.

Your cardiac rehabilitation team may also suggest some easy physical activity at home. If your doctor okays it, walking is a fine exercise. Taking a daily walk may be particularly good for recovering heart attack or heart surgery patients because it can be easily adapted to suit individual needs. Walking also helps reduce swelling that might have resulted from grafts taken from the leg and used for bypass surgery. Start with modest goals that your doctor recommends. Then try to walk a little farther each day or increase the duration by five minutes or so each week. Rest frequently as needed. (For more information about starting a regular walking program, see pages 242–44.)

Whether you are exercising at home or in a cardiac rehab facility, avoid overexertion, but try not to be too cautious, either. Let your doctor guide you. If you experience any of the following problems while exercising, stop immediately and call your doctor:

- chest pain that is different from pain associated with your operation
- shortness of breath
- dizziness
- weakness

Heart attack survivors and heart surgery patients who develop chest discomfort, a rapid heartbeat, arrhythmias, or extreme blood pressure changes during exercise tests are not allowed to start any exercise program until these problems are brought under control.

With their doctor's permission, others may eventually take up different kinds of regular exercise that they enjoy, such as tennis, aerobic dance, or swimming. By following a regular program, it's likely that you will wind up in better shape than you were before your heart attack or heart surgery. We delve deeper into the benefits of regular exercise, and how to establish a routine that you can commit to, in Chapter Ten.

Resuming Routine Activities

Shortly after your heart attack or heart surgery, you probably began to do some easy activities, such as walking slowly in the hospital corridors. As you continue to recover, you may begin to resume some easy to moderate activities, such as walking out to the mailbox. Your doctor will probably allow you to gradually add more activities. You can probably do light household chores, such as dusting, after four weeks. Heavy lifting and moving, sports, and many household chores are strenuous activities. Avoid them until your doctor permits them. (Heavy lifting means lifting anything that weighs more than 10 pounds.) You will probably be cleared for any activity you like three months after your surgery.

Bathing

If you have had heart surgery, check your incision to make sure it looks as if it is healing cleanly. Keep it dry most of the time, although it is all right if it gets wet while you are bathing. Upon leaving the bath, pat it dry carefully, especially in the first six weeks after the operation.

During the first weeks after a heart attack or heart surgery, you may need help getting in and out of the bathtub and help with washing, as well. Avoid either very hot or very cold water. The heart responds to extremes of temperature by working harder. In the first few months after heart attack or heart surgery, the goal is to let the heart rest and heal.

Intimacy

A large number of heart patients and their partners worry about when they will be able to resume their sex life—or even if they should. They are frequently afraid that having sex will put too great a strain on the heart, triggering another heart attack or sudden death. That simply isn't true. In fact, sexual intercourse exerts about as much strain on the heart as walking briskly up a couple of flights of stairs. That amount of activity is well within most heart attack patients' capabilities by the time they leave the hospital.

After the first phase of recovery is complete—about a month after an uncomplicated heart attack or heart surgery—feel free to resume the same forms of lovemaking that you found pleasing before. Above all, take your time. Don't feel pressured into following some imagined schedule for resuming lovemaking. The right time will be when you and your partner are ready. That time is different for every couple.

Some couples find that slowly easing back into a physical relationship works well for them. At first, you might want to consider expressing your feelings simply by cuddling and holding one another in a relaxed, loving atmosphere. That mood may not just "happen," given the many responsibilities and pressures most adults feel during the day, so try planning for it. Set aside time for a special "date" together. Be sure to plan on a time when you will both feel relaxed and refreshed, even if you need to rest earlier in the day to do so. Choose a time when you aren't likely to be interrupted or distracted by other responsibilities (at home, consider turning the telephone down so you won't hear it ring).

Your "date" might be as simple as sharing a special dinner together, watching a romantic movie, or sitting in front of the fireplace, looking through a box of old family pictures. Do as much in advance to prepare for your evening together as possible. That way you can concentrate on each other later. Try renting the movie that morning. Serve food that you prepared ahead of time, or arrange to have it delivered from a favorite restaurant. Arrange the wood in the fireplace.

Depression and fear about performance are two other factors that can reduce sexual desire and capacity. Depression tends to exacerbate previous sexual problems between partners. Some ideas that can help couples ease back into a satisfying sex life are noted in the box on page 110.

Sex and Heart Disease

A person who has had a heart attack or heart surgery may usually resume sexual activity after the first phase of recovery is complete. (This is usually about three to four weeks after the event.) Some doctors suggest it is appropriate when both the patient and his or her partner feel ready. Even then, couples often feel some anxiety at the notion of resuming sex after one partner has had a heart attack.

It can help to prepare in advance. One way both partners can do this is to maintain and improve their physical conditions. Since mood swings are common in heart attack survivors, it also helps if both partners can stay relaxed and tolerate those emotions.

Some general guidelines for resuming sex are:

- Choose a time when you are rested, relaxed, and free from stress brought on by the day's schedules and responsibilities.
- Wait one to three hours after eating a full meal, so that digestion can take place.
- Select a familiar, quiet setting that is free from opportunities for interruptions.
- Take medicine before sexual activity if prescribed by the doctor.
- Consider trying new positions; you may find some are easier than others.
- Take it easy. Allow adequate time for foreplay, to become used to each other again after spending some time apart. It may be right for you just to be intimate without experiencing a climax or orgasm the first few times you are together.
- If you experience a rapid heartbeat or difficulty breathing for twenty or thirty minutes after intercourse, have angina pain, or feel very tired the next day, consider slowing the pace down a bit. In time, the partner who has had a heart attack or heart surgery is usually able to resume the same activity level as before.

If you continue to worry about your heart attack or your heart surgery and its impact on sexual activity, discuss the matter with your doctor. You'll find that having your fears addressed openly and directly can ease your mind and go far to resolve your fears. If your doctor seems unwilling or uncomfortable discussing the matter with you, seek another qualified counselor. Your questions deserve answers.

Getting Behind the Wheel

Driving represents independence. For those who drove before a heart attack or heart surgery, being able to drive afterward is a big concern. Safe driving requires alertness and quick reactions. It's important to have a very clear idea of your true strength and abilities in this area before you return to driving. Survivors of heart surgery or uncomplicated heart attack are commonly permitted to get behind a steering wheel again three to four weeks after the surgery or heart attack. But everyone is different. Be sure to check with your own doctor before you resume driving. If you have had a particularly disabling heart attack with complications, it may be wise to have your driving evaluated by an independent party first. Specialized businesses that do just that exist in many areas. Call your local rehabilitation center for more information.

You may ride in a car if you like. If you ride for a long period, however, be sure to stop every hour at least and walk around for about five minutes to get your blood circulating.

Going Back to Work

How soon you go back to work will depend on the type of job you have. Your doctor can discuss this with you. Generally, you can expect to be away from your job for about three months, until you make a full recovery.

Long-Term Goals

Four months after your heart attack or heart surgery, you may be ready to work on long-term goals associated with your improving health. These may involve diet, exercise, monitoring conditions such as high blood pressure, and, if you haven't already, quitting smoking. We will address those goals and more later in this book.

CHAPTER SIX

Assessing Your Progress

At some point, usually about six weeks after your heart attack, you and your doctor or rehabilitation nurse will evaluate your progress. At this time, you can make sure you're on the right track. The medications are doing the job. Your physical recovery continues. In short, you're on your way to resuming an active, productive life. Now is also a good time to reflect on changes you are making in your habits. These include changes in diet, regular exercise, quitting smoking, or control of high blood pressure. It's also time to fine-tune those efforts for maximum success.

A follow-up appointment is a good opportunity to ask your doctor questions that have come up since you left the hospital. It's also a good time to discuss anything that's bothering you. It's important to review your efforts with a health-care professional after the heart attack. That way you can be clear about your rehabilitation goals and why they are so important to your continued good health. If you aren't sure of your goals or find it hard to make the changes "stick," now is an excellent time to ask your doctor for help. You can also rededicate yourself to the effort. This chapter can help.

The Six-Week Checkup

What can you expect at the six-week checkup? You may be asked to take an exercise or walking test. This test will give an estimate of your current level of physical conditioning. (If you have severe heart disease or unstable angina, you will not be asked to take this test.) If you experience ischemia (a lack of blood supply) at a relatively low level of exercise, an angiogram or other test may be required. This will indicate whether ischemia is worsening. The doctor is also likely to measure your weight, blood cholesterol level, and blood pressure, as well as make other routine physical checks.

The Exercise Test

An exercise test six weeks after your heart attack can give your doctor an idea of your strength and endurance. The results help the doctor determine when you can return to work, if that is a concern. The exercise test usually involves walking at a slight uphill grade on a treadmill. During the test, electrocardiographic leads will be placed on your body. The leads are connected to an electrocardiograph (EKG), which monitors your heart activity (see page 37). The test is symptom-limited. That means that it stops if the EKG shows abnormalities or if you feel any chest pain. To get the most accurate results, you may be asked to stop taking medications for a brief time before the test.

Using the results of the exercise test, your doctor will determine if you can tolerate a certain level of activity. If so, you will know things are going well. You will probably be allowed to pursue light to moderate activities at home, increase your current exercise prescription, or return to office work. (People whose work requires heavy physical labor or a great deal of responsibility—such as piloting airplanes—must meet higher exercise standards.)

Your doctor will compare your heart rate, blood pressure, EKG, and rate of perceived exertion with certain standards before prescribing an exercise program. If abnormalities are found at a relatively low exercise tolerance level, you may need further evaluation and treatment. You may require supervision during exercise until your tolerance increases. At all times, of course, you should exercise at a reasonable and comfortable intensity. It is never a good idea to exercise until you are out of breath or feel pain or discomfort.

❦ *When Magda got on the exercise treadmill and started walking, she wasn't sure it was something she wanted to do. What if she got bad news? What if she couldn't garden anymore?*

As she walked, she tried to concentrate on the progress she'd made in the weeks since her heart attack. A lot had changed. She walked some every day. She watched what she ate. She took her medicines faithfully. All in all, pretty good, she thought.

Meanwhile, the treadmill pace was picking up slightly. Magda hardly noticed. Suddenly, the nurse interrupted Magda's thoughts. She said Magda had passed with flying colors. The treadmill was slowing down, and Magda could get off in a moment. What a relief! ❦

Other Tests

To check your blood chemistry, a blood sample will be taken and analyzed in a laboratory, just as it was when you were admitted to the hospital. When the test results are returned, your doctor will compare them with the earlier results. Then you'll know whether your efforts to change your diet, exercise, and monitor a diabetes condition (if you have one) are starting to pay off. If the changes aren't as great as your doctor would like at this early stage, you may be given medication. You may also be asked to change the emphasis or degree of your rehabilitation efforts.

Medication Review

If you are taking drugs to control angina pectoris, high blood pressure, arrhythmias, heart failure, or other conditions, your doctor may want to adjust your prescription at this time. Beta-blockers, nitrates (such as nitroglycerin), calcium channel blockers, digitalis, vasodilators, aspirin, and ACE inhibitors are examples of drugs your doctor will review. If you are responding well to treatment, some dosages may be reduced or eliminated. If you have experienced uncomfortable side ef-fects, the drug dosages or the drugs themselves may need to be changed to minimize those effects.

Now is also the time to ask your doctor any questions you have about taking your medications. If you aren't sure or can't remember why you are taking a certain medication, ask your doctor to explain it to you. Knowing exactly why you take a drug helps fix its importance in your mind and makes compliance easier. Be sure you are taking all medications exactly as your doctor prescribed them. If you have not al-ready done so, create a reminder system to help you keep track of which medications to take and when to take them. Tell your doctor about all medications you're taking, not just those he or she has pre-scribed. Even over-the-counter medications should be checked out with your doctor and pharmacist before you take them. They may be dangerous in combination with other drugs you are taking or they may neutralize the effects of those drugs.

🍂 *"I'm feeling pretty good, except for this flu going around." Hilary was in her doctor's office for a six-week checkup. "I know I'm not supposed to mix my heart medicines with other kinds of medicines. Can you tell me what I can take safely and what I can't?"*

"I'd be glad to go over that with you now," the doctor replied. "If you have questions later, or are thinking about taking some-thing else, please give me a call first. I need to know about all the over-the-counter preparations you take. And of course, if you should see another doctor for a different problem while tak-ing your heart medications, be sure to tell that doctor about all your medications. Feel free to call me and ask any other doctor you see to do the same. We'll work together to make sure you're taking the medications that are right for you."🍂

It may be a good idea to write down your questions before your ap-pointment. You may also want to bring along a notebook so that you can jot down answers or suggestions you hear. (Ask a family member to join you during this part of the appointment. He or she can also benefit from hearing this information and may help you remember more of the conversation and instructions later.) If you find any part of your routine hard to follow, tell your doctor about it. He or she may be able to adjust your medications or dosage schedule so that it is easier for you to follow.

Based on the medical findings of your checkup, you'll probably want to review or fine-tune your "lifestyle prescription" as well. Let's take a closer look at some elements of that prescription.

How Are You Doing?

By now, you have learned a lot about the mechanisms of coronary heart disease (CHD) and its prevalence (see Chapter One). You have learned that, over a lifetime, day-to-day habits make a big difference in whether CHD develops. These habits include eating right, exercising, and avoiding smoking. You can also take care of conditions that can lead to development of atherosclerosis and CHD. These are important ways anyone can learn to fight this disease.

As part of your recovery, you've been asked to think about some or all of these issues and to make healthful changes in your behavior. You probably received a lot of help and information about these changes while you were in the hospital. But you may find it harder to stick with a new plan now that you're on your own. You may feel discouraged or overwhelmed by the extent of the changes you've been asked to make. Such feelings are common.

There's no doubt about it: changing old habits can be hard—even when you are strongly motivated. But sooner than you think, the changes you've made will begin to make you feel better and stronger. You may even have received good news at your checkup. Were the results of your exercise test improved? Were your blood cholesterol levels lower? Maybe your cough is clearer if you quit smoking. (See Chapter Eight for more information about quitting smoking.) Was your blood pressure lower? If so, give yourself a pat on the back! What you're doing *is working*.

If not, you may need to review these areas. Are you having trouble maintaining your commitment to these changes? If so, talk with your doctor about ways to rekindle your enthusiasm and rededicate yourself to a more healthful, active life. Now is an excellent time to ask yourself, "How am I doing?"

Exercise

A personalized exercise prescription from your doctor probably provides instructions for:

- warm-up and cool-down phases
- an aerobic or conditioning phase
- the duration and frequency of your exercise sessions
- the type of exercise appropriate for you (such as walking)

Are you still following those instructions? If you aren't following them consistently, stop and think about what the problem might be. Then discuss it with your doctor or rehab nurse. Always tell your doctor about *any* physical discomfort that exercise causes, from chest pains to foot or bone problems.

People for whom an exercise routine is new may stop exercising for a number of reasons. Most of these can be easily overcome with a little effort. Here are some common reasons people give for not exercising:

- bad time of day
- exercise hurts
- exercise is boring
- can't see any progress
- not enough family support
- no encouragement from doctor

Most of these excuses are easily resolved once they are identified. Bad time of day? Find another time that is more convenient for you. Bored or uninterested? You never need to feel locked into one kind of exercise. You can choose from a number of different activities. Just be sure your workout reaches the intensity or energy expenditure that is right for you. Even playing with the kids or working in the yard may qualify. Keep experimenting until you find the right fit.

You haven't seen any progress? Periodic exercise tests at the hospital or outpatient clinic will show improvement clearly. You might also keep a log that shows how much you exercised during each session and how it made you feel. Over time, you'll notice a difference in your stamina in these records. Read your notes periodically.

Do you feel like your efforts aren't supported by family members or your doctor? Then look for support elsewhere. Talk with a friend who exercises regularly or take an exercise class. Join an interest group that will put you with others who exercise. (Try a group such as "mall walkers," people who meet at indoor malls to exercise before the stores open.) And, as we've already stated, always promptly discuss physical discomfort related to exercise with your doctor.

Finally, remember that exercise should be enjoyable. Treat it like play! Think of your workouts as time you owe yourself for fun. Go ahead and be flexible—to a point. If you walk for exercise, for example, perhaps you'll want to change your usual route occasionally. Instead of driving, try walking to a nearby park. Consider brightening your routine by listening to your favorite music or radio station on a portable disk or cassette player while you walk. (If you listen to talk radio, you might take your regular walk during a favorite program.)

🍎 *"Your blood pressure is down, Steve. Your cholesterol levels are also improving. I'm glad you're finding it easier than you thought it would be to adjust your diet. Tell me, how is your new exercise program coming along?"*

Steve was in his doctor's office for a six-week checkup after his heart attack. He was doing better at eating lower-fat, lower-sodium foods, but exercise was a problem. He thought about a walking program. But he just wasn't the type to stride out into the neighborhood and walk around for half an hour. He confided to the doctor that he hadn't even tried exercising. In fact, he still dreaded the whole thought of it.

The doctor was sympathetic. "Not everyone likes the same kind of exercise," he said. "What do you like to do?"

Steve laughed. "What do I like to do? Watch TV!" he said. "But that's not very good exercise, is it?"

"Ah, but it can be," the doctor said. "I've heard of some creative people who've figured out how to power a TV by connect-

ing it to a stationary bicycle. You have to pedal to watch! That's not for everybody, of course. But there are other ways to exercise while you watch TV. Have you thought about buying exercise equipment that you could work out on while you watch TV? A treadmill or stationary bicycle would be perfect. Or you could buy an aerobic exercise video and work out in your family room."

These ideas appealed to Steve. He thought about why he hadn't even wanted to try walking. It wasn't the walking he minded really. He just thought it a bit ridiculous to walk for twenty or thirty minutes with no particular destination in mind. It sounded boring. But if he could walk while watching TV, that would be different. It was like killing two birds with one stone. The more he thought about it, the more he liked the idea of a treadmill. He decided to pursue the idea when he got home. His wife and daughters would use a treadmill, too, he thought. It sounded like a good investment. ❦

Eating Plan

Following a low-fat, low-cholesterol eating plan is a great idea. It can have very positive effects on blood cholesterol levels, blood pressure, and weight loss efforts. It can also help keep diabetes under control. Such an eating plan may require changes in the way you shop for, prepare, and eat food. Making these changes can be easier than you think, particularly if others in your household are as committed to them as you are. You may want to begin by making small changes. Then you can make more changes as you learn more. (See Chapter Nine for more information on nutrition.)

A low-fat eating plan is made up of low-fat foods that are as tasty and satisfying as the high-fat foods you may be accustomed to. (Many people think that foods cooked with low-fat methods actually have a more intense flavor.) If you aren't familiar with this style of cooking and dining, it may take you a little while to adjust to it. Give yourself time to become comfortable shopping for and preparing foods in a new way. After all, you probably didn't learn to cook in your present style overnight either.

Help yourself out. Talk with friends who follow a low-fat, low-cholesterol eating plan. Pick up some low-fat, low-cholesterol cookbooks or cooking magazines. They are usually full of recipes and tips for lowering the fat content of foods while maintaining a high "tastiness quotient." (Often they provide some welcome encouragement, too.) Quick and easy cooking methods, such as stir frying and a new emphasis on seasoning with herbs and spices, can help you make the adjustment.

A registered dietitian may be able to evaluate your diet with you. He or she can suggest useful ways to reduce the fat and cholesterol you consume. Strategic changes in some foods you eat regularly may make a big difference. For example, try substituting oatmeal for scrambled eggs in the morning. That one change can have a profound effect on the cholesterol level of someone accustomed to eating eggs every day. Reaching for salt-free pretzels (which are baked) instead of potato chips (which are fried) can make a big difference to someone who is "addicted" to snack food. Switching from whole milk to skim is another easy way to help keep your cholesterol under control.

Maybe your latest blood cholesterol levels have not fallen as much as your doctor would like. Then you may need to review your current diet and any changes you have made in it. If you haven't been committed to making those changes, now is the time to discuss it with your doctor or a registered dietitian. If you have been diligent about making dietary changes but they have not had the desired effect, you may need to modify your eating plan a little more or begin to take medications.

Many people's blood cholesterol levels can be controlled through diet alone. However, if a stricter diet doesn't help in your case, you may have an inherited tendency toward high cholesterol. Your doctor may put you on cholesterol-lowering medications if you're not on them already. Other family members should also be tested, in case they have the same problem. They too will benefit from a low-fat, low-cholesterol eating plan.

Remember, the changes won't all happen overnight. And you can still have that piece of cake on special occasions. But if you are aware of the kinds of changes you need to make and try to make them consistently, you *will* make progress. Remember, even a small drop in your blood cholesterol levels can make an important difference in your health. Keep going!

Quitting Smoking

As we'll see in Chapter Eight, smoking is closely related to the development of heart disease as well as cancer. Continuing to smoke cigarettes after a heart attack is very dangerous. People who smoke are more likely than others to suffer *additional* heart attacks and to suffer *more severe* heart attacks. If you have not yet quit smoking, it should be a top priority for you now.

There is some good news: People who have had a heart attack are usually so motivated to quit that they have a very high success rate. Fifty percent of those who quit cigarette smoking after a heart attack stay off tobacco permanently. They begin to reap the benefits of better health very soon after quitting. If you've tried to quit but failed, don't give up! It may take several tries before you succeed. However, with each attempt you've learned a little more about why you smoke and what your trouble spots are. With that information and continued resolve, you will be successful.

Controlling Diabetes

Diabetes mellitus is the inability of the body to produce or react properly to insulin. Insulin is a substance that allows the body to process glucose (sugar). This disease, for which there is no cure, can start in childhood or adulthood. Diabetes seriously increases the risk of heart disease and stroke, as well as other health problems. More than 80 percent of persons with diabetes die of some form of heart or blood vessel disease.

The adult form may be delayed or controlled with diet and exercise. It is often associated with obesity. Adult-onset diabetes may be delayed if weight is kept under control. If you have diabetes or are at risk for developing it, you may need to make some changes. Pay particular attention to adopting a low-fat, low-cholesterol eating plan, exercising regularly, and keeping blood pressure under control. It's also very important that you not smoke cigarettes. If your blood glucose level isn't what it should be, talk over your options with your doctor, and then follow his or her advice closely.

Overcoming Depression

A period of depression is common after a heart attack (see Chapter Twelve). You may feel angry, guilty, or deeply worried about what the future holds. These emotions are understandable. In most cases, they pass rapidly as you begin to feel better. Sometimes, however, depression continues. The person who is depressed may not even realize it. The severity of the depression is not related to the severity of the heart attack. A person who had a mild heart attack may have a very deep depression afterward. Another person, who had a much more medically serious heart attack, may bounce back quickly.

Most often, depression strikes within a couple of days of the heart attack and lasts a few days. But some people become depressed after they go home. They may worry about leaving the security of the hospital. They may fear most activity because they think it might trigger another heart attack. That fear may lead them to avoid previous activities and other people, fueling depression. In other cases they may be surrounded by overprotective family and friends. Too much care and protection can damage an adult's self-esteem and hinder recovery. Being alone, however, is also not desirable.

If you feel depressed, be sure to talk to someone you trust about what you are feeling. Depression makes people withdraw. When that happens, they may not participate in all the important aspects of their recovery program. They may not get enough exercise or sleep, both of which can help counter depression. They may not eat right or resume activities they enjoyed before their heart attack. In short, such a person is at risk of becoming an invalid—and it doesn't have to be that way. Depression is treatable. Ask your doctor.

Taking Stock

Now that the immediate crisis of the heart attack has passed, you may be facing a new problem: Your initial enthusiasm for making serious lifestyle changes may have dimmed somewhat. It can be hard to remain motivated day after day. Now is a good time to take stock of your achievements thus far and to remind yourself of the progress you are making.

CHAPTER SEVEN

The Risk Factor Connection

How does heart disease develop? In the early part of this century, it was rare in the United States and Europe. But as nations became industrialized, people became less physically active. We ate richer foods and faced different kinds of stress than we did in the past. During this period rates of coronary heart disease (CHD) and high blood pressure became epidemic. Since 1968 those rates have fallen steadily. Our habits have begun to change again—this time for the better. More people are quitting or never starting smoking, choosing a leaner diet, managing high blood pressure, and getting more exercise. The rewards are tangible. Although far too many people still die of cardiovascular disease, death rates are dropping. From 1983 to 1993 death rates from cardiovascular diseases fell by more than 23 percent.

The pattern of heart disease development observed across the century in this country and Europe tells medical researchers something important. Heart disease is not the inevitable consequence of aging or a matter of bad luck. Personal behavior plays a very important role in its development. Some risk factors for heart disease cannot be changed. However, many others can be modified or eliminated. In fact, in many cases modifiable risk factors may determine whether or not one gets heart disease at all.

Notice, as you read this chapter, how often certain risk factors reappear under different guises: obesity, cigarette smoking, high blood pressure, high blood cholesterol levels, physical inactivity, drug abuse.

As an experiment, take a notepad and track just one risk factor that nags you. See how often it pops up as a contributing factor in the development of other problems. Risk factors associated with development of atherosclerosis and heart disease criss-cross in all sorts of ways and contribute to all sorts of health problems. Once you have a heart attack, you should *not* give up on the notion of reducing your risk factors. The same risks that produced the first heart attack are likely to produce another one. By eliminating or modifying some or all of these known health risks, you can really do a lot to improve your overall risk profile.

What Is a Risk Factor?

A **risk factor** is a condition associated with an increase in the risk of developing an illness, in this case, heart disease. Risk factors are established through extensive medical research and analysis. The first large study to identify risk factors for heart disease was the landmark Framingham Heart Study. This research study began in 1948 and continues today. It has tracked the cardiovascular health of literally thousands of men and women living in Framingham, Massachusetts. The Framingham study is long term and exceptionally comprehensive. It has provided trustworthy statistics that have identified and confirmed the effect of a number of risk factors associated with heart disease.

Other major research studies, such as the Multiple Risk Factor Intervention Trial (called MRFIT for short) and the Seven Countries study, have also provided important information that verifies the effects of various risk factors on heart health. In the MRFIT study—appropriately named, because only men were participants—investigators found that a dietary link exists between higher blood cholesterol levels and an increased risk of CHD. The Seven Countries study showed that national differences in cholesterol levels and heart disease rates were a function of differences in national diet patterns. Both studies gave doctors even more evidence that heart disease risk could be modified through changes in behaviors, including eating behaviors.

Risk factors for heart disease are not created equal. **Major risk factors** are those that medical research has shown to be definitely related to an increased risk of heart disease. Medical research has proven a connection between major risk factors and heart disease. **Contributing factors** are also associated with the development of heart disease. They show the troubling tendency to be somewhere in the picture when heart disease develops. However, the link between contributing factors and heart disease is often indirect and isn't precisely understood.

Some risk factors cannot be changed. Others can be eliminated with effort. Still others that cannot be completely eliminated may be modified, reducing their "risk value." Major risk factors that cannot be changed include heredity, being male, and increasing age. Major risk factors that can be eliminated or modified include cigarette/tobacco smoking, high blood cholesterol levels, high blood pressure, and physical inactivity. Factors that contribute to the development of heart disease include diabetes mellitus, obesity, and, according to some studies, stress. The more risk factors you have, the higher your risk of developing heart disease.

The Many Causes of Heart Disease

Only rarely does heart disease develop because one risk factor, such as extremely high blood pressure, is wildly out of control. Doctors have found that heart disease usually develops from a complex mosaic, or cluster, of risk factors. Atherosclerosis is the principal manifestation of heart disease, causing angina and heart attack.

By themselves, risk factors in any one person may not be extreme. Most people with high blood pressure who have heart attacks, for example, have only mild to moderate elevations above normal. However, the perceived severity of any one risk factor becomes worse in the presence of other risk factors. It is the *interaction* of all risk factors that creates the true risk profile for anyone.

For example, a young man has a total blood cholesterol level of 200 mg/dl (milligrams per deciliter of blood), which is considered borderline high. He has no other risk factors for heart disease. By current estimates, this man would probably not be expected to develop heart disease until he is 70 years old or more, when his age (another risk factor) catches up with him.

However, by adding just *one* other risk factor to his profile, cigarette smoking, his profile changes dramatically. With that single addition, this young man is more likely to develop CHD 10 years earlier, by age 60. By smoking he has altered his profile to look more like that of a person with a blood cholesterol level of 275 mg/dl, which is a very high reading. Suddenly, bringing down his borderline cholesterol level becomes much more urgent. (So does his quitting smoking, of course.) If this man also had high blood pressure and were diabetic, he could be expected to show signs of heart disease at the very early age of 40.

🐓 *"Yeah, I'll have a Kaiser roll, buttered, and regular coffee with extra cream."*

Martin called out his breakfast order to the fellow behind the deli counter. He was running a little late. "That's gridlock in this city for you," he grumbled to himself. It looked as though he wouldn't have time for his usual cigarette before he sat down at his desk.

Martin worked on the building's third floor. He raced into the lobby and began stabbing at elevator buttons. Behind him was a stairway. But the 48-year-old never took the stairs. In fact, he rarely exerted himself at all, even at home, on the weekends. He told himself he didn't like to get too hot.

Over the years, it was clear, Martin gradually had established cherished but unhealthful habits that he unconsciously followed every day. These habits included smoking, a lack of exercise, and an unbalanced diet that heavily emphasized rich, fatty foods at the expense of vegetables, fruits, and carbohydrates. He saw nothing wrong with it; after all, he could look around his office and see dozens more just like him. But without knowing it, Martin was setting himself up for a heart attack and increasing his risk for stroke as well. Lately, Martin felt mild pain in his chest whenever he ran for the subway. But so far, he hadn't bothered to get his symptom diagnosed. 🐓

Controlling Risk Factors

Some interventions affect several risk factors at once. By working with your doctor, you can find ways to streamline your efforts and maximize results. For example:

- *Increasing physical activity* modifies several other risk factors for heart disease. Exercise can help lower high blood pressure and increase the amount of HDL or "good" cholesterol in the blood. It can also help persons with diabetes control blood sugar levels and help efforts toward weight loss.
- *Changes in diet* can help lower blood pressure and cholesterol levels and also aid in weight loss.

Before starting a modification program, you'll want to consider which risk factors you can eliminate or modify and those that you'll have to live with. Obviously, if you have risk factors that you cannot change, such as a family history of early heart disease, you will want to concentrate more energy on those that you *can* affect.

Information is power. You need to know your own risk factors and their relative importance in your own health profile. This is critical to proper management of your illness. Your doctor will help you identify risk factors affecting your heart health. He or she will ask you detailed questions about your health history and your personal habits. You will probably be asked to take certain tests. Once you have a good idea of what your risk profile is, you'll be in the best position to do something about it. This chapter will help you get to know your own risks and to understand why it is so important to control or eliminate those that you can.

After a heart attack, most people feel vulnerable. Understandably, they are worried about their health and its impact on their future. There is one way to reduce these feelings: Resolve to work with your doctor or other health-care professional to make positive lifestyle changes, starting now.

You do have some control over what happens from now on. You can make changes for better health.

Three Risk Factors to Live With

Three major risk factors for heart disease can't be changed or eliminated. They are age, being male, and having a family history of premature heart disease (heart disease that appears in men before age 55 and women before age 65). It is important to acknowledge these risk factors. Although they can't be changed, they affect the severity of other risk factors in your profile that *can* be modified or eliminated.

Family History

If either—or both—of your parents or other close relatives had early heart attacks, or if you have an older brother or sister who has been diagnosed with early CHD, you are more likely to develop CHD yourself. In some scientific studies, premature CHD in a close relative has been found to be the single best predictor of future CHD risk. Signs of premature CHD include not only heart attack in men before age 55 and women before age 65 but also angina pectoris, findings of CHD on an angiogram, and sudden cardiac death. The number of relatives and their ages at disease onset influence the strength of this important association. The more of your close relatives who fit this profile and the younger they were when stricken, the more serious this risk factor is for you. A family history of CHD tends to complicate the presence of other risk factors in the profile. The effects of high blood cholesterol, smoking, and high blood pressure on persons with a family history of heart disease are even more dangerous than they would be for those without a family history of the disease.

Coronary heart disease tends to run in families. If you are a heart attack survivor, you may find it in your own family tree. Studies have found that susceptible family groups with premature heart disease tend to exhibit other risk factors for CHD more frequently than do families without a history of premature CHD. These groups may be more susceptible to developing CHD because of these risk factors.

African-Americans as a group have a significantly higher incidence of high blood pressure and heart attack than do white Americans, Hispanic-Americans, or Asian-Americans. On average, African-Americans exhibit moderately high blood pressure at twice the rate of whites of the same age. African-Americans also exhibit severe high blood pressure readings that are three times those of white Americans.

African-Americans and those with a family history of heart disease need to take particular care of their controllable risk factors because their heredity is a major risk factor for them. If your risk profile fits these descriptions and you have children, do them a favor: Practice habits that will keep their risk of developing CHD as adults as low as possible. Teach them to be physically active and to see a doctor regularly for checkups. Encourage them to eat a balanced, low-fat, nutritious diet.

Being Male

It's a fact that American men have a greater incidence of heart attack than women do, and they suffer heart attacks earlier in life. Men also die of heart attack more often than women do. However, CHD is a very serious problem for women, too. It is the leading cause of death in women.

Determining why men are at a greater disadvantage for heart disease requires a comparison to women's risk. In youth and through middle age, women tend to have lower blood cholesterol levels, lower proportional weight, and lower blood pressure than men do. As women age, though, these values, which are closely associated with atherosclerosis and heart disease, tend to creep upward, until they approximate those of men.

After menopause, women's incidence of heart attack also begins to approach that of men. There may be a couple of reasons for this. One is that estrogen appears to have a protective effect on the heart and blood vessels of women. This is a somewhat variable effect, however, and hasn't been proven conclusively in medical studies. **Estrogen** is a female sex hormone. Its production in the body drops dramatically after menopause—at the same time that women's cholesterol levels and risk of heart attack begin to rise. (Heart attack risk also rises sharply in women who have had complete hysterectomies, which induce surgical menopause.) Estrogen replacement therapy (ERT) is prescribed for many women after menopause or a hysterectomy to prevent brittle bones. ERT has a demonstrated protective effect against heart disease, too. (See discussion of ERT on pages 80–82.)

Age

Studies have shown that risk of CHD and heart attack increases with age, regardless of sex. Being 45 years and older for men and 55 years and older for women is considered a risk factor for CHD. Only about 5 percent of all heart attack victims are under 40 years of age; about 45 percent are under 65 years. More than half of all heart attack victims are 65 years or older. The risk of suffering a heart attack increases every 10 years of your life, regardless of your other risk factors.

Why atherosclerosis and CHD tend to develop with age isn't completely understood. Atherosclerosis may develop as the result of long-term exposure of blood vessels to other risk factors, such as high blood cholesterol levels or elevated blood pressure.

Major Controllable Risk Factors

Cigarette/Tobacco Use

Most people are aware of the health problems associated with cigarette smoking. Most assume that lung cancer is the only risk associated with smoking. Certainly, lung cancer can be a terrible consequence of smoking cigarettes. But smoking carries a very high risk of heart attack and stroke as well. In fact, more smokers die from CHD than from lung cancer! Of the estimated 417,000 premature deaths attributed to smoking each year, more than 43 percent are linked to cardiovascular disease. Less than 30 percent are attributed to lung cancer.

People who smoke are at much greater risk of all sorts of health problems than are nonsmokers. Smokers have fully twice the risk of developing cardiovascular disease and having a heart attack that nonsmokers do. Their heart attacks are also likely to be worse than those of nonsmokers; that is, they are more likely to die as a consequence. Smoking is the most preventable cause of premature death. It is also a risk factor for sudden cardiac death—the kind of heart attack that kills the victim outright before he or she has a chance to get treatment at a hospital. Smokers are two to four times more susceptible to sudden cardiac death than nonsmokers.

❦ *"I like to smoke. I feel fine. What's the problem?" Jed was sick of being hassled by the others in his Masters swim group. Like Jed, these middle-aged men met regularly to swim at a public pool. They occasionally entered meets, competing against other Masters swimmers. Unlike Jed, the others in his group didn't smoke. They were trying to convince Jed that his smoking habit had consequences, despite his commitment to regular exercise.*

A doctor in the group laid it out for Jed as everyone headed for the parking lot after a workout. "OK, you asked for it. Here's the truth: If you and I were alike in all other respects, you'd still have twice the risk of having a heart attack that I do. That's because you smoke and I don't. But remember, neither of us starts at particularly low risk. We're already at extra risk because of factors we can't control: We're male and we're aging like everyone else on the planet. You have another risk factor that you can't control: Your father died of a heart attack at 53. It doesn't get more personal than that. A smoking habit is a major risk factor you can control. Don't you want to, just to keep your odds down, just in case?

"Look, quitting smoking isn't easy. I realize that. But smoking isn't so great when you consider how it makes you feel every day: more tired, harder to get your breath, harder to work out, and, at the back of your mind, worried. C'mon, pal. I know people our age who've quit. Let them give you a before-and-after picture of what quitting can mean. Just try. I'll call you with some numbers when I get back to my office. And I'll see you next week!" ❦

How does smoking exert its terrible influence? Basically, three mechanisms are at play. Smoking delivers nicotine into the bloodstream. **Nicotine** is a substance found in tobacco that produces several effects in the body. It increases the heart rate while the person is smoking. At the same time, it increases the heart's demand for oxygen. It also raises blood pressure temporarily. Nicotine acts directly on the heart muscle and is thought to make smokers more susceptible to developing ventricular arrhythmias, which can be deadly.

Smoking also delivers carbon monoxide into the bloodstream. Normally, hemoglobin in the blood picks up oxygen in the lungs and delivers it to cells throughout the body. But if carbon monoxide is present, hemoglobin takes that up instead. The body doesn't "recognize" carbon monoxide, nor can it make use of it. The particular nourishment that oxygen provides the body can't be substituted. Every cell suffers for this. But the heart, which needs so much oxygen to do its job, may suffer the most. Researchers suspect that carbon monoxide is the major factor in cigarette smoking that stimulates development of CHD.

The conflicting demands on the heart made by nicotine and carbon monoxide through smoking are cruel. On the one hand, nicotine makes the heart beat faster. On the other, carbon monoxide in the bloodstream ensures that the heart gets less of the oxygen it needs!

As bad as they are, nicotine and carbon monoxide aren't the only problems that make smoking such a dangerous risk factor for CHD. Smoking is believed to contribute to a "sticky blood" condition. Blood platelets, the circulating components that help blood clot over wounds, are stickier in smokers than in nonsmokers. Thus, blood tends to clot even when it isn't supposed to. This condition contributes to the development of atherosclerosis and helps create thrombi and emboli. These rogue blood clots block blood vessels and can cause stroke or heart attack, among other problems.

That's not all. Smoking also aggravates angina and decreases exercise tolerance, one indicator of CHD. Smoking has been linked to coronary artery spasm in women who otherwise do not show evidence of CHD. **Coronary artery spasm** is the involuntary, temporary closure of an artery, causing symptoms of angina pectoris and sometimes heart attack.

Any of these effects would be bad enough. But smoking has an even more damaging effect on people who are already predisposed to heart attack because of other factors in their risk profile. Smoking worsens the effect of these factors. Blood pressure, for example, is harder to control in smokers than in nonsmokers. Smoking decreases HDL ("good") cholesterol levels in the blood. Even if smokers carefully follow a low-cholesterol diet, their good efforts toward managing their cholesterol levels may literally "go up in smoke." Smoking may cancel the beneficial effects of their diet.

Pipe and Cigar Smoking

Most studies have found that pipe and cigar smokers are also at greater risk of developing CHD than nonsmokers. Their risk is somewhat lower than that of cigarette smokers. Pipe and cigar smokers who do not inhale smoke do absorb nicotine into their system through the mouth. This amount is less, however, than that which cigarette smokers inhale.

Passive Smoke

People who inhale other people's cigarette smoke over the long term are also at greater risk of developing heart disease than are nonsmokers. Such persons might be the spouses of smokers, office mates of smokers, or anyone who is often in a smoke-filled room. This kind of smoke has also been called **second-hand smoke** and **environmental tobacco smoke.** Like cigarette smoking itself, passive smoke carries a health risk and should be avoided.

High Blood Cholesterol Levels

High levels of cholesterol in the blood may be the most important risk factor in the development of atherosclerosis. These levels should be brought down within normal ranges through changes in diet and exercise, and, if necessary, through medication. Even small reductions in this area are beneficial and can lower the risk of future cardiovascular disease.

A blood cholesterol level reading reflects the amount of cholesterol circulating in the bloodstream. There are different kinds of cholesterol. High-density lipoprotein (HDL) is considered "good" cholesterol because it is thought to remove excess cholesterol from the circulatory system. Low-density lipoprotein (LDL) is considered "bad" cholesterol because it tends to collect in artery walls and contribute to the development of atherosclerotic plaque. Triglycerides are often measured along with HDL and LDL cholesterol in cholesterol tests. Triglycerides are blood fats. The connection between atherosclerosis, the underlying cause of heart disease, and cholesterol is discussed more fully in Chapter One, pages 3–34.

Scientists believe that adults without evidence of CHD should have a blood cholesterol level no greater than 200 milligrams per deciliter (mg/dl) of blood. The higher the cholesterol level, the greater the risk of heart attack. A person with a cholesterol reading of 240 mg/dl is twice as likely to suffer a heart attack as a person whose total blood cholesterol level is 200 mg/dl or less. People whose cholesterol levels are high—within the 240–300 mg/dl range—benefit directly from every little bit they can whittle off that score. Every 1 percent reduction in serum cholesterol will yield a 2 percent reduction in the risk of CHD.

Generally speaking, the lower your cholesterol level, the better. Doctors do not yet know whether, at some point, a very low cholesterol reading becomes unhealthy. They do know that HDL and LDL cholesterol levels are important. Individuals with high cholesterol readings overall may not be at greater risk of developing heart disease if they have a high HDL cholesterol component (35 mg/dl or higher) in their profile. But a pattern of high LDL and low HDL cholesterol indicates the opposite: a greater risk of developing atherosclerosis. In many of those with high LDL levels, the factor is familial rather than purely diet-related.

If your own blood cholesterol levels are "just a little bit" above 200 mg/dl, you may be tempted to think that your cholesterol problem isn't really worth worrying about. But you'd be wrong. Half of all patients with CHD have only "modestly" elevated cholesterol levels—that is, levels above 200 mg/dl but lower than 240 mg/dl. Cholesterol lowering should be much more vigorous in those with CHD. For this reason, doctors will order a complete lipoprotein analysis for all patients with CHD. This analysis includes measurement of total cholesterol, total triglycerides, and HDL cholesterol. LDL cholesterol is calculated from those measurements. Classification of these patients is based on LDL cholesterol. The optimum LDL cholesterol is 100 mg/dl or lower. That corresponds to a total cholesterol of less than 160 mg/dl. Ideal HDL levels are 35 mg/dl or greater.

❦ *Tim stared moodily at the breakfast the waitress delivered to the table next to his: nicely salted fried eggs, a Danish pastry, hash brown potatoes, hot coffee with cream. He loved eating breakfasts like that himself. Or he did until last month.*

That was when he had a medical checkup. The doctor found that Tim had high blood cholesterol. It was complicated by obesity.

The doctor told Tim the diagnosis. Then he discussed Tim's overall condition. Although his blood cholesterol levels didn't seem that high to Tim, he learned it was important to get them under control. The doctor explained that as a 62-year-old man with high blood cholesterol, Tim was at pretty high odds for a heart attack. The doctor suggested that Tim watch his diet carefully and get some exercise. If that didn't work, Tim might have to take medicine to lower his blood cholesterol levels.

Tim had started a regular walking program. He walked near his home two or three times a week and at the mall with other walkers every Wednesday morning.

Tim and his wife Jackie were also trying to cut the fat out of their diet wherever possible, one meal at a time. It wasn't always easy, especially when the couple ate out. But the prospect of a heart attack kept Tim's priorities in line. Today was his first follow-up appointment. He would see whether his efforts were working.

When their order arrived at the table it looked pretty good to both of them. They split a mushroom omelette made with egg substitute and low-fat cheese. They also had whole-wheat toast with jam. They both ordered cranberry juice and coffee with skim milk.

"I still miss those sturdy breakfasts—more like 'break-feasts'—now and then," Tim told his wife. "But I have to admit I feel a little more energetic after lighter meals like these. I don't mind getting on the scale so much, either. Eating right this past month has taken off five pounds, and it wasn't even hard. I think I'll get some good news at my checkup today." ❦

A high triglyceride level (400 mg/dl or above) often accompanies a low HDL level. A high triglyceride level can be important, however, as a marker for high blood sugar (a precursor of diabetes) in women.

High Blood Cholesterol Levels and Other Risk Factors

When a high blood cholesterol level is combined with other risk factors in an individual profile, the likelihood of developing further CHD increases dramatically. Obesity tends to raise LDL levels, and smoking depresses the level of HDL cholesterol in the bloodstream, for example. Either condition worsens the overall blood cholesterol score. Yet there are remedies. A reasonable weight-loss diet, exercise, and quitting smoking can begin to help correct these imbalances. And they can do so in a relatively short amount of time.

Dietary Fats and Blood Cholesterol Levels

While some people have an inherited tendency to develop high blood cholesterol levels, most of us simply eat too much of the wrong things—fatty things. Most Americans eat a diet that is too rich in fat. Currently a daily diet composed of less than 30 percent fat is recommended by health and nutrition experts. The average American daily diet is 34 percent fat.

There are different types of fat. **Saturated fat** is derived from whole-milk dairy products, eggs, animal fats, and tropical oils (such as coconut, palm, and palm kernel). Many foods that are high in saturated fats are also high in cholesterol. (**Dietary cholesterol** comes only from animal products, such as egg yolks, organ meats, dairy products, beef, poultry, and fish.) Saturated fats increase total blood cholesterol levels and LDL cholesterol. Many saturated fats can be identified quickly by the fact that they are usually solid at room temperature.

Polyunsaturated and **monounsaturated fats** are normally liquid at room temperature. Plant oils are generally polyunsaturated or monounsaturated. These oils cause less damage than saturated oils and should be substituted for saturated oils whenever possible. These oils work very well in salad dressings and in cooking. Fish oils are also polyunsaturated but a different type than plant oils. Monounsaturated and polyunsaturated oils should be used in place of saturated fats whenever possible. Remember that all types of fats have 9 calories per gram. Carbohydrates and protein have only 4 calories per gram. Therefore, high-fat diets promote obesity no matter what types of fats are eaten. So, the use of any oil should be limited. *All* fats in the Amer-

What Do Your Cholesterol Numbers Mean?

A high blood cholesterol level with a low HDL cholesterol level can be bad news. It's one of the four major risk factors that medical research has shown to be associated with an increased risk of heart attack. The other three are cigarette smoke, high blood pressure, and lack of adequate physical activity.

So it's important to have your blood cholesterol and HDL cholesterol levels checked regularly, along with your other risk factors. (It is recommended that this practice begin at age 20.) If your blood cholesterol is less than 200 mg/dl and your HDL level is equal to or greater than 35 mg/dl, have another test within five years. Be sure to discuss your cholesterol level with your doctor. (Mg/dl is short for the measurement units "milligrams per deciliter.")

Your total blood cholesterol is probably the first number your doctor will talk about. It's the most common measurement of blood cholesterol. It's also wise to ask your doctor to discuss your LDL and HDL cholesterol levels and explain what they mean.

Your total blood cholesterol will fall into one of these categories if you have not had a cardiac event:

Total Blood (Serum) Cholesterol	*Classification*
Less than 200 mg/dl	Desirable
200–239 mg/dl	Borderline high risk
240 mg/dl and above	High risk

If you have had a cardiac event, your doctor will look closely at your LDL cholesterol level. Your LDL cholesterol level greatly affects your risk of heart attack. In fact, LDL cholesterol is a better predictor of heart attack risk than total blood cholesterol. If you have not had a cardiac event, your doctor may classify your LDL cholesterol level according to these categories:

LDL Cholesterol	*Classification*
Below 130 mg/dl	Desirable
130–159 mg/dl	Borderline high risk
160 mg/dl and above	High risk

If you have had a heart attack or other cardiac event, your goal for LDL cholesterol should be 100 mg/dl or lower.

HDL cholesterol is thought to be protective against heart attack. A high level of HDL cholesterol in the blood is therefore desirable. Average levels of HDL cholesterol vary between men and women. For men, average HDL cholesterol levels range from 40 to 50 mg/dl. For women, average HDL cholesterol levels range from 50 to 60 mg/dl. An HDL level less than 35 mg/dl is considered low for men and women.

HDL Cholesterol	*Classification*
Less than 35 mg/dl	High risk

ican diet should be limited for maximum dietary health and prevention of CHD.

Controlling High Blood Cholesterol Levels
Many people with high blood cholesterol levels can bring those levels down to less than 200 mg/dl by cultivating different eating habits. This means following a sensible diet and eating a wide variety of foods (see Chapter Nine on diet). Consuming too many calories a day also raises LDL levels and lowers HDL independently of fat intake. A registered dietitian can help you develop an eating program you will feel comfortable with.

Blood cholesterol levels can often be lowered about 10 to 15 percent through changes in diet *alone*. Total fat intake for all adults should be kept to less than 30 percent of total daily calories. If you have had a heart attack, you need to pay particular attention to saturated fats and cholesterol in your diet. Saturated fats should be limited to less than 7 percent of your daily calories. Polyunsaturated fats should make up no more than 10 percent of your daily calories. Cholesterol intake should be kept to less than 200 milligrams per day. To find out about the foods you eat, read the labels on the food products you buy. There are many easy-to-use books and pamphlets that can provide you with values for fresh and prepared foods.

Exercise should also become part of your program to reduce high blood cholesterol levels. Exercise raises HDL, the good cholesterol, and can accelerate weight loss. Smokers should stop smoking, which lowers HDL (among other negative effects). If lifestyle changes like these aren't enough to bring down cholesterol levels adequately, a more restrictive diet may be needed. If that doesn't work either, drug therapy may be required. Even so, with the other changes you're already making, you will probably need fewer medicines than you would otherwise.

Some studies have focused on diets in which fat intake is severely limited. They have found that these radical changes to a very low-fat diet along with increased activity levels may partially "erase" atherosclerotic deposits in vessels to some extent. To achieve that kind of improvement takes a great deal of diligent effort over a number of years. Still, the findings indicate a profound connection between what we put in our bodies and what we do with our bodies and our health.

☙ *Grace studied her granddaughter's face. She was so young, not yet eight years old! Her mother was taking such good care of her, feeding her a balanced diet with lots of wholesome foods. She even loved her fruit or juice snacks. It had been quite different for Grace, growing up. No one thought much about diets then. You just ate the kinds of things your family had always eaten. Her mother had always made sure everyone got plenty of meat—and all the trimmings. A clean plate was every kid's goal back then. But now Grace knew that was when her weight problem must have started.*

As an adult, Grace had become obese. She had tried some weight-loss diets. None had worked for very long. Early on, a doctor had told her that her weight contributed to her high blood pressure and high cholesterol, as well as diabetes. But Grace took her medication and didn't worry much. Years later, Grace was told that these problems were getting worse. They were largely responsible for the coronary artery disease she developed in her 50s.

So Grace was at it again. Now she was determined to be a good example to her darling grandchild while she was at it. She was on a healthy diet this time. This one didn't limit her to strange foods or lots of one kind of food. Instead she ate a variety of nutritious foods in the right proportions. With the help of a registered dietitian and her doctor, Grace was changing her eating habits. She was eating a low-fat, low-sodium diet—and liking it. Learning the right portion sizes for meat was a real eye-opener. She realized she had been eating almost twice as much meat as she needed. She also switched to skim milk and low-fat dairy products. She really couldn't tell much difference in taste. The difference was in how she felt. Grace could clearly see the connection between what she ate and all her health problems. She was keeping track of her weight, blood pressure, blood sugar levels, and cholesterol levels. And they were all coming down, helped by what she was eating and doing! Grace chuck-

*led to herself. "Now my granddaughter and I enjoy the same
foods when she visits. I'm drinking her kind of milk now," she
thought.* 🍂

High Blood Pressure

The comprehensive Framingham Heart Study identified high blood
pressure—hypertension—as a risk factor for cardiovascular disease.
High blood pressure is a problem because it makes it harder for the
heart to circulate blood through the body's vast network of blood vessels. Over time, that extra work enlarges and weakens the heart. High
blood pressure is hard on the arteries, too.

High blood pressure is an especially dangerous condition because its
symptoms are "silent." Silent symptoms cause no outward distress
even as the disease damages organs. Yet most people do not know their
own blood pressure levels—and they should. A person might have high
blood pressure for years and not know it until he or she suffers a heart
attack, stroke, kidney failure, or other illness as a consequence. Yet
high blood pressure is easily identified through a simple test and can be
managed with the right diet, exercise, and sometimes medicine.

🍂 *Murlene fidgeted. She had come to the mall to shop, not sit.
Her friend Beth, however, noticed that the local hospital had set
up a table near the biggest department store. Hospital staff offered free blood pressure screenings to anyone who asked for
them. So here they sat. "Beth never could pass up a deal," Murlene thought resignedly. Personally, she didn't see the point.
Murlene felt fine.*

*Having her blood pressure measured only took a moment,
though. The friendly nurse slipped a heavy green cuff around
Murlene's upper arm. Then she inflated the cuff. Murlene felt
a slight pressure, but it wasn't unpleasant. The nurse explained
that this briefly stopped the flow of blood through the arteries in
Murlene's arm. In a moment the nurse released the pressure.
At that point she started to listen through a stethoscope to the
sounds Murlene's blood made as it again began to flow through
her arteries. Listening and looking at her watch, the nurse*

recorded two numbers on a piece of paper, and it was over. The nurse removed the cuff from Murlene's arm.

"Your blood pressure appears to be high today," the nurse said. "It's high enough that I recommend that you contact your doctor and have it checked again within the week. If you have another high reading, you'll need to work with your doctor to bring it within normal ranges. Your blood pressure is 153 over 110. An optimal reading would be less than 120 over less than 80."

"But how serious could this be? I feel fine!" Murlene protested.

"Your high blood pressure puts you at risk for a number of very serious diseases, including stroke and heart disease. I know it's a little hard to believe, especially if you feel fine right now. But you aren't fine, believe me. That's why we have these screenings periodically—to alert as many people as we can who may not realize they have high blood pressure. High blood pressure can't be cured, but it can be controlled."

It was true that Murlene hadn't seen her doctor in several years. She supposed it might be time to have a checkup anyway. And now she was a little curious about this blood pressure thing.

"These pamphlets will tell you more about the effect of this condition on the body when it is left uncontrolled," the nurse said. "Read them, and talk about them with your doctor. Don't wait." 🐦

Some factors associated with high blood pressure can't be changed, such as age, sex, race, and heredity. Others *can*, including sodium consumption, weight, activity level, and alcohol consumption. Doctors are heartened by the fact that changes made in these areas can have a significant impact on the control of high blood pressure. In fact, for people with mild high blood pressure, weight loss (when appropriate) and exercise may be all that are needed to control the condition.

High blood pressure is not a rare disease. It afflicts about one in every four American adults. About 50 million Americans have this condition. Twenty years ago only about half of that group would have been aware of it, and less than one fifth would have taken any steps to control it. Today more than 65 percent of those with hypertension *are* aware of having it, and it is controlled in approximately 10.5 million. These efforts pay off. It's no coincidence that during the same 20-year period, deaths due to CHD have dropped by more than 40 percent. Remember, CHD is America's number one killer. High blood pressure is one of the major risk factors for CHD. So these statistics are significant. If everyone with high blood pressure identified it and brought it under control, these numbers could be even more impressive. Clearly, the link between high blood pressure and CHD is a strong one. And, clearly, taking care of high blood pressure is good for the heart.

High Blood Pressure and Coronary Heart Disease

People with CHD and high blood pressure often find that their episodes of angina are less intense after they bring their blood pressure under control. High blood pressure is brought down slowly.

What is blood pressure?

Everyone has blood pressure. Blood pressure values may vary a little from person to person and still be considered "normal."

Blood pressure readings record values for two important and related forces. When the heart beats, it pushes blood into the arteries and circulatory system. When the heart pauses between beats, the force of the arteries as they press against the blood in the system exerts milder pressure. The higher **systolic** number in a blood pressure reading represents the higher pressure required to force blood from the heart into the arteries and throughout the circulatory system. The lower **diastolic** number represents lower pressure when the heart rests between beats. A blood pressure reading always lists the systolic number first and the diastolic number second.

When is blood pressure considered high?

A systolic pressure of less than 120 mm Hg (millimeters of mercury) and a diastolic pressure of less than 80 mm Hg is considered optimal for adults. A systolic reading of 120 to 129 and/or a diastolic reading of 80 to 84 is considered "normal." "High normal" is a systolic reading between 130 and 139 and a diastolic reading between 85 and 89. Higher numbers—140 to 159 systolic and/or 90 to 99 diastolic—indicate a high blood pressure condition that needs to be monitored. Systolic readings of 160 or higher and/or diastolic readings of 100 or higher indicate a need for treatment. As the numbers increase, the risk for cardiovascular disease also increases. Not all high blood pressure conditions are the same, although all should be monitored and treated appropriately.

It used to be that doctors divided high blood pressure conditions by the terms *mild, moderate,* and *severe* (see box, page 144). However, these words failed to convey the very real health danger involved in having even so-called mild or moderate high blood pressure. More and more doctors are using terms that better convey the sense of urgency that surrounds treatment of high blood pressure. Like other kinds of emergencies, high blood pressure is now often described as a Stage One (mild), Stage Two (moderate), Stage Three (severe), or Stage Four (very severe) category.

A single high blood pressure reading may not be cause for alarm. Generally, a high blood pressure reading should be confirmed on at least two subsequent visits during one to several weeks. If, however, the initial reading shows a systolic pressure of 210 or greater and/or a diastolic pressure of 120 or higher, your doctor may make an immediate diagnosis and start treatment right away. Such readings indicate that you have a blood pressure problem.

How does it start?

In most cases, a cause for high blood pressure is never known. Hypertension without a known cause is diagnosed as **essential hypertension.** Hypertension of this kind can't be cured; it is a permanent condition. However, it can be successfully controlled.

How is it treated?

Treatment strategies vary from person to person. A low-sodium diet and moderate exercise are enough to control hypertension in many cases. In obese people, a weight-loss diet often helps bring high blood pressure under control. In some cases, blood pressure remains high even after these measures have been given a fair try. At that point, drug therapy is probably needed. Be sure to follow your doctor's instructions for controlling your blood pressure.

Physical Inactivity

Many of us have heard a lot about the benefits of exercise. Such bene-fits are usually described vaguely as making people feel better and look better. That makes getting regular exercise a rather "neutral" subject for many people. It's not an issue for them if they feel pretty good at the moment and are satisfied with the way they look. In fact, there's a lot more to the story than that. Physical inactivity is not a choice we make without consequences. We now know that regular physical exer-cise, done over the long term, has a demonstrated positive influence on heart health that cannot be ignored. And the other side of the coin—a sedentary lifestyle—has a demonstrated negative effect.

Physical inactivity—lack of regular exercise—is a major risk factor for development of coronary heart disease. It also contributes to other risk factors for CHD, including obesity, high blood pressure, and a low level of HDL cholesterol. That is why exercise is so often a very im-portant part of cardiac rehabilitation (see Chapter Ten on exercise).

How Regular Exercise Helps the Heart

Regular aerobic exercise improves an individual's ability to use oxygen efficiently. That capacity means that your body can do more work with less oxygen. Such efficiency also means that your heart doesn't have to work as hard to get the same results. Exercise is important in primary

---

Blood Pressure Classification

Category	Systolic (mm Hg)	Diastolic (mm Hg)
Normal	<130	<85
High normal	130–139	85–89
High blood pressure*		
Stage One (mild)	140–159	90–99
Stage Two (moderate)	160–179	100–109
Stage Three (severe)	180–209	110–119
Stage Four (very severe)	≥210	≥120

*Based on the average of two or more readings taken at each of two or more visits fol-lowing an initial screening.

prevention of CHD (never getting coronary heart disease). It is also helpful for secondary prevention in those with established heart disease. Men and women who have had a heart attack but have increased their exercise capacity find that they are able to exercise longer without developing angina pain. They are able to do more kinds of activities more comfortably. If persons with cardiovascular disease who exercise regularly do have a heart attack, their conditioning can help them survive more often and more easily than those who are not physically active.

Even modest levels of physical activity, when done regularly, exert a positive influence on health. Exercise can help control blood cholesterol problems, improve HDL and LDL levels, control glucose imbalances in those with diabetes, and reduce body fat as well as overall body mass. Exercise can also help lower blood pressure in some people who are susceptible to high blood pressure.

Regular exercise is good not only for the heart but also for the bones and overall flexibility. It can help combat depression and help you sleep better at night. Less scientifically, it appears that regular exercise enhances your general awareness of your body. This can promote other healthful behaviors and help curb your desire to smoke a cigarette or overeat or drink too much.

How Much Exercise Do I Need?
Not everyone can or should follow an intensive exercise program. Your physician will guide you using your own health history. *If you are more than 40 years old, have a history of heart disease, have had a heart attack, or have any other health concerns, you must get your doctor's approval before starting a regular exercise program.*

Intense activities are especially beneficial when performed regularly. Such activities include brisk walking, hiking, aerobic exercise, jogging, bicycling, swimming, singles tennis, touch football, and basketball. For cardiovascular conditioning, these activities should be performed 30 to 60 minutes at a time, three or four times a week.

While more intense exercise tends to provide proportionally more benefits, studies have proven that even low-intensity activities, performed every day, can have some long-term health benefits, too. They too can help lower the risk of further cardiovascular disease.

Low-intensity activities include pleasure walking, lawn bowling, gardening, yard work, housework, dancing, and golfing. What kind of effort do we mean? Golfing, for example, offers the best opportunity for exercise when you leave the electric cart behind. Try walking the course—or least part of it—for a good workout.

Even if you can't exercise as much as recommended, some exercise is still better than none. Exercise and heart disease is discussed at greater length in Chapter Ten.

Contributing Factors

Contributing factors play a significant part in the development of heart disease by differing degrees. They are less closely related to the development of atherosclerosis. They may contribute to the development of other risk factors that are directly related to such formations, however. They may be directly linked to heart disease but in a less pronounced way. Diabetes mellitus, obesity, and stress fall into this category. Oral contraceptives, hormonal factors, and the use of cocaine appear to play a role as well.

Diabetes Mellitus

Diabetes is the inability of the body to produce or respond to insulin properly. Insulin enables the body to use glucose (sugar). Some people develop diabetes in childhood. Most adults who have diabetes developed it as adults (about 80 percent). In adults, the disease usually appears in middle-aged or overweight people. People who have a mild form of adult diabetes may not know for years that they are afflicted with it.

Diabetes increases the risk of kidney damage, blindness, and nerve and vessel disease. It also seriously increases the risk of cardiovascular disease. The Framingham Study found that the presence of diabetes doubled the risk of developing cardiovascular disease. More than 80 percent of people with diabetes die of some form of cardiovascular disease.

In time, diabetes can hurt the heart not only by damaging blood vessels but by damaging heart tissue as well, which predisposes the diabetic person to heart failure. With regard to cardiovascular risk, women appear to be more negatively affected by the presence of diabetes in the profile than men are, at least until menopause. However, for both men and women, the presence of other risk factors definitely has an effect on the overall risk of developing cardiovascular disease.

Studies have found diabetes to be less strongly associated with heart disease in other parts of the world. This may be because other parts of the world do not have diets as high in fat as we do in the United States. This suggests that other risk factors play a larger role in the development of the disease in people with diabetes than diabetes itself does. Physical inactivity, cigarette smoking, obesity, poor diet, and a lack of treatment of the condition may all contribute to the ultimate development of heart disease in the person with diabetes. It is possible that by controlling these other factors, heart disease will be less likely to develop in those with diabetes. It may be that persons with diabetes need to watch these risk factors more carefully than others.

Some people who do not have a full-blown diabetic condition may be told that they have "impaired glucose tolerance." This is the same thing as "borderline diabetes." Up to 17 million Americans may be glucose-tolerance impaired. This group must also take care of their condition with careful treatment and monitoring by a doctor.

Diabetes is generally associated with a family history of the disease and with obesity. Some people who are susceptible to developing diabetes mellitus because of a family history may be able to delay or prevent onset by controlling their weight. Where their weight is carried also has some predictive value. People who carry their excess weight around the middle (the so-called "apple" body type) have been shown to be more likely to develop diabetes and heart disease than people who carry their weight around the hips (the so-called "pear" body type).

Obesity

A person is considered obese when he or she is more than 20 percent overweight (based on height, bone structure, and age). (A weight chart appears on page 216.) Obesity is strongly associated with a number of health problems. High blood pressure, high blood cholesterol levels, adult-onset diabetes, and coronary heart disease are all more common in people who are obese than in others.

Obesity is an important, modifiable risk factor for heart disease. Studies show that when weight comes down, associated health problems tend to subside. For people with Stage One or Stage Two high blood pressure, for example, weight loss to normal ranges is very important. In fact, it is often an effective way of achieving and maintaining lower blood pressure, all by itself.

Where weight is concerned, even small movements up or down the scale make a difference. Being even 10 percent above your recommended weight is a strong predictor of heart disease, especially if you are less than 50 years old. But by the same token, losing a modest amount of weight can be helpful. Obese persons who lose 10 percent of their weight on a nutritious diet will notice positive changes. Losing some weight can help extremely heavy people control problems with glucose tolerance. It can also help lower blood pressure, lower blood cholesterol levels, and lengthen life. Even if greater weight loss cannot be sustained, studies show that it is still worthwhile—and recommended—to achieve modest weight loss.

We know instinctively that it's easier to avoid becoming overweight or obese than it is to lose a lot of weight permanently. However, whether you are trying to maintain a normal weight or trying to achieve one, the same basic principles apply. Select a healthful diet, eat in moderation, and incorporate enjoyable exercise into your routine. It is also important to have realistic expectations. Joining a support group or working with the help of your doctor or a registered dietitian can also help you realize your goal. These principles and others are discussed in greater depth in Chapter Nine. At best, healthful habits that prevent obesity should be instilled during childhood. If you're past that, don't despair. With consistent effort, these habits may be developed at any age.

Stress

Stress is a familiar emotion to most of us. However, researchers still aren't sure of the exact relationship between stress and heart disease. The effect of stress on the body varies tremendously from person to person, which makes it very hard to measure in a consistent, useful way. There does seem to be a connection between heart attack and a person's day-to-day stress levels, behavioral habits, and socioeconomic level.

A person who has a lot of negative stress in his or her life may start smoking or smoke more, start drinking alcohol or drink more, eat more, and so forth—all in response to stress. Whether any resulting cardiovascular disease is the result of the consequences of those habits or can be directly tied to the stressful feelings themselves still isn't known. More research is needed.

Other Factors

Other factors may contribute to the development of cardiovascular disease. Some studies have indicated that oral contraceptives, estrogen replacement therapy, and use of cocaine may play a role as well. Let's take a brief look at each of these.

Oral Contraceptives

The amounts of estrogen and progestin in oral contraceptives used to be higher than they are now. Studies in which the older formulations of oral contraceptives were used indicated that users had an increased risk of cardiovascular disease. This was especially true for heavy smokers and women with high blood pressure.

Today, oral contraceptives contain lower amounts of estrogen and progestin. Scientists are now studying the effects of these lower dosage pills on the women who take them. Early results indicate a lower risk of cardiovascular disease among healthy, nonsmoking women who take the low-dose pills. The effect of the pills in women who smoke or who are older than 35 is unclear. So, if you are under 35 and have no other risk factors, you and your doctor may decide that the risk is acceptable. However, if you have other risk factors, you should think very carefully about changing to a different method of birth control. Women who smoke should not use oral contraceptives. *Smoking and use of oral contraceptives can be an especially dangerous combination for women.* If you can't give up smoking, use some other form of birth control, no matter what your age.

Estrogen Replacement Therapy

Estrogen replacement therapy (ERT) is usually prescribed for menopausal symptoms or osteoporosis (a condition in which bones become brittle and porous and are more prone to fractures). For reasons that aren't yet clear, ERT also appears to be protective against heart disease in women. ERT seems to cut risk of developing CHD by one third to one half. **Estrogen** is a sex hormone that declines in women after menopause—at the same time that their risk of heart attack begins to rise sharply. About 10 years after menopause, women's risk of heart attack nearly reaches that of men. Similarly, heart attack risk has been proven to rise sharply in women who have had complete hysterectomies. (See discussion of ERT on pages 80–82.)

Cocaine Use

The illicit use of cocaine is widespread in the United States and other industrialized countries. It is estimated that between 25 and 30 million Americans have tried cocaine, and 5 to 6 million use it regularly. Cocaine has long- and short-term health consequences that can be devastating. It is a very unpredictable drug that has been closely linked to heart disease, especially heart attack and sudden death.

Cocaine affects the heart in several bad ways. Using cocaine elevates blood pressure levels briefly but astronomically as it is taken. The effect is even worse when combined with smoking cigarettes. Increasing blood pressure rapidly and dramatically in this way is very hard on the arteries, which bear the brunt of the additional pressure. Taking cocaine can also create dangerous arrhythmias in the heart. Seizures, spontaneous vessel collapse (coronary artery spasm), and tachycardia (rapid, shallow heartbeats) all may be triggered by cocaine use. Its exact effect varies among individuals because the drug itself varies widely in strength, dosage, and ways in which it is taken (including with other drugs that may be taken at the same time). It can happen as easily in first-time users as in regular users, and it doesn't matter if you take a lot or a little—the risk is the same. Cocaine can be deadly.

Autopsy reports have confirmed that cocaine use speeds the development of atherosclerosis. It can bring on arrhythmias in the heart muscle, leading to sudden death. Cocaine can also damage the heart muscle cells, perhaps because it stimulates the release of too much calcium into the cells. In some cases, cocaine use has ruptured the aorta—the result of an astronomically high blood pressure surge.

Cocaine's deadly effects on the heart are varied. The drug can damage the heart by wreaking havoc on blood pressure, as we have seen. Cocaine stimulates the development of atherosclerotic plaque but not in the same way that diet or other conditions do. Researchers believe the plaque develops in response to vessel damage caused by repeated vasoconstrictions. Vasoconstrictions are spontaneous, temporary blood vessel collapses that stop blood flow. Vasoconstrictions can occur during cocaine use, usually in vessels with some evidence of atherosclerosis. Cocaine use leads to the "sticky blood" problem we discussed earlier. So-called sticky blood clots more easily and can create blockages in blood vessels that cause heart attack or stroke, depending on where they occur in the body.

Like cigarette smoking, cocaine increases the body's demand for oxygen by stepping up the heart rate and blood pressure while simultaneously reducing the oxygen supply. Oxygen supply is reduced because taking cocaine acts in some ways like an anesthetic (which was its original use). This effect slows down electrical impulses across the heart. That in turn slows down the heartbeat and reduces blood flow—and so moves less oxygen through the system. (Conduction problems can also create the deadly arrhythmias that often kill cocaine users.)

Because heart attack as the result of cocaine use is not typical, treatment of its victims has been difficult. Calcium channel blockers seem promising, since cocaine tends to stimulate the release of too much calcium from the cells into the body. Nitroglycerin relieves vasospasms when administered promptly.

Summary

Twenty years ago the factors that lead to development of heart disease were largely unknown or unheeded by the American public. Heart disease reached epidemic proportions. Today that situation is changing. Medical researchers putting together the pieces of the heart disease puzzle are finding that the individual is central to the developing picture.

Four individual risk factors for heart disease cannot be changed: age, being male, family history of premature heart disease, and race. Their existence increases the importance of concentrating on the many other risk factors that can be changed through different behaviors. Though individual risk factors are very important in the development of heart disease, keep in mind that overall risk is really based on the interaction of the individual risk factor components of the profile. Therefore, even seemingly mild or moderate risk factors may be more dangerous in some people than in others because of the presence of other risk factors.

However, by modifying the risk factors that you can control, you will lower your risk of heart attack. If you have already had a heart attack, you can help prevent another one. Work with your doctor to make positive lifestyle changes starting today. You'll feel better and look better—and you'll know why!

CHAPTER EIGHT

Cigarettes and Heart Disease— Calling It Quits

Did you know that the majority of deaths in the United States can be attributed to fewer than a dozen conditions? Many of these conditions are preventable. Cigarette smoking, as we've noted several times in this book, is the nation's number one preventable cause of death and disability. In 1983 the Surgeon General of the United States declared smoking "the most important of the known modifiable risk factors for coronary heart disease."

That opinion hasn't changed. People with established heart disease, or who have had a heart attack, particularly have an incentive to stop smoking as soon as possible. Here are a few important reasons why.

- Smokers are at fully twice the risk of dying of coronary heart disease as nonsmokers.
- Smokers who have had one heart attack are more vulnerable to a fatal subsequent attack than are nonsmokers or people who have quit.
- On average, smokers die five to eight years earlier than nonsmokers.

But health problems associated with lighting up don't stop there. Most people are aware that smoking cigarettes greatly increase a person's chances of developing cancer as well as heart disease. People who smoke are 10 times as likely as nonsmokers to develop some form of cancer. They are particularly susceptible to cancers of the lung, mouth, throat, esophagus, pancreas, kidney, bladder, and cervix. They suffer more bone fractures. Smokers are also more likely to develop emphysema and bronchitis, lung conditions that make breathing very difficult. Emphysema can lead to death.

Let's take a closer look at smoking and cardiovascular disease. Smoking can cause **fibrillation**, an extremely dangerous condition in which the left ventricle of the heart beats shallowly and ineffectively. Fibrillation, in turn, can result in sudden death. Unfortunately, sudden death may be the first indication that an individual even had heart disease. Of all types of heart disease, sudden death is the most closely related to cigarette smoking. The more cigarettes smoked, the higher the risk.

Young male smokers are particularly susceptible to this manifestation of heart disease. They are four times more likely than their non-smoking peers to suffer sudden death. Older male smokers in their 50s are twice as likely as their nonsmoking peers to suffer sudden death. There is no apparent relationship between smoking and sudden death in women. Doctors aren't sure why.

Sudden death and heart attack aren't the only cardiovascular problems that smokers can suffer. Smoking can cause hemorrhage in blood vessels. Vasoconstriction, or the spontaneous closure of a blood vessel, can also be a consequence. Vasoconstriction can be severe enough to cause a heart attack or angina pectoris. Smokers with angina pectoris feel chest pain during physical activity sooner than their nonsmoking peers do.

People who smoke are also much more likely to develop peripheral vascular disease, which affects blood vessels in the arms and legs. Smoking is the major risk factor for development of this disease. Atherosclerosis in these vessels affects circulation to the limbs. In extreme cases, circulation may be cut off or slowed to such a degree that the limb must be amputated.

Smoking is also a risk factor for stroke, especially hemorrhagic stroke, which is difficult to treat. Stroke is the third leading cause of death in this country, behind only diseases of the heart and cancer. And cigarette smoking is closely associated with the development of all of these terrible diseases.

Clearly, smoking plays a primary role in the development of a number of the major illnesses that cause premature death. It is a noxious habit, with punishing long-term consequences. In this chapter we'll look at some of the mechanisms that make smoking so dangerous—and so hard for many people to shake. We'll also review the most common ways that people break a smoking habit for good.

Remember this. There can be good news beyond the scary consequences of smoking. People who quit enjoy better health. Their risk of developing many of the diseases or conditions we've just mentioned can drop markedly. Three years after quitting, the risk of death from heart disease and stroke for people who smoked a pack a day or less is almost the same as for people who never smoked. And smoking is perhaps unique in that there is absolutely no risk involved in quitting—quitting smoking is a completely positive step.

❦ *Roy had been a smoker almost as long as he could remember. He'd started smoking as a kid in Nebraska. He smoked in the Navy, too. He still smoked. How was he going to quit?*

He'd tried before, but nothing seemed to work. During those attempts Roy woke up with a headache, feeling terrible, and really wanting a cigarette. When he told his doctor about the other times he'd tried to quit, the doctor listened carefully.

"I think you have a strong physical addiction to the nicotine in cigarettes, Roy," the doctor observed. "You smoke heavily. The morning headaches and cravings tell me that your body is looking for more nicotine after a night without it. Your other attempts to quit didn't address that craving properly.

"I suggest you try something different this time. I want to put you on a nicotine patch. You mustn't smoke while you're on the patch. The patch will help reduce your craving for nicotine slowly. It should help you get the upper hand on your addiction."

"Do you think just wearing a patch will work?" Roy asked.

"That and some support from people around you. You should consider joining a stop-smoking group. We have one here at the hospital. We'll get you a schedule of the meetings and a description of the group itself. Together, the patch and the group may just do the trick."

"Okay, doc. It's worth a try." ❦

How Smoking Affects the Body

Smoking is a complex behavior. It affects most people in several ways—physical, psychological, and sociological. Each aspect influences an individual smoker to a greater or lesser degree, making it hard to quit. This interrelationship affects the kind of intervention method that works best for you. We'll take a closer look at your options later in this chapter. For now, let's see what smoking does to the body—the health consequences and the addictive aspect.

What's in a Cigarette?

More than 4,000 substances have been identified in cigarette smoke. These substances are absorbed into the bloodstream when someone smokes. There they have the potential to damage vessels as they tumble along in the blood. However, of all the identified particles, nicotine and carbon monoxide, a gas, are considered the most dangerous elements of cigarette smoke. When a cigarette is inhaled, several things happen in the body at once.

Nicotine

Nicotine is the physically addicting substance in cigarettes. Found in the tobacco leaf, nicotine is absorbed into the body through cigarette smoke. Nicotine affects the brain, as we'll see in a moment. It also affects blood pressure and increases heart rate. When people smoke, their blood pressure climbs dramatically but temporarily. Blood flow increases to the coronary arteries but decreases everywhere else in the body.

When a cigarette is finished, blood pressure drops to previous levels. Doctors have not established that smoking, over time, causes a high blood pressure condition (hypertension). They do know that smoking aggravates an existing high blood pressure condition. In people with high blood pressure, smoking increases the likelihood that they will develop coronary heart disease (CHD).

Doctors are concerned about the temporary response of increasing blood pressure, repeated thousands of times in a smoker's history. They believe this response can have an adverse effect on health, promoting wear and tear on the vessels. Damaged vessels provide an opportunity for atherosclerosis to start or accelerate.

Carbon Monoxide

The vascular system delivers oxygen to every cell in the body. Carbon monoxide is a gas that is a byproduct of smoking. In the bloodstream, carbon monoxide "bumps" oxygen. Less oxygen reaches the cells that need it. The combined effect of nicotine and carbon monoxide is particularly hard on the heart. At the same time that nicotine stimulates the heart to work harder (an increased heart rate), the heart muscle actually receives less oxygen to do the job.

Other Effects

Smoking has other effects on the cardiovascular system as well. Researchers have learned that smoking makes blood platelets stickier, for reasons that aren't understood. Sticky platelets have several adverse effects. They might not last as long as normal platelets. They reduce the time it takes for blood to clot. They also make blood thicker. Thicker blood can aggravate the blood vessel walls and give atherosclerosis a chance to flourish.

Smoking affects blood cholesterol levels. It decreases HDL cholesterol, the "good" cholesterol. Smoking is closely associated with the development of atherosclerosis. Coronary atherosclerosis is found more frequently and in a more severe form in smokers than in nonsmokers. It is also found more often in a relatively unusual but critical place—the aorta, the largest artery in the body.

Cigarette Smoking Combined with Other Risk Factors

Cigarette smoking is an independent risk factor for heart disease. It also has a "synergistic" effect on other risk factors in the total risk profile. When cigarette smoking is added to the risk profile, other risk factors are considered even "riskier" than they would be otherwise.

The Dose-Response Relationship

The dose-response relationship of cigarette smoking to heart disease is strong. The more you smoke, the more likely it is that you will develop the disease. How do you measure your dose of cigarette smoke? Take a look at the following factors:

- the number of cigarettes you smoke each day
- the number of years you have smoked
- how deeply you inhale the smoke
- how young you were when you began smoking

All of these influence the dose-response relationship between smoking and heart disease.

What About Pipe and Cigar Smoking?

People who smoke pipes and cigars are less likely to develop CHD than are people who smoke cigarettes. Most pipe and cigar smokers don't inhale smoke into the lungs, the way most of the noxious substances in cigarettes enter the body. Their risk, however, is still higher than that of nonsmokers. Pipe and cigar smokers, moreover, also put themselves at risk for other diseases, such as mouth cancer.

What About Low-Tar and Low-Nicotine Cigarettes?

No cigarettes are safe. There is no scientific evidence that switching to low-tar and low-nicotine cigarettes lowers the risk of heart disease. Smokers who have switched to such cigarettes tend to inhale smoke more deeply and smoke more often to compensate for the decreased amount of nicotine they inhale with each cigarette. But that means they are also inhaling more of *all* the substances that make cigarettes so dangerous to health. Smoking so-called low-tar and low-nicotine cigarettes may actually increase the risk of contracting a disease.

Why Do Smokers Smoke?

Most smokers start smoking to fill a perceived need. Commonly, they start in response to peer pressure or out of a desire to "fit in" with others. Not surprisingly, studies have found that most smokers started at a young age—often as young as 10 or 11 years or in their later teenage years.

Advertising plays into these perceived needs with a vengeance. Take a look at cigarette advertising today. You'll see glossy images depicting power, wealth, and beauty. Not shown are the millions of people whose health has been compromised by a lifelong habit of cigarette smoking. You won't see smokers with emphysema gasping for breath. Nor will you see smokers recovering from a near-fatal heart attack. But those are some of the real stories behind cigarette smoking.

Adolescents, who already feel a strong a need to fit in, may be most vulnerable to cigarette advertisers' messages. In 1994 a case in the California courts challenged R. J. Reynolds Tobacco Company regarding its "Joe Camel" cartoon advertising campaign. The suit alleged that Reynolds unlawfully targeted underage smokers with Joe Camel ads. Studies show that smokers who take up the habit early in life find it especially hard to stop smoking years later when they are adults.

The nicotine in cigarettes keeps smokers physically hooked. (They may feel that they need the other elements of the smoking ritual as well, such as smoking with a cup of coffee or smoking at a certain time of day.) Nicotine affects not one but two centers in the brain. In this respect, it is unique. One brain center releases chemicals into the body that deliver a pleasurable sensation. The other releases chemicals that increase attention and alertness. These effects are temporary. They subside when the nicotine level in the body fades.

Who Smokes?

Overall, the number of people who smoke cigarettes in the United States continues to drop. In the past 30 years the number of Americans who smoke has declined by an estimated 37 percent. That's wonderful news. Some groups that smoked heavily in the 1960s, such as white-collar workers, have largely quit. However, other groups that didn't smoke before have started. Today more people who have not completed high school smoke than do those with a college degree. And more women are smoking than ever before. Teenagers—especially white teenage women—are taking up the habit in record numbers.

Women and Smoking

Until 1991 the percentage of women who smoked was dropping in a way that was consistent with the overall decline in smoking seen in this country. Since 1991, however, the rates have vacillated. Among women ages 18 and over, the percentage of women who smoked rose from

23.1 percent in 1990 to almost 27 percent in 1992. In 1993 the rates were down. The Centers for Disease Control and Prevention (CDC) is the government agency that collects these statistics. According to the CDC, there is some evidence that young white women, especially those between 18 and 24 years of age, use smoking as a means of weight control. Other ethnic groups do not.

Women are at particular risk of heart attack or stroke if they smoke and take birth control pills. Studies show that women are much more likely to have a heart attack or a stroke than are women who neither smoke nor use oral contraceptives. The message to women is clear: If you smoke, *stop*. But if you continue to smoke, don't take the Pill. Talk with your doctor about alternative forms of birth control.

Quitting Isn't Always Easy

Cigarette smoking is an addictive, complex behavior. Smokers reach for cigarettes for a number of reasons. One is their physical addiction to nicotine. Some people are more susceptible to nicotine addiction than others. People who start smoking as children or teenagers tend to be more physically addicted than other smokers. They also tend to feel withdrawal sensations more strongly when they do quit. People who feel the need to smoke first thing in the morning are likely to be very dependent on nicotine.

Nicotine enters the body in cigarette smoke inhaled into the lungs. From the lungs, it enters the bloodstream. Nicotine is a fast-acting drug. It reaches the brain in only seven seconds. The effect of nicotine in the brain is to create feelings of pleasure and alertness in the smoker. No other drug causes this same combination of feelings.

Smokers also become psychologically "addicted" to the act of smoking. This component of the smoking experience is more important to some smokers than to others. Many smokers reach for cigarettes because of a mood. That mood can be happy, anxious, or anything else. Such people are responding to a psychological need. Similarly, some people feel the desire to smoke when drinking a cup of coffee or an alcoholic beverage. Others feel the need to smoke at work. That's because these activities are frequently paired in the smoker's experience. This need is established over time, as the act of smoking becomes habit. The more you've smoked in the past, the more practice and reinforcement you've had for a "psychological addiction" to smoking.

Third, people develop a dependency on tobacco for social psychological reasons. They smoke because they are around others who smoke. They may notice that they tend to smoke more in the company of others than they do alone. A spouse, friends, or coworkers may smoke, so they light up as well.

Every smoker responds differently to the dependencies associated with smoking—physical, psychological, and social psychological (social pressure). To some degree, all three are at work within every habitual smoker. For most smokers, however, one element or another is more prominent than others. To stop smoking successfully, it's important to recognize your own habits and motivations for continuing to smoke. As a first step, keep a daily record or logbook of your smoking activity for several weeks or months. Learning what makes you vulnerable to lighting a cigarette will help you later, when you decide to quit—for good.

❦ *Sylvia twiddled her fingers in her lap. She chewed her lip. She stared at the person at the other end of the room, who was lighting up a cigarette. "I shouldn't have come to this party," she muttered darkly to herself.*

Sylvia was trying to quit smoking. She hated the cough she had developed. It made her feel like she was old and worn out. So yesterday she threw out all her cigarettes and declared herself a new person. But she wasn't prepared for this—a cocktail party. She was surrounded by friends who didn't know she'd quit and kept asking her if she needed a light. The fact was, Sylvia loved to smoke at parties. That was how she'd started, in college.

When a fourth person offered her a cigarette, Sylvia took it. She lit up and waved away the smoke, coughing a little. She realized that quitting smoking was going to be a lot more work than throwing away a box of cigarettes. But she still knew she needed to do it. Sylvia resolved to call her doctor tomorrow and get some help from a professional. She would find out how people quit successfully. After all, she'd been a good student in col-

lege. She would use those smarts now to learn how to quit and stay quit. Meanwhile, Sylvia looked on the bright side: She'd already learned that she needed to practice refusing cigarettes at parties. ❦

Quitting Successfully

Everyone who smokes cigarettes can quit—even you! Quitting smoking is easier for some people than for others. You are never too old to quit smoking. Although older smokers may have difficulty quitting, the highest rate of quitting is actually observed in those over 65. The same pressures that may have encouraged you to start smoking may encourage you to *continue* smoking. As a smoker you probably feel additional pressures to keep smoking. These include nicotine dependency, social pressure, and familiarity of the habit. Smokers who quit successfully go through three phases when they quit. First, they prepare themselves to quit. Then they choose the smoking intervention that's best for them. Finally, they take the nonsmoking maintenance phase as seriously as the first two. In fact, successful ex-smokers learn that quitting smoking is not the ultimate goal. The real goal is to *stay off* cigarettes.

Avoid the "Total Failure" Trap

No doubt, quitting smoking is hard. There are many temptations to face over a long period of time. But some people expect a "perfect effort" right away. If they yield to temptation and smoke a cigarette after several days or weeks of being smoke-free, they may declare the whole effort a failure. Then they start smoking again in earnest.

Others who quit smoking and then start again just give up. They decide that if they've tried once and failed, they will certainly fail the next time, too. So, they think, why bother?

The fact is, there are fallacies to such thinking. If you break down and have a cigarette after your quit date, don't give up. You have not necessarily doomed the entire stop-smoking effort. True, you've made it a little harder to say no to the next temptation. But smoking is a habitual behavior. Habits are hard to break. So be realistic and understanding of yourself. If you backslide and have one cigarette, or more, try to see it for what it is. It is one slip in a long journey. Keep going!

That said, most people who want to quit smoking do *not* succeed on their very first try. Successful quit-smoking efforts seem to involve a learning curve. In that curve the smoker becomes more and more aware of which techniques work for him or her and which do not. On average, smokers try to quit smoking three times before they finally succeed. So, don't get discouraged if you've tried to quit smoking in the past but failed. You actually have a *better* chance of success this time if you've tried and failed a couple of times already. Every failed attempt teaches you something and brings you closer to the attempt that *will be* successful. That's the attempt that will make you an ex-smoker for good.

How to Quit Smoking

Quitting smoking is hard but not impossible. Motivation to quit is perhaps the most important component of the effort. If you've been diagnosed with heart disease, you're probably well motivated to quit smoking. Use that motivation to help you quit. If you were hospitalized after a heart attack, you have successfully gone a number of days without smoking already. Why not take advantage of that momentum and keep going!

Three Stages

A number of methods are available to the person who wants to stop smoking. What works for one person may not work for another, so a certain amount of experimentation may be necessary before you find the method that's right for you. But any successful method involves three steps:

- preparation
- intervention
- maintenance

Each stage is equally important to the total success of the stop-smoking effort.

Preparation

You'll need to do a little homework before you quit smoking. Become informed, both about your own smoking habits and the interventions available for treatment. Try to match the two as closely as possible. During the preparation stage, discuss your desire to stop smoking with a doctor or another health-care professional. That person is in an excellent position to recommend an appropriate intervention and en-courage you. He or she can also help you identify additional motiva-tions for quitting.

Monitor your habit.

Do you have a strong physical addiction to the nicotine in cigarettes? Or do you have a stronger psychological dependency on the smoking ritual? It's quite possible that you've smoked for years but don't know what triggers your desire to smoke. You'll find out if you keep a log of your smoking activities.

For several weeks, keep a detailed record of your smoking habits in a small notebook. Take exact note of *when* you smoked (time of day), *why* you lit a cigarette, and how you felt afterward (motivation). Also write down *where* you were and *who* you were with (social pressure/en-vironment). Do this every day. Get to know your habit as it really is. Your log may yield surprising results. You may identify a pattern in your smoking habit that you were unaware of. You'll also learn how much you smoke each day on average. This information will help you choose an appropriate intervention method.

What you learn in the process of keeping a record of your smoking habit helps you later. During the intervention and maintenance stages, this knowledge will help you stay in control of your desire to smoke. You'll know which situations create the greatest temptations *for you* to smoke. As a result, you'll be better able to avoid them or to work around them.

Identify your goals.

Recognize that the ultimate goal of your program is not to *quit* smok-ing. Rather, it is to *stay off cigarettes.* Quitting—the intervention stage—is an intermediate step on your way to this goal. Recognize too that the desire to quit smoking represents a major life decision. Treat it with respect. Feel very comfortable with the decision and committed to it before you go any further.

Set a quit date.

Your quit date is the day you stop smoking forever. (You could call it your own liberation day.) Think about choosing a day that is personally significant in some way. The positive association you already have with the day reinforces the importance of the step you're taking. Choose your birthday, a "lucky" day, your anniversary, or the day you start a new job. Any might serve the purpose. (Many people find support in quitting during the Great American Smoke-out. This is a national quit day sponsored by the American Cancer Society. It occurs each year on the third Thursday in November.) In any case, choose a date that's far enough away for you to get used to the idea of quitting and learn some maintenance skills beforehand. Once you've set a quit date, tell your family and friends about your plans, and enlist their support.

Make a follow-up appointment with your doctor.

After you've chosen a quit date, contact your doctor. Set a follow-up appointment for about a month after your quit date, or for a date he or she suggests. Make this appointment *before* you quit. At the follow-up appointment you'll have an opportunity to discuss problems or concerns, such as withdrawal symptoms. If you're doing well, your doctor will be glad to congratulate you and encourage your continuing efforts. You may want to schedule other follow-up appointments as necessary.

Intervention

The most effective way to stop smoking is to combine intervention techniques. It's best to consider *both* the physical and psychological dependencies associated with the habit. Have you had severe withdrawal symptoms, such as irritability, sleeplessness, or depression after quitting? If so, your physical dependence on nicotine may be especially strong. Your doctor can help you identify and find ways to get around that problem.

Does your habit have a strong psychological aspect? Do you like having a cigarette in your mouth? Do you think that smoking calms you down? If so, you can learn to substitute other activities for smoking at those times. For example, you might suck on a cinnamon stick instead of a cigarette. Or try taking a quick walk around the block or the office when you start to feel tense. You might find it helpful to join a support group for people who have quit smoking. (Your local hospital, church, VA hospital, or health clinic may sponsor such a group.) These kinds of strategies come in handy while you're becoming a nonsmoker.

Choose a strategy.
After determining the kinds of situations that predispose you to smoke, choose an intervention method. The best method for you will address those situations and help you cope with them in ways other than smoking cigarettes. Specific intervention methods, their advantages, drawbacks, and estimated success rates, are discussed elsewhere in this chapter, beginning on page 170.

Maintenance
Quitting smoking is one thing. Staying off cigarettes can be quite another. To stay smoke-free, you'll need to use a number of strategies until they become second nature. Smoking is a complex behavior. You'll find that a multifaceted approach to break the habit works best. Find ways to incorporate strategies from each of the areas described below in your own battle plan.

Find social support.
You'll need the continuing support of family, friends, and coworkers to kick the smoking habit permanently. Some people find that it helps to spend free time in public places designated as no-smoking areas, such as museums, libraries, and movie theaters. A smoke-free workplace is obviously desirable. If yours isn't, declare your own desk or office a "smoke-free zone." Now is the time to continue to draw on the support of your doctor through follow-up visits or telephone calls.

Talking with other ex-smokers can help, too. Self-help groups such as Smokers Anonymous can put you in touch with people who are having the same experiences that you are.

Relapses triggered by social situations are common. As an ex-smoker, prepare in advance for situations or places in which you'll be tempted to smoke. These may be at home, at work, in a restaurant or bar, or at parties. You may encounter people who do not support your desire to stop smoking. You'll need to be prepared to remain firm. It may help to rehearse with yourself how to refuse a cigarette.

Develop coping skills.

Another way to manage the urge to smoke after you've quit is to develop some strategies, or coping skills. These strategies can help you over the rough spots or withdrawal symptoms. Again, think of some workable strategies *before* you smoke your last cigarette. Perhaps you always smoked a cigarette after a meal, for example. To help you break that habit, you might brush your teeth with a mint-flavored toothpaste immediately after eating instead.

Take a moment now to think of when or where you most love to smoke. Those situations will probably be the ones that give you the most trouble. Imagine ways to get through those situations now. Don't let them surprise you! Ask family, friends, and especially ex-smokers for their ideas, too.

You might also cope with your urge for a cigarette by rewarding yourself for not smoking. At the end of each week, for example, you might put aside money that you would have spent on cigarettes. Keep it separate from other funds to remind you that it's special "reward money." Use it to buy something else you enjoy. This could be music by a favorite recording artist, a collectible, a toy for a grandchild, a pair of movie tickets—anything, as long as you enjoy it!

Understand yourself.

Remember: most smokers don't quit smoking on their very first try. Usually they succeed by the third or fourth serious attempt. Each failed attempt, then, brings them closer to success.

Have you tried to quit smoking before but were unable to do so? If that's the case, take a look at your past efforts to quit. You may have chosen an intervention that didn't meet your needs adequately. Before trying the next time, tell your doctor what you think didn't go right in your last attempt. Together, find ways to modify your tactics for your next attempt at quitting.

Identify with a new crowd.

Many smokers start their habit both to fit in with a crowd and to be "different." This is especially true if they started at a young age. They continue to identify themselves in a fundamental way as "smokers" and to identify others as "nonsmokers." The natural desire to fit in, which we all share, may even be reinforced by a particular cigarette brand. Cigarette advertisements inspire consumer loyalty by delivering a carefully constructed image of their customers. Such people are portrayed as slim, beautiful, rugged, athletic, sexy, or "cool."

After you quit smoking, actively promote yourself as a nonsmoker or ex-smoker. (As an ex-smoker, you'll join millions of other Americans. According to some studies, 25 percent of all American adults have quit.) Get used to this new identity. Think of all of the advantages that will be yours because you're now an ex-smoker. You'll have lower insurance premiums, fresher breath, cleaner teeth, and more energy. Write these advantages down in a list. Post the list where you can see it often. Be proud of the "new you."

Avoiding Relapses

Smokers who are trying to quit may resume smoking because of anxiety, stress, or depression. Good or bad feelings may also trigger the urge to light up. Others relapse because they find themselves back in a social situation in which they typically smoked (such as a party). Smokers who are more likely to relapse are described in the box on page 169. Smokers who reach for a cigarette out of habit or to handle stress need to learn other kinds of coping skills. Such skills will lend them the power to resist smoking when the temptation is greatest. To work, coping skills must be individualized to the smoker's particular vulnerabilities. You may need the help of a doctor or other professional to identify these triggers initially. You may want to write down your list of at-risk situations. Carry the list in your wallet so that you'll become very familiar with it.

Which Smokers Are More Likely to Relapse?

Everyone can quit smoking—even you. It's true that some people are more likely than others to relapse after quitting smoking. If you see yourself described below, you may need extra help or extra vigilance to stay off the habit. Talk with your doctor, your stop-smoking program leader, or another professional if you need to.

- You're an older smoker.
- You started smoking at a young age.
- You're a heavy smoker.
- You have issues in your life that cause you anxiety.
- Your spouse smokes.
- Your friends smoke.
- You aren't prepared to handle withdrawal symptoms.
- You have an attitude of "positive resignation." That's to say, you're easily deterred from your stop-smoking program.

To Prevent a Relapse

Make sure a substitute for smoking is available to you when you need one. Try relaxation exercises or deep breathing exercises. Try keeping something nearby that you can manipulate in your fingers. It should be about the same size and shape as a cigarette. Pop a stick of gum in your mouth. Do whatever you find works for you. (It may take some experimentation to find it.) Identify high-risk situations before they present themselves. Pay special attention to emotions that are likely to accompany the desire for a cigarette.

Don't try to rely on one technique, such as chewing gum, to see you through all situations. Try to take advantage of *all* strategies that apply to you. Keep in mind the problem of nicotine withdrawal symptoms as well as the psychological and social dependencies that are part of your smoking habit.

Don't try to quit alone. Ask for support from your closest companions. If they are unable to give you the support you need, try a support group or stop-smoking program. Check with your doctor regularly for help and encouragement.

Keep your motivation high. Know exactly why you want to quit, and review those reasons regularly, especially if you slip. Keep the list posted, or carry it with you in your pocket or purse. Remember the health complications of smoking.

Know what to expect before you start the process of quitting. If you've had a relapse, you know more about which situations are sensitive for you than you did before. You'll be better able to plan ways to get around them the next time. If certain situations trigger an urge to smoke, change the activities in some way to break the pattern. (For example, maybe you used to bring coffee and a roll to your office for breakfast, and lit a cigarette afterwards. Try eating breakfast at home instead and skip the coffee until you've been at work an hour.) It's also a good idea to know what sorts of withdrawal symptoms you're likely to encounter as your body rids itself of nicotine. A list of withdrawal symptoms appears in the box on page 171.

Smoking Interventions

Smokers smoke for different personal reasons. It makes sense to individualize interventions, too. Some evidence indicates that heavy smokers may need to emphasize strategies that address the addictive nature of nicotine. Lighter smokers may find strategies that address the social or psychological aspects of their habit work better for them.

Physical, psychological, and social psychological addiction to cigarettes and the available interventions vary. That's a good reason to keep trying to quit even if you were unsuccessful before. You may not have been using a method that was suited to you. Go back to the beginning and become very familiar with your smoking habits by keeping a notebook (see page 164). Your doctor can help you choose an intervention method. He or she may be able to administer a quick screening tool, called the Fagerstrom checklist. The checklist evaluates the probable strength of your nicotine addiction. You can then use that information to choose an intervention that's right for you. The success rates noted below refer to year-long smoking abstinence, unless noted otherwise.

Symptoms of Nicotine Withdrawal

Cigarettes are impressive nicotine delivery systems. After you quit, your body takes some time to readjust to life without nicotine. That adjustment period is often accompanied by feelings of discomfort. Discomfort from nicotine withdrawal is different from person to person. Some people are more susceptible to the effects than others, especially heavy smokers.

Common signs of nicotine withdrawal include:

- irritability
- depression
- weight gain
- restlessness
- anxiety
- insomnia
- impatience

If you're troubled by any of these signs or others that you suspect are related to nicotine withdrawal, discuss them with your doctor when you meet after your quit date.

Self-Help

From 10 to 17 percent of all ex-smokers quit on their own after several attempts. Or they find the motivation they need while discussing quitting with their doctor during a checkup. Often they have experienced a health problem, such as shortness of breath, angina pain, or heart attack. Such an event underscores for them the importance of quitting smoking.

They may enhance their effort by reading materials about stopping smoking that they received at a doctor's office or self-help books on the subject. They may watch videos or use other supplementary information. The American Cancer Society and the American Lung Association offer kits designed to help smokers quit. Other materials about how to quit smoking are available from the American Heart Association; the National Institutes of Health; the National Heart, Lung, and Blood Institute; the National Institute on Drug Abuse; and the Centers for Disease Control and Prevention.

People who quit on their own may get brief instructions on how to quit and then do it. They make up their own way of quitting, choosing coping mechanisms that address their specific needs. Many try chewing gum, exercising regularly, or changing daily habits that involved smoking.

Clinics/Behavioral Therapy

Behavioral therapy includes a variety of techniques. It may involve one person working with a therapist or several people participating in a support group. At best, behavioral therapy is tailored to individual needs and combined, if necessary, with a program to ease physical symptoms caused by nicotine withdrawal. Behavioral therapy alone is estimated to have a 20 to 30 percent success rate. The rate goes up when the technique is combined with other intervention methods. Smokers learn to find substitutes for smoking and get support. They learn coping skills through role-play situations. They also address underlying issues, such as why someone finds smoking enjoyable and why that person wishes to stop smoking.

❦ *"I've tried this before. I can't quit!" Jo was talking to Henry, the leader of the stop-smoking group her doctor had recommended. Her angina was getting worse. Her doctor wanted her to quit smoking.*

"One step at a time, Jo," Henry said soothingly. "You don't have to quit today. In fact, I don't want you to quit today. You need to think about the other times you tried to quit and why they didn't work. You need to think about your smoking habit as it really is. What triggers your need for a cigarette? When you've thought about it, we can set a quit date together. I suspect you smoke mostly in response to social and environmental situations. You've told me how you smoke in your car and after meals. We can devise a plan that addresses those particular needs. Don't give up! I know your angina attacks are worrying you. If you quit smoking, you'll do your health a big favor. Your motivation this time may very well make this attempt successful." ❦

A Word About Group Programs

The typical group program meets several times over the course of several weeks. At each meeting group members watch a short film or share a reading assignment on different aspects of quitting smoking. A group discussion follows. Typical topics might include why people smoke and how it affects them. Another popular topic is intervention. Is it better to quit "cold turkey" or "fade" (smoke fewer cigarettes on successive days or weeks)? These group discussions help members learn to recognize and cope with withdrawal symptoms. The meetings also help them manage stress and handle obstacles such as weight gain. Maintenance strategies are often discussed, as is assertiveness.

In the past group programs were often managed by private companies. Today hospitals, health clinics, state health departments, VA hospitals, churches, large corporations, exercise clubs, and community colleges have group programs to help people quit smoking. The American Cancer Society, the American Lung Association, and the American Heart Association often have similar programs available to the community at the local level. Lay leaders rather than therapists usually conduct these well-organized classes, which typically have a strong emphasis on health education. Often the programs are offered at very little cost to the participant.

Commercial quit programs typically cost more to join and use various methods to encourage smokers to quit. An objective report of graduate success rates may be hard to come by. In a commercial quit program, the company has an investment in claiming a high success rate. What is meant by a commercial program's "success rate" may not be known. Often such programs count people as "successes" if they merely attend all sessions.

Nonprofit programs are likely to be as successful as commercial programs. Many have a proven success rate and are less expensive. If you do try a commercial quit program, ask around about its success rate before you sign up. Also find out what method the company uses to encourage participants to quit smoking.

Some private quit-smoking businesses use aversive techniques. Aversive methods make smoking very unpleasant. Aversion therapy can teach smokers to imagine bad sensations when smoking or good ones when the urge to smoke is overcome. More typically, the smoker may be forced to breathe stale, smoky air, puff rapidly, or smoke until nauseated. These techniques are successful for some people but are dangerous for people with serious cardiovascular problems. We do not recommend them.

Individual Counseling

Individual counseling offers more "hands-on" support for those who feel they need it. Counselors can help prepare the smoker to stop and intensify the motivation to quit. They can also help the smoker pay attention to his or her own smoking habits and devise substitute behaviors to use instead. Counselors also provide solid follow-up support during the maintenance phase as needed.

Nicotine Replacement Therapy

Nicotine replacement therapy is appropriate for a certain group of smokers. It seems to work best with smokers who have a very strong physical addiction to nicotine in cigarettes. These people may exhibit especially severe withdrawal symptoms. In nicotine replacement therapy smokers receive controlled doses of nicotine in the form of nicotine gum or a nicotine patch. The amount of nicotine delivered to the body is reduced over a period of weeks or months. Finally it is stopped altogether.

Nicotine replacement therapy helps some smokers concentrate on their psychological dependency on cigarettes before they have to give up nicotine. They taper off nicotine slowly before stopping consumption completely.

When combined with some form of behavioral therapy, nicotine replacement therapy has a success rate of between 15 and 40 percent. However, this method of quitting smoking is not for everyone. You and your doctor will decide if it's right for you.

Nicotine Polacrilex

Nicotine Polacrilex, or nicotine gum, is a drug administered in sugar-free gum form. Some people don't like to call it "gum" because it has little in common with chewing gum. Nicotine Polacrilex is a medication. It is not chewed in the same way that chewing gum is chewed.

When the urge to smoke arises, the patient chews a piece of gum.

Each piece, or dose, delivers about 2 milligrams of nicotine to the system. This is far less than the nicotine in an average cigarette. The patient must chew slowly to administer the drug properly and to avoid side effects. It takes about half an hour to release all the nicotine in one piece of nicotine gum when chewed properly.

Nicotine taken this way is absorbed more slowly than nicotine from a cigarette. Chewing nicotine gum does not give a smoker the same sensation that comes from smoking a cigarette.

On average, patients may chew 10 or 12 pieces of gum per day. Under no circumstances should more than 30 pieces be chewed in one day. Gradually, over several months, the patient reduces the number of times a day he or she chews the gum. Finally, the patient stops completely. No patient should remain on nicotine replacement therapy for more than six months.

Smoking while you're on nicotine replacement therapy can be dangerous. Don't! Also, avoid caffeinated drinks, such as coffee and colas, because caffeine dilutes the drug's effect.

Side effects of nicotine replacement therapy are greatly minimized when the gum is chewed and used exactly as directed. Chewing the gum rapidly or swallowing it causes side effects. If chewed too fast, the gum releases nicotine too quickly. This may irritate the mouth and cause sleeplessness, dizziness, irritability, headache, stomach ache, indigestion, nausea, vomiting, sore throat, an aching jaw, or hiccups. You may also salivate excessively.

Nicotine gum is not appropriate for everyone. Those who should definitely not take nicotine Polacrilex include anyone with any of the following:

- a recent heart attack
- life-threatening arrhythmias
- severe or worsening angina pectoris
- pregnancy or nursing
- throat or mouth problems
- peptic ulcer
- joint disease

Nicotine gum may be a good choice for heavy smokers (those who smoke more than 25 cigarettes a day). It is best for those who have experienced severe withdrawal symptoms in previous attempts to quit smoking. The therapy helps them concentrate on other aspects of their dependency while they slowly wean themselves from nicotine. Like its cousin, the nicotine patch, nicotine Polacrilex delivers the nicotine but not carbon monoxide or tar—other dangerous elements in cigarette smoke. For best results, it should be part of a multifaceted stop-smoking program. Used alone, it has a success rate of just 6 to 10 percent.

Nicotine Patch

The nicotine patch (or "transdermal patch") is a relatively new intervention that has received a lot of attention. It is easy to use and has few side effects. Its success rate is very high—50 percent—when combined with behavioral therapy.

The patch works by steadily delivering nicotine through the skin ("transdermally") into the bloodstream. The patch is typically worn on the upper arm, under clothing. It is changed once a day. Nicotine patches are available in two types. One version delivers nicotine for 24 hours, while the other lasts 16 hours and is removed at bedtime. Both work equally well. However, the 24-hour patch seems to benefit those who wake up craving a cigarette, while the 16-hour patch lessens the side effect of insomnia that some patch wearers experience.

Nicotine patches are typically worn for two or three weeks. They may be used for up to five months if necessary. Over time, the nicotine dose from the patch is cut back, easing withdrawal symptoms. Like nicotine gum, the patch delivers less nicotine than cigarettes, while cutting out the carbon monoxide and tar that cigarette smoking also delivers. Wearing the patch doesn't completely eliminate the craving for a cigarette, nor does it change the daily habits that may trigger the urge to smoke. That's why the patch works best when combined with behavioral therapy.

There are side effects associated with the patch. It may irritate your skin or cause an allergic reaction. By delivering nicotine 24 hours a day, the patch may result in sleeplessness or bad dreams. Switching to a 16-hour patch, which is removed before you go to bed, may clear up the problem.

The nicotine patch isn't for everyone. Pregnant women and children shouldn't use it. People who have had a heart attack recently or who have angina pectoris or cardiac arrhythmias should discuss the matter with their doctor first. The patch may not be a good idea for people with such problems.

In Conclusion

Nicotine replacement therapy isn't for everyone. Nicotine gum is not designed for persons who have had a recent heart attack, who have developed unstable angina, who have cardiac arrhythmias, or certain other health problems. This group probably should not use the patch either. Nicotine replacement therapy does seem to help heavy smokers—those who smoke more than 25 cigarettes a day—cope with smoking withdrawal symptoms. Success rates using this method are greatly enhanced when therapy is combined with behavioral therapy and strong follow-up with a doctor.

Other Methods for Quitting

A number of other quit-smoking techniques are available in the marketplace. However, there is no scientific evidence that the methods that follow work as well as some practitioners have reported.

Acupuncture

The Chinese practice of acupuncture involves pressing or piercing spots on the body with special needles to lessen pain elsewhere or ease symptoms of disease. It can be painful. It isn't clear whether acupuncture helps people quit smoking or reduces their withdrawal symptoms.

Two types of acupuncture are used to help smokers quit. In one, part of the nose is pierced to generate feelings of disgust with tobacco smoke. In the other method, part of the ear is pierced. This is said to reduce the craving for nicotine.

However, independent studies have not found that use of a particular site makes a difference as to whether someone stops smoking. When acupuncture was applied to different sites, whether correct or incorrect, the results were the same. This suggests to scientists that a "placebo effect" may be at work. It may be that acupuncture works for some people because they believe it will help them rather than because of its intrinsic value.

Acupuncture has a reported success rate of 8 to 32 percent. However, these percentages are from anecdotal reports and have not been independently verified. For long-term success, smokers who choose this intervention method should also learn coping skills to handle the psychological and social dependencies associated with smoking.

Hypnosis

Hypnosis is perhaps the most widely advertised quit-smoking technique in the phone book. Many commercial programs using hypnosis claim a high rate of success. However, no scientific data are available to support such claims. In reality, hypnosis is probably about as successful as spontaneously quitting on your own, which has a 5 to 10 percent success rate.

Hypnosis for quitting smoking may be performed individually or in a group setting, at just one session or at a series of sessions. While hypnotized, the smoker may be encouraged to change his or her ideas about smoking or to form negative associations with the habit. After the session is over, the smoker is supposed to subconsciously recall those thoughts, which will help him or her quit the habit.

Hypnosis can have highly variable success rates, depending on the expertise of the hypnotist and the suggestibility of the subject. It can be a very expensive form of therapy. People who quit smoking easily because of hypnosis also tend to go back to smoking more readily (unless they have strong social support to back them up).

Medications

At one time it was thought that clonidine, an antihypertensive drug, could help smokers kick the habit. Occasionally this drug is still prescribed for quitting smoking. However, success rates are low. Women seem to respond to this drug a little better than men do. Clonidine must be prescribed by a doctor.

A popular over-the-counter drug, lobeline, has long been available to people trying to stop smoking. There is no scientific evidence that lobeline works any better than a placebo, however.

Silver acetate, a harmless but bitter compound, is sometimes prescribed as part of aversion therapy to make smoking distasteful to the smoker. No solid evidence exists that suggests that silver acetate helps people quit smoking for good. Aside from prescribed nicotine gum or the nicotine patch, we do not recommend medications as a method of quitting smoking.

It *Is* Possible to Quit

It isn't easy to quit smoking, but it *is* possible—for everyone. As we've seen, it takes most people three serious attempts to quit smoking before they succeed. With each attempt, however, they learn more about their habit. And they can use what they learn in their next attempt. A number of intervention methods and programs are available, many of them low in cost. You can design a customized program that's right for you. Your doctor or other health-care professional can help.

CHAPTER NINE

Nutrition

Few of us are dispassionate about the food we eat. Most of us resist changing diets that we have lovingly developed over years to reflect favorite tastes and satisfy unique hungers. Yet the evidence from scientific studies is building to show a strong link between health and daily diet. Although a heart attack does indicate a heart problem, we now know that for many it is a "stomach problem" as well.

To a great degree, what we eat influences our blood cholesterol level. A **high blood cholesterol level** is a serious risk factor for heart disease. In this chapter we'll look more closely at cholesterol levels, fat, and how they fit—and don't fit—into a healthful diet.

Diet can influence the development or prevention of heart disease in other ways as well. Persons who are **overweight** (10 to 15 percent above their recommended weight) tend to have high blood cholesterol levels. (See weight chart on page 216.) Even if an overweight person doesn't have a high blood cholesterol level, however, **obesity** itself is a contributing risk factor for heart disease. **A diet high in sodium** can elevate blood pressure levels in some people with a tendency to high blood pressure. **Chronic high blood pressure** is also a risk factor for heart disease. We'll look at these problem areas and how diet affects them, too.

Your doctor may have told you to modify your diet to lower your blood cholesterol levels, bring down your blood pressure, or lose weight. Relax! You won't be restricted to a routine of alfalfa sprouts and dry toast. On the contrary, the most nutritious diets incorporate a wide variety of foods in moderate amounts. You won't have to give up all your rich food favorites. You may eat them less often or substitute some nonfat, low-fat, or low-sodium ingredients. To get the benefits you want, you'll eat some foods less often than before and other foods more often than before. And you'll undoubtedly make favorites of some new dishes and flavors as you go.

Blood Cholesterol Levels

The number one cause of coronary heart disease (CHD) and heart attack is coronary atherosclerosis—the fatty plaque that collects in the inner walls of coronary arteries. If plaque goes unchecked, it can pinch off blood flow through the vessel or cause a clot. When that happens, blood is prevented from reaching heart tissue, and episodes of angina pectoris and heart attack may occur. High levels of blood (or serum) cholesterol contribute to the development of atherosclerosis. Low-density lipoprotein (LDL cholesterol), often called the "bad" cholesterol, moves excess cholesterol through the bloodstream. It is believed to be the main culprit in the formation of atherosclerosis. The level of cholesterol in the blood can be reduced with changes in diet and medication. When serum cholesterol is reduced, LDL levels go down, too. The risk of developing atherosclerosis and heart disease also drops.

Lowering your total blood cholesterol level is particularly important if you've already had a heart attack. According to statistics, you're more likely to have another heart attack than others are of having a first event. Anyone with a high blood cholesterol level should lower it to an acceptable range. This is important, regardless of age, sex, or other risk factors for heart attack. Many people can reduce their high cholesterol levels without drugs. They do this by increasing their activity level and changing some aspects of their daily diet.

Cholesterol

Cholesterol is a soft, waxy substance found circulating in the bloodstream and in every cell in the body. Cholesterol enters the bloodstream from two sources: our own bodies and the foods we eat. Our bodies manufacture all the cholesterol we need—about 1,000 milligrams (mg) a day. More cholesterol comes from foods from animal sources.

Despite its bad reputation, cholesterol is necessary in small amounts for the body to function normally. The body uses cholesterol to form cell membranes, some hormones, and other needed tissues.

Like cholesterol, a certain type of fat can raise blood cholesterol levels when ingested. There are three kinds of fats or—more precisely— fatty acids in the foods we eat. Doctors and dietitians distinguish between the types and qualities of fats because each affects the body differently. Saturated, polyunsaturated, and monounsaturated fats each have a different degree of saturation. Saturated fat has the greatest effect on blood cholesterol and LDL cholesterol levels. *Saturated fats and dietary cholesterol raise blood cholesterol levels.* When saturated fats are reduced in the diet, blood cholesterol levels usually fall, too.

Saturated Fats

Saturated fats are found primarily in foods from animal sources. They are also found in some plant sources. Palm oil, palm kernel oil, coconut, and cocoa butter all contain saturated fats. In general, the same foods that contain dietary cholesterol add saturated fat to the diet: meats, poultry, fish and seafood, and whole-milk dairy products. Lard (rendered beef fat) is primarily a saturated fat. Saturated fats are found in some plant foods as well, notably the tropical oils. Palm and palm kernel oils, coconut oil, and cocoa butter are all saturated fats. (These oils are commonly used in commercially prepared bakery goods.)

One way to identify saturated fats is by their appearance at room temperature: Most saturated fats set, or harden, at room temperature. Polyunsaturated and monounsaturated fats, which are preferable to saturated fats in the diet, remain liquid at room temperature.

Polyunsaturated Fats

Oils high in unsaturated fats remain liquid at room temperature and in the refrigerator. These oils come from plant sources. Safflower, sesame, sunflower, corn, soybean, and a few other nut and seed oils are polyunsaturated. Scientists think polyunsaturated oils lower cholesterol by helping remove it from the bloodstream and artery walls. Used in place of saturated fats, polyunsaturated fats can help lower blood cholesterol levels.

Monounsaturated Fats

Monounsaturated oils are liquid at room temperature. They may start to solidify when refrigerated. Olive, canola, peanut, and avocado oils are all examples of primarily monounsaturated oils. Studies indicate that these fats can help reduce cholesterol levels also—but only if the diet is very low in saturated fat. Monounsaturated oils are also more desirable for use in cooking than saturated fats. But remember, always use restraint when cooking with fats of any kind.

Both polyunsaturated and monounsaturated fats may help lower total blood cholesterol levels when substituted for saturated fats. But note: This is *not* a recommendation to consume a lot of polyunsaturated and monounsaturated fats! *All* fats should be used sparingly. Fats are high-calorie foods. Any time you ingest more calories than you use—no matter what the source—you create body fat. And being overweight or obese contributes to the risk for heart disease. Fat created from excess calories in the diet may raise blood cholesterol levels.

Hydrogenated Oils

Fats that start out as liquids but were processed to become semisolid— and more saturated—are said to be **hydrogenated**. Polyunsaturated and monounsaturated oils can be hydrogenated. They are often found in commercially prepared foods.

Hydrogenated fats, because they are partially saturated, tend to raise total blood cholesterol levels. The greater the degree of hydrogenation, the more saturated the fat. Consume hydrogenated fats sparingly.

Triglycerides

Triglyceride is the chemical form of most of the fat we eat as well as the fat manufactured by the body from excess calories. Triglycerides are absorbed into the bloodstream, where they circulate as a natural component of the blood. In a healthy person, some triglycerides and other fatty substances move into the liver. Some are taken up by muscle for energy. Others are stored in fat tissue for future use.

Does a high triglyceride level in the blood increase risk for CHD? Triglyceride levels in humans vary widely. People with heart disease often have high triglycerides. People with high triglyceride levels often have high cholesterol and a lower level of high-density lipoprotein (HDL) cholesterol (the "good" cholesterol). They may also suffer from diabetes, obesity, and high blood pressure. The primary treatment for people with hypertriglyceridemia (a high level of triglycerides in the blood) is weight reduction for those who need it and the AHA's Step Two Diet (see information on pages 189–205). Exercise is often effective in reducing triglyceride levels. If these approaches are not effective, medications will be prescribed.

Omega-3 Fatty Acids

Fish contain a special kind of polyunsaturated oil called **omega-3 fatty acids.** Researchers have found that eating fish regularly is a smart part of a "heart-healthy" diet. Several large studies suggest that people who eat more fish have less CHD. Studies of populations who eat large amounts of fish, however, have not confirmed these results.

One thing is clear. Eating fish in place of other protein foods laden with saturated fat is a good idea. Omega-3 fatty acids aren't a magic cure-all for atherosclerosis and heart attack. Omega-3 fatty acids lower triglyceride levels in the blood. But they appear to have little effect on LDL cholesterol, the "bad" cholesterol associated with the development of atherosclerosis. Nor does fish oil raise blood levels of HDL cholesterol. The benefit is more indirect than that.

The AHA recommends that adults eat fish more frequently than meat or poultry. That's because fish is low in saturated fat. Fish oil supplements, on the other hand, are specifically *not* recommended. More studies are needed to look closely at the health benefits of fish oils and omega-3 fatty acids.

There is another reason to avoid fish oil capsules. Regular consumption of fish oil capsules can prevent blood from clotting even when it should, which could be dangerous. Excessive bleeding can be a negative side effect of consuming fish oil capsules.

Fat Substitutes

There are many ways to reduce the amount of fat in the diet. One is simply to eat less fat. Another is to substitute nonfat and low-fat items for high-fat foods (see page 193). Some people are also turning to substances called fat substitutes, which are getting a lot of media attention.

Fat substitutes aren't necessary if you follow a balanced diet and eat foods that are naturally low in total fat, saturated fat, and cholesterol. If you use a fat substitute, be sure to check the nutrition label. Foods made with fat substitutes often contain as many calories as their counterparts with fat. Some are also high in sodium. Also, be sure not to use fat substitutes in place of nutritious foods. Remember, a healthful, balanced diet is the goal.

Sodium

Like atherosclerosis, high blood pressure (hypertension) is linked to coronary heart disease. Chronic high blood pressure both increases the work of the heart and damages the arteries. In most cases, the cause of high blood pressure is never known. Hypertension is an important risk factor that must be controlled carefully. Sodium intake can increase blood pressure in some people. Most Americans eat more sodium than they need. To control or prevent high blood pressure, they may need to increase their physical activity. They may also need to go on a salt-restricted diet. People on a salt-restricted diet avoid salty foods and use salt only sparingly for cooking.

Some people are susceptible to high blood pressure but aren't yet hypertensive. Sometimes they can avoid developing it simply by watching what they eat. Otherwise, consuming too much sodium may ultimately "trigger" the emergence of high blood pressure.

Exercising and changing your diet may be enough to bring blood pressure back to a normal range. When it isn't, you may need medication. People who take medication to help control high blood pressure should still exercise and follow a low-salt diet. Diet and exercise can often help reduce the amount of medication a person needs to control high blood pressure. People with high blood pressure need to work with a doctor or other health-care professional to bring it into normal ranges.

Sodium is a chemical element found in nature. Table salt, or sodium chloride, is a compound that is almost half sodium. Sodium occurs naturally in many foods. It is often added to food as well, usually as table salt. Sodium is used as a preservative as well as a flavor enhancer. Commercially prepared foods often contain liberal amounts of sodium or salt. To find out whether a commercial food product contains a lot of salt, read the nutrients label and ingredients list carefully. The following words in an ingredients list indicate the presence of sodium in a product: soda (which refers to baking soda), sodium, Na, and salt.

A number of over-the-counter medications, such as antacids, are prepared with sodium. If you need to control your sodium intake, check the labels of any medications you take. Look for a low-sodium version. If you don't find one, ask your pharmacist if one is available.

Dietary Guidelines

Eating a nutritious diet that's low in fat, saturated fat, cholesterol, and sodium can make a big difference to your health. Sometimes changing your dietary habits means updating your recipe box. These days it's easy to find cookbooks that emphasize low-fat, low-saturated fat, and low-sodium cooking. Often it's just a matter of making some simple adjustments to old favorites. The American Heart Association publishes several cookbooks based on its dietary guidelines, including the comprehensive *American Heart Association Cookbook, Fifth Edition*, the *American Heart Association Low-Fat, Low-Cholesterol Cookbook*, the *American Heart Association Low-Salt Cookbook*, and the *American Heart*

Association Quick and Easy Cookbook, available in bookstores. The recipes in these books show you just how tempting healthful eating can be.

❧ *Connie was famous in her family for her Sunday afternoon "munchies." She provided enough chips and dips to last a whole football game. But since Louis had been diagnosed with heart disease, Connie faced a dilemma. She hated to give up a family tradition. But she wanted to give Louis, and the rest of the family, more healthful options.*

Connie decided she could continue the tradition while adjusting some of its particulars. She could still serve chips and dips—but she experimented with lower-fat and lower-sodium options. Instead of potato chips, Connie set out a bowl of finger-sized carrots, celery sticks, zucchini spears, and green onions. For more color, she included cherry tomatoes. For those who wanted a little more crunch, she provided a smaller bag of baked tortilla chips. She also served salt-free pretzels instead of jumbo-sized bags of fried chips. She stayed away from hot cheese dips. Instead she offered up a creamy black bean dip that was very low in fat and microwavable. Instead of sour cream dip, she put out low-fat cottage cheese mixed with a dollop of fresh salsa. She also served salsa by itself. A pretty pitcher of water containing ice and lemon slices stood next to the food. All the food and drinks were nicely arranged on a side table at the back of the room. Her new spread looked much better than what she used to just lay out on the coffee table in front of the TV. "Will they eat it?" she wondered.

Everyone ate everything, even her son Jimmy. His only comment was, "This is sort of weird." That made her laugh. In fact, Connie realized that her avid football fans liked the food. What was more amazing to her was that it actually cost less to set out this new spread.

Connie started another family tradition. Before the game, she had the whole family take a brisk walk around the neighborhood together. She promised they'd be back in time for the kickoff. ❧

The American Heart Association has two eating plans designed to help you lower your blood cholesterol levels. The Step One Diet is for healthy people whose cholesterol levels are slightly elevated. The Step Two Diet is recommended for people with CHD. That's the one we focus on in this book. It's a practical, easy-to-follow eating plan that emphasizes a wide variety of foods. The Step Two Diet gives particular attention to the amounts and kinds of fats and the amount of sodium in the diet. People with stubbornly high blood cholesterol levels or blood pressure may need to restrict their intake of fat and sodium to a greater degree than that outlined in this diet. Persons with certain medical disorders, such as diabetes, may need to modify this diet with a doctor's help or choose a different eating plan. Pregnant women may also need a different diet. Growing teenagers may require more calories from the fruits, vegetables, and breads groups. Consult your doctor, a registered dietitian, or a nutritionist before beginning any new eating program for yourself or your family.

For maximum nutrition and health benefit, the AHA Step Two Diet is based on the following daily guidelines, which reflect the latest findings of medical researchers. Keeping track of these ground rules in your own daily diet may take some calculating and record-keeping at first, but over time it will become familiar—almost second nature.

- **Total fat intake** should be 30 percent or less of calories. Of these:
  —**Saturated fat intake** should be less than 7 percent of calories.
  —**Polyunsaturated fat intake** should be up to 10 percent of calories.
  —**Monounsaturated fat** should be up to 15 percent of total calories.
- **Cholesterol intake** should be less than 200 milligrams per day.
- **Sodium intake** should be no more than 2,400 milligrams per day.
- **Carbohydrates, especially complex carbohydrates** (such as breads and grains), should comprise 55 percent or more of all daily calories.
- **Total calories** consumed should be enough to achieve and

maintain a healthy body weight, according to height and gender (refer to the weight chart on page 216).

- **Enjoy a wide variety of foods** every day for a balanced diet that provides all needed nutrients.

Reducing the dietary cholesterol and saturated fat in your diet is an important step on your "road to wellness." A good way to start is by choosing a wide variety of foods and eating them in balanced amounts. Read over the AHA Step Two Dietary Recommendations (pages 194–205). You'll see that at least half your daily caloric needs should be met with complex carbohydrates—breads, pastas, grains, beans, and peas. Fruits and vegetables are important, too. Consume at least two servings of fruit and three servings of vegetables every day. Prepared simply, with a minimum of fat or oil, these foods will fill you up and pack a nutritional wallop, besides. Round out your diet with prudent selections from the dairy products and meat, poultry, or fish groups. (For more information about reducing fat and cholesterol in the diet, see the boxes on pages 192 and 193 and sections about specific food categories, such as meats, that follow.)

Limit Cholesterol and Saturated Fats

The AHA currently recommends limiting cholesterol intake for those with very high blood cholesterol levels and those who have had a heart attack to less than 200 milligrams a day. (Note that one egg yolk contains approximately 213 milligrams of cholesterol. The average American's daily consumption of cholesterol is about 310 milligrams.)

Egg yolks, meats, poultry, fish, seafood, and whole-milk dairy products all contain cholesterol. Egg yolks and organ meats (liver, sweetbreads, kidneys, etc.) are especially high in cholesterol. Limit your consumption of these foods. Foods from plant sources—fruits, vegetables, nuts, seeds, and grains—do not have cholesterol. However, they may contain a certain amount of fat. It's important to remember this distinction when reading food labels. It's not just cholesterol that we need to watch. Too much fat in the diet (especially the saturated kind) carries consequences of its own.

Americans tend to eat too many foods high in saturated fats. On average, saturated fat makes up 11 percent of our total daily calories. Reducing saturated fat is important. When you reduce saturated fat in the diet, you also reduce the level of cholesterol in your blood. The AHA's Step Two diet recommends that less than 7 percent of all daily calories come from saturated-fat sources. That's about half of what many Americans now eat regularly. Reducing total fat, saturated fat, and cholesterol sometimes requires an aggressive approach to dietary changes. (See the box on page 192 for some easy tips to get you started.) A registered dietitian can help people in this situation. He or she can design an eating plan that provides all the necessary nutrients, keeps saturated-fat intake low, and meets personal tastes. (Your doctor can help you find a registered dietitian if you need one.)

Hydrogenated oils are processed from polyunsaturated or monounsaturated oils until **hardened and partially saturated.** Like any other fat, these oils should be limited in the diet. You can do this easily by substituting liquid oil for solid shortening in cooking whenever possible. Check the labels of commercially produced bakery products for hydrogenated fats. Compare brands and types of margarine before you buy; they are not all "created equal." Stick margarine is more hydrogenated than the softer tub margarine. When possible, use a spread instead of a stick.

Butter Versus Margarine

Scientists have found that hydrogenation not only saturates fats but also changes their chemical structure somewhat. The new structure creates a fat molecule known as a **trans fatty acid**. Trans fatty acids also seem to raise blood cholesterol levels but not as much as saturated fats.

If margarine is partially hydrogenated, is it still a good substitute for butter? Butter is high in saturated fat and cholesterol and contributes to the development of atherosclerosis. Most margarine, even when hydrogenated, does not contain animal fat and therefore does not contain cholesterol. Moreover, people who choose margarine over butter may also choose between products that are more or less hydrogenated. The softer the margarine, the less the hydrogenation, and the better for the heart.

The AHA does not recommend using butter instead of margarine.

On the contrary, the AHA suggests using as little fat of any type as possible. Try to choose soft margarine over stick margarine, especially for spreading and cooking. For baking, choose a stick margarine that lists liquid vegetable oil as the first ingredient. Choose margarine that contains no more than 2 grams of saturated fatty acids per tablespoon.

Substituting margarine for butter is just one way to reduce the saturated fat in your diet. We've listed more in the box on page 193.

Shake the Salt Habit

How much sodium is too much? The AHA recommends that healthy adults consume no more than 2,400 milligrams of sodium a day. The same restrictions apply whether sodium appears naturally in food or is added in cooking: Three grams is the limit.

The chart below lists typical sources of sodium and the amounts of dietary sodium they represent. As you can see, a pinch of salt here and there doesn't take long to add up!

$1/4$ teaspoon salt = 500 milligrams sodium
$1/2$ teaspoon salt = 1,000 milligrams (1 gram) sodium
1 teaspoon salt = 2,000 milligrams (2 grams) sodium
1 teaspoon baking soda = 1,000 milligrams (1 gram) sodium

Most Americans consume far too much salt with their food. Cutting back can be an effort, especially at first. It's easy to overlook sources of sodium in the diet (especially if they're "hidden" in prepared convenience foods) or to suppose that some foods you eat are less salty than they really are.

The American Heart Association Step Two Diet is naturally low in sodium. However, people with high blood pressure may need to restrict their salt intake further. Before starting any diet, get the approval of your doctor, a registered dietitian, or other health-care professional first. Be sure the diet provides all the nutrients you need every day.

Whether you choose to follow a specifically low-sodium diet or not, it's easy to find ways to reduce your average daily consumption of salt. The key is to establish a few ground rules.

Many recipes that call for salt don't really need it. (There's no reason

Reducing Saturated Fat and Cholesterol in the Diet

Here are a few tips you can use every day to help reduce the amount of cholesterol you consume.

- Eat no more than 5 ounces of cooked poultry, fish, and lean meat per day.
- Trim away all visible fat on meat before cooking. Drain or skim off fat from cooked meats before using the juices in soups, stews, gravies, etc.
- Remove skin and fat under the skin from poultry before cooking. If you're roasting a whole chicken or turkey, leave the skin on until the bird is cooked to avoid drying the meat out. Remove the skin before carving and serving.
- Limit your consumption of organ meats. Organ meats are very high in cholesterol. They include liver, brains, chitterlings, kidney, heart, gizzard, sweetbreads, and pork maws.
- Try meat as a side dish instead of a main dish occasionally. Give pasta or beans a chance to shine at dinner instead. A 1-cup serving of cooked beans, peas, or lentils, or 3 ounces of soybean curd (tofu) can replace a 3-ounce serving of meat, poultry, or fish.
- Limit your consumption of egg yolks. Egg yolks are high in cholesterol. Limit egg yolks and whole eggs to no more than 2 a week. Egg whites, which have no fat, are not limited. Limit your consumption of baked goods made with egg yolks, such as egg noodles, egg bagels, or commercially prepared baked goods. Check ingredients lists, and be sure to include eggs from these sources as well as those used in cooking in your weekly total.
- In cooking, use 2 egg whites, or 1 egg white plus 2 teaspoons of unsaturated oil, in place of 1 whole egg, or use a cholesterol-free egg substitute.
- Use skim or 1% fat milk and nonfat or low-fat dairy products. If you're used to whole-milk products, make this change slowly. Start with 2% fat milk, then try 1% fat milk, then skim.
- Choose natural or processed cheeses with no more than 3 grams of fat per ounce.
- Use 6 to 8 teaspoons of fats and oils each day for cooking and baking and in salad dressings and spreads. (The amount can vary, depending on individual needs.)
- Use little or no fat when cooking: boil, broil, bake, roast, poach, steam, sauté, stir-fry, or microwave.

to add salt to boiling water for pasta, for example.) Try leaving out the salt and see if you notice a difference—you probably won't miss it. In baking you may not be able to eliminate salt entirely, because it contributes to the chemical process that makes dough rise. However, you can usually halve the suggested amount of salt without compromising the quality of the final product.

Canned or prepared foods are frequently loaded with salt. Look for

Fat Substitutes

You can reduce the saturated fat in your diet without giving up your favorite foods or flavors. The list below is a handy reference for making substitutions for fatty ingredients.

When your own recipe calls for:	Use:
1 cup whole milk	1 cup skim or nonfat milk plus 1 tablespoon unsaturated oil
1 cup heavy cream	1 cup evaporated skim milk; $1/2$ cup low-fat yogurt and $1/2$ cup low-fat cottage cheese
1 cup sour cream	$1/2$ cup low-fat yogurt and $1/2$ cup low-fat cottage cheese; 1 cup ricotta cheese made from partially skimmed milk (thinned with yogurt or buttermilk, if desired); 1 cup chilled evaporated skim milk whipped with 1 teaspoon lemon juice; 1 cup low-fat buttermilk; 1 cup low-fat yogurt
Cream cheese	Nonfat or low-fat cream cheese (add chopped chives or pimiento and herbs and seasonings for variety).
1 tablespoon butter	1 tablespoon polyunsaturated margarine; $3/4$ tablespoon polyunsaturated oil
1 cup shortening	2 sticks polyunsaturated margarine
1 egg	2 egg whites; 1 egg white plus 2 teaspoons unsaturated oil; Cholesterol-free egg substitute according to package directions
2 eggs	3 egg whites; Cholesterol-free egg substitute according to package directions
1 ounce unsweetened baking chocolate	3 tablespoons unsweetened cocoa powder or carob powder plus 1 tablespoon of polyunsaturated oil or margarine (carob is sweeter than cocoa, so reduce sugar in recipe by one fourth).

no salt-added varieties of canned and frozen vegetables, or use fresh. Instead of buying prepared soups, entrees, or desserts, make your own. That way you can control the amount of salt they contain.

Unsalted peanuts, cashews, sunflower seeds, and almonds are all easy to find these days. Dried beans, peas, and lentils have naturally little salt, unlike their canned counterparts. They should be used whenever possible. You need only spend a little more time to prepare them than the precooked variety.

Use herbs and spices in place of salt. Be creative! You can love many flavors. "Salty" is only one. Cultivate a few alternatives. It's possible to buy no-salt spice and herb blends or create your own. Then put them where you can easily reach them—in the cupboard or next to the stove, for example. On the table, replace salt with them.

Fresh herbs add an unmistakably gourmet touch to even the simplest meals. A few snips of fresh tarragon, rosemary, oregano, or thyme can turn pasta or baked chicken into something special. Herbs don't need a lot of care and are easy to grow. Try planting an herb garden at your back door or in small pots on a sunny window sill.

When you dine out, order food that is prepared simply—grilled, broiled, roasted, or steamed—rather than fried or served in a heavy sauce. If you're not sure how a dish is prepared, ask the server. And don't be afraid to make special requests. It's perfectly acceptable to say, "I'd like that prepared without salt, please." Most restaurants are happy to comply.

Dietary Recommendations

The following section describes the American Heart Association's dietary recommendations by food category. This information can help you visualize acceptable serving sizes for each category of food. You'll also discover more useful tips that can help you develop a healthful, flavorful diet you'll want to keep for life.

Meat, Poultry, and Fish

Servings from this food group are high in protein, B vitamins, iron, and other minerals.

Servings per day: No more than 5 ounces of cooked lean meat, poultry, or fish

Serving size: 3 ounces cooked (4 ounces raw) of lean meat, poultry, or fish

A kitchen scale is a good investment as you learn to estimate serving sizes accurately. You may also learn to do the same visually. A 3-ounce portion from this food group equals:

- The size of a deck of playing cards or the palm of your hand
- 2 thin slices of roast beef
- One-half of a chicken breast or a chicken leg with thigh (skin removed)
- ³/₄ cup flaked fish, such as canned tuna packed in water

Choose from:

- Fish, fresh, frozen, or canned (in water or rinsed if packed in oil)
- Shellfish, such as shrimp or crawfish. Although some shellfish tend to be higher in cholesterol than most other types of fish, they are also lower in saturated fat than most meats. They are acceptable once or twice a week.
- Chicken, turkey, Cornish hen, eaten without the skin
- Lean beef. The leanest cuts are from sirloin, loin, or round.
- Lean or extra-lean ground beef
- Ground turkey
- Lean ham (but ham and Canadian bacon are higher in sodium than other meats)
- Wild game (venison, rabbit, pheasant, duck). Farm-raised game is higher in fat than wild game.

Remember that it's possible to substitute other proteins for meat in some dishes. You'll get the same nutrition but often with less fat and fewer calories as well. Try ¹/₂ cup of tofu (bean curd) or ¹/₂ cup of cooked beans, lentils, or peas instead of a serving of meat in entrees, salads, casseroles, and soups.

Organ meats are very high in cholesterol. However, liver is also very high in iron and vitamins. One serving (3 ounces) is acceptable once a month.

Always remove all visible fat from the meat you prepare. Trim away fat from beef, pork, or lamb before cooking. Remove skin and fat under the skin in poultry, unless you plan to roast a whole bird. Then leave the skin on while the bird is in the oven, but remove it before serving.

Prepare meats simply, without heavy sauces or frying. Broiling, boiling, roasting, and grilling are all good methods.

Fruits and Vegetables
Foods in this category are high in vitamins, minerals, and fiber. They are also naturally low in fat and sodium. They do not contain cholesterol.

Servings per day: 2–4 of fruit *and*
3–5 of vegetables
Serving size: 1 medium-size piece of fruit
½ cup diced fruit
or ¾ cup fruit juice
1 cup leafy raw vegetables
or ½ cup cooked vegetables
¾ cup vegetable juice

Enjoy plenty of fruits and vegetables. They provide a wealth of nutrition without a heavy caloric cost. And the range is astonishing—from crunchy carrots to creamy papayas, deep-yellow squash to sweet citrus. More than anything else in the diet, fruits and vegetables keep menus fresh. They change with the seasons and add an incredible variety of tastes, colors, and textures to meals.

You can enjoy most vegetables, when prepared without added fat or eaten raw, in unlimited quantities. There are a few exceptions. You'll find certain starchy vegetables, such as potatoes, listed with breads because their caloric values are similar to those of that food group. Olives and avocados count as fats because of their exceptionally high fat content. Coconut should be avoided altogether, because it is high in saturated fat.

Potassium serves a number of important functions in the body. This mineral is important for growth, cell maintenance, contraction of muscles, and the balance of water between cells. Certain medications prescribed for heart disease, notably some diuretics, reduce the amount of potassium in the body. Doctors often recommend that patients taking diuretics eat more foods containing potassium to compensate for that loss. Bananas, cantaloupe, grapefruit, oranges, tomato or prune juice, honeydew melon, prunes, and potatoes are all good sources of potassium. So is molasses, a natural sweetener.

Breads, Cereals, Pasta, and Starchy Vegetables

Items from this food group are low in fat and cholesterol. They are high in B vitamins, iron, and fiber.

Servings per day: 6–11

Serving size: 1 slice bread

           1/2 bun, bagel, or muffin

           1/4 cup nugget or bud-type cereal

           1 cup flaked cereal

           1/2 cup cooked cereal, dry peas or beans, potatoes, or
               rice or other grains

           1/4 to 1/2 cup starchy vegetables

           1 cup low-fat soup

Good low-fat bread choices include wheat, rye, raisin, or white bread; English muffins; bagels (not egg bagels); pitas (pocket bread); and baked tortillas.

Snack breads can be trickier to choose wisely. They are often prepared with saturated fat, so read labels before you buy. (Even better, try making your own.) Fig and other fruit bars, molasses cookies, and graham, rye, saltine, and oyster crackers are all acceptable in limited quantities. Look for crackers with unsalted tops, flat breads, unsalted pretzels, and air-popped popcorn without butter.

Hot or cold cereals are usually good choices except for granola, which may be high in saturated fat. Read labels when choosing instant cereals and ready-to-eat rice or pasta dishes. These products are often high in sodium.

Quick breads, biscuits, muffins, corn bread, fruit breads, pancakes, French toast, and waffles are acceptable as long as they are low in fat. To be safe, try making them from scratch. The commercial versions are often loaded with fat and salt and may not be as full-flavored as homemade. If you do buy prepared bakery items, read labels carefully.

Starchy vegetables appear in this category because their calorie count per serving more closely resembles those of the bread category than those in the vegetable food group. Starchy vegetables include potatoes, lima beans, peas, winter squash, corn, yams, and sweet potatoes.

Soups are super! Avoid the cream-based variety, and instead opt for broth- or tomato-based types. Vegetable, chicken noodle, bean, split pea, and lentil are all good, low-fat choices. Always read labels, and choose low-fat and low-sodium products. Better yet, make your own soups so that you can control the fat and sodium content yourself. Chill homemade soups so that the fat rises to the top and hardens, then skim it off, reheat, and enjoy.

Fiber

Fiber is an important component in a healthful diet. Dietary fiber, which the body cannot digest, comes from plant-based foods. The two types of dietary fiber are soluble and insoluble. The American Heart Association Step Two Diet recommends eating foods that are high in both types of fiber. Fibrous foods are filling, with fewer calories than many other choices. They also add roughage to the diet, aiding digestion and elimination.

When used in a low-saturated fat diet, soluble fiber can lower total blood cholesterol and LDL cholesterol (the bad cholesterol). Eating soluble fibers regularly lowers cholesterol levels from 3 to 5 percent in some people. Doctors aren't yet sure why this happens. It may be that people who eat more foods high in soluble fibers may eat fewer foods high in saturated fats. Foods high in soluble fibers include corn, oats, barley, rice bran, beans, peas, citrus, strawberries, and apples.

Because of its soluble fiber, oat bran has attracted much media attention recently. While oat and wheat bran can have a place in a healthful diet, many packaged foods that promote these brans should be avoided. Often they don't contain significant amounts of the bran, but they do have too much added salt and fat. Read labels carefully before you buy. Most important, remember that no food alone is a "wonder drug" against developing cholesterol. A nutritious diet that emphasizes a *variety* of foods is a much better hedge against atherosclerosis and heart disease.

Insoluble fibers in themselves don't appear to lower total blood cholesterol. However, they do fill you up and contribute to proper bowel function. Foods containing significant amounts of insoluble fibers include whole-wheat breads, cereals, cabbage, beets, carrots, brussels sprouts, turnips, cauliflower, and apple skin.

Carbohydrates

Most people who strive to reduce their daily fat intake to less than 30 percent of total calories wind up boosting their daily carbohydrate consumption to a small degree. And that's good. Carbohydrates, which are quick-energy foods, should comprise a little more than half of all daily calories consumed. There are two types of carbohydrates: complex and simple. Complex carbohydrates—the starches—offer the body a better nutritional deal and are recommended in the AHA Step Two Diet over simple carbohydrates. Eating plenty of complex carbohydrates also helps persons prone to low blood sugar avoid hypoglycemia.

Simple carbohydrates are basically one form of sugar or another. Table sugar, brown sugar, and confectioner's sugar are all examples of the simple carbohydrate **sucrose**. **Fructose**, another type of simple carbohydrate, is represented by the sugars in honey, fruits, and vegetables. Commercially prepared products usually use sugar in the liquid form of **glucose**, which includes dextrose, corn syrup, and glucose syrup.

Complex carbohydrates include vegetables, fruits, and grains, and both soluble and insoluble fibers as well as starches. Foods high in complex carbohydrates are generally low in calories and high in vitamins, minerals, and other nutrients the body needs. They also add roughage to the diet. Studies have shown that some population groups that eat a diet high in carbohydrates have low blood cholesterol levels. The connection between complex carbohydrates and heart health is still under investigation.

Dairy Products

Items in this category are high in protein, calcium, phosphorus, niacin, riboflavin, and vitamins A and D.

Servings per day: 2 or more for adults over 24 years and
children 2–10 years old
3–4 for young people 11–24 years old, and
women who are pregnant or breastfeeding

Serving size: 1 cup skim or 1% fat milk
1 cup nonfat or low-fat yogurt
1 ounce low-fat cheese
$^{1}/_{2}$ cup low-fat cottage cheese

Skim milk and other nonfat and low-fat dairy products are recommended in a low-fat, low-saturated fat, low-cholesterol diet. They contribute important nutrients that can be hard to find from other sources. In particular, milk products are an excellent source of calcium. Getting enough calcium in the diet is especially important for women to prevent **osteoporosis**, a condition in which bones become brittle and porous and are more prone to fracture.

Whole-milk products are high in saturated fat, so it's important to choose nonfat or low-fat dairy products. Good choices include fortified skim milk, buttermilk made from skim milk, powdered nonfat milk, and canned evaporated skim or nonfat milk.

Choose low-fat cheeses as well, but proceed carefully. Even so-called lower-fat cheeses can remain high in total fat content and saturated fats. Read labels carefully and stay within your daily totals. Avoid cheeses with more than 3 grams of fat per ounce.

If you're used to whole-milk products, you may notice a difference when you switch to lower-fat versions. To make the transition easier, go slowly. Don't drink whole milk today and skim milk tomorrow. Taper off gradually over the course of a few months. Switch first from whole milk to 2% fat, then 1% fat, then skim. These products all have the same nutrients, but skim milk lacks the saturated fat, cholesterol, and calories you don't want.

Cook with "lighter" milk, too. However, don't substitute nondairy products for milk products. They're often made with tropical oils, which are heavily saturated and should be avoided. For desserts, instead of ice cream, choose nonfat or low-fat frozen yogurt, low-fat ice milk, a fruity sherbet or sorbet, or a nonfat or low-fat pudding.

Fats and Oils
Foods in this group are high in fat and calories and should be used sparingly. Some are high in vitamins A and D.

Servings per day: No more than a total of 6 to 8, depending on caloric needs

Serving size: 1 teaspoon vegetable oil or regular margarine
2 teaspoons diet margarine
1 tablespoon salad dressing
2 teaspoons mayonnaise or peanut butter
3 teaspoons seeds or nuts

⅛ of a medium avocado

10 small or 5 large olives

It's best to choose from among vegetable oils and margarines with no more than 2 grams of saturated fat per tablespoon. Acceptable margarines list liquid vegetable oil as the first ingredient. Oils that are acceptable are canola, corn, olive, safflower, sesame, soybean, and sunflower. Salad dressings should have no more than 1 gram of saturated fat per tablespoon.

It's easy to add fat to foods almost unconsciously. Here are a few effective ways to take control of the amount of fat in your diet:

- Choose nonfat or low-fat salad dressings for salads, dips, or marinades.
- Use hydrogenated (partially solid) fats sparingly. The shortenings you do use should be made from vegetable rather than animal products.
- Cook with little or no fat. Avoid frying foods or using heavy sauces. Instead, stir-fry, microwave, broil, roast, poach, or steam your food. For flavor, add herbs and spices instead of salt and butter to your meals. When you eat out, choose simply prepared foods.
- Remember that fats are often "hidden" in baked goods and snack foods. But they count just as much as the fats you use in cooking and spread on breads or vegetables.
- The tropical oils—coconut, palm, and palm kernel—are vegetable oils. They do not have cholesterol. However, they are high in saturated fat, the kind linked most closely to the development of atherosclerosis. Avoid tropical oils. They are frequently used in commercially prepared crackers, snacks, and other baked products. Be sure to read ingredients lists and nutrition labels carefully before you buy.
- Avocados and olives are counted as fats, not vegetables, for the purposes of the AHA Step Two Diet because they are very high in fat compared with other vegetables.

Desserts, Snacks, and Beverages

Desserts, snacks, and beverages don't qualify as a major food group, of course. But it's important to acknowledge them because they're often high in calories and saturated fat. Besides which, the calories and fats they contribute are often unaccounted for in a daily menu plan. That's why they're often considered "diet wreckers." Everyone, of course, slips now and then, sneaking a mid-morning snack here or indulging in a heavy dessert there. In a diet for life, we need to acknowledge that slips and special events happen. The important thing is to prepare for them when possible and to limit the damage afterward.

🍎 *It was 11:30 p.m. Everyone was asleep. Everyone, that is, but Rich. He was prowling the kitchen. He'd been on a diet for a few weeks. He was slowly changing his eating habits for the better. He ate fewer things that were high in fat or salty. He'd already lost a few pounds. But every now and then, he thought he'd go crazy if he didn't have something rich-tasting. He'd been "good" all day today. If he slipped a little in the middle of the night, that would be OK, he told himself.*

Then why was he still prowling and not eating?

Actually, Rich didn't want to cheat. But he was determined to eat something. He sat down at the table. He considered his options. Ice cream. Yes, that sounded good. But all that fat and cholesterol! What else? Maybe he could get that creamy goodness some other way. He thought. He stared at a bunch of bananas on the counter. A banana split? No. What about a banana split without the ice cream? Hmm. A banana, sliced, in a bowl, with some skim milk? Maybe a light sprinkling of sugar? That would be sweet, creamy, filling—really, a little like ice cream. He decided to try it.

Ten minutes later, Rich was having his treat and feeling good. Cholesterol—low. Fat—also low. Calories—low, compared with the ice cream he'd have grabbed in other times. And this dish was so good, he'd make it again. He was really getting the hang of this! 🍎

Desserts

Desserts aren't automatically evil. If you plan for and choose them carefully, they can continue to play some part in your mealtime routine. Where eating is concerned, almost everything is relative. The key is to eat in moderation, make wise choices, and adjust your diet to maximize the health benefits it can offer.

Some desserts are better for you than others. It's important to choose desserts that for the most part are low in saturated fat, cholesterol, and calories. Good choices are fruit, whether fresh, frozen, canned, or dried; nonfat or low-fat yogurt with fruit; angel food cake; frozen nonfat or low-fat yogurt; sherbet or ice milk; flavored gelatin; and sorbets (ices).

For a special occasion—and notice how closely related the words *occasion* and *occasional* are—it's okay to indulge. But rich foods are high in saturated fat and calories. Try to stick with homemade desserts made with oils or soft margarines instead of shortening or butter. In ready-made desserts, look for something that is nonfat or low in fat. If you're dining out, share a dessert with a friend.

Snacks

Snacks, like desserts, can fit into your eating plan if you select carefully. Choose snacks from other acceptable foods in the diet: fruit or fruit juice; raw vegetables with low-fat dips; plain popcorn or unsalted pretzels; low-fat crackers, rice cakes, or cookies; or hard candy. Your choice should be low in saturated fat, salt, and cholesterol. Try to avoid impulse choices, such as candy bars at the checkout counter.

If you find you're routinely hungry at a certain time of day, such as late afternoon, *plan* to have a snack at that time. But factor it in with your other calories and fat considerations. Many people reserve part of their lunch to eat as a snack later in the day, when they get hungry again. That way, their snack is already factored into their daily diet totals. Also, drink plenty of water throughout the day—at least eight glasses. (Coffee, tea, or soft drinks don't count.) Water is good for you and will help fill you up.

Beverages

Water is always a good beverage choice, with meals or between. Other good choices include fruit juice, low-sodium vegetable juice, coffee, tea, mineral water (flavored or plain), low-sodium broth, or low-sodium bouillon. Fruit punches and carbonated soft drinks are not as good from a nutritional standpoint. They can add calories and extra sodium to the diet.

There has been a great deal of discussion in recent years as to whether light to moderate drinking of alcoholic beverages can protect you against coronary heart disease. Studies have shown a slight protective benefit. Light consumption of alcohol apparently raises HDL cholesterol levels slightly, but that accounts for only some of the benefit.

However, light to moderate drinking also has potential negative effects. In a number of people, systolic blood pressure rises with even moderate drinking. And of course, heavy drinking is another story entirely. It has unquestionably adverse health consequences. People who drink heavily have a *higher* death rate from CHD and all other causes as well.

So, if you don't already drink, *don't start!* If you do drink, don't increase consumption on behalf of your heart. The benefits are negligible compared with the health risks. If you are a man, limit yourself to no more than two drinks (1 ounce of ethanol) a day of wine, beer, or liquor. If you are a woman, limit yourself to no more than one of these drinks a day. And stay within your caloric guidelines. Any mild beneficial effect is lost above two drinks a day—and other health problems may ensue.

The following amounts count as one drink (half an ounce of pure ethanol):

2 ounces 100-proof whiskey
3 ounces 80-proof whiskey
8 ounces wine
24 ounces beer

Caffeine

Caffeine, consumed most commonly in tea, coffee, and cola drinks, produces a temporary change in the constriction and dilation of blood vessels. Researchers have studied the effects of heavy caffeine consumption on health. They've tried to determine whether it plays a part in the development of heart disease. So far, a link has not been proven definitively. For now, moderate caffeine consumption appears to be safe.

Putting It All Together

In the previous section we reviewed the guidelines for heart-healthy eating. Now it's time to assess your own situation and put this information to practical use! What changes do *you* need to make, and how will you make them?

First, you'll need to find where your problem areas lie. Next you'll need to plan how to attack these areas. You do that by setting your own dietary goals. After all, planning for success is a big part of being a success—no matter what your goals. Your doctor or a registered dietitian can help you. Your goals will be determined by your current eating habits, blood cholesterol levels, whether or not you need to lose weight, and other health concerns.

After that, you'll need to educate yourself and become more knowledgeable about the foods you eat. Which foods are higher in saturated fat? Which contain cholesterol? How salty is too salty? At first, you'll probably need to keep some kind of record of what you normally eat. This will help you establish a dietary baseline. Then you can start to cut back in areas where you need to, while making sure you get all the nutrients that a balanced diet provides. Let's look next at some of the ways you can begin to sort out these matters for yourself.

Keeping Track

Let's face it: Most of us consider eating one of life's great pleasures. It can be hard at first to look at food somewhat critically. But keeping track of the amount of saturated fat, cholesterol, and sodium in the foods you eat is self-help at its most basic. Fortunately, it is easier than ever to monitor the components of the foods you eat.

Reading Nutrition Labels

The recent Nutrition Labeling and Education Act requires food products to carry new easy-to-read labels called *Nutrition Facts*. The new labels are easy to read (see sample label on page 208). Of course, no one food can make you healthy. Use the information in nutrition labels to help you choose from a wide variety of foods to make up a healthful diet.

Serving Size
Is your serving the same size as the one on the label? If you eat double the serving size listed, you need to double the nutrient and caloric values. If you eat half the serving size shown here, cut the nutrient and caloric values in half, too.

Calories
Are you overweight? Cut back a little on calories! Read the label to see how a serving of the food adds to your daily total. A 5'4", 138-pound active woman needs about 2,200 calories each day. A 5'10", 174-pound active man needs about 2,900. How about you?

Total Carbohydrates
When you cut down on fat, you can eat more carbohydrates. Carbohydrates are contained in foods like bread, potatoes, fruits, and vegetables. Choose these often. They give you nutrients and energy.

Dietary Fiber
Grandmother called it "roughage," but her advice to eat more fiber is still up-to-date. That goes for both soluble and insoluble dietary fiber. Fruits, vegetables, whole-grain foods, beans, and peas are all good sources and can help reduce the risk of heart disease and cancer.

Protein
Most Americans get more protein than they need. Foods that contain animal protein also contain fat and cholesterol. Eat small servings of lean meat, fish, and poultry. Use nonfat or low-fat milk, yogurt, and cheese. Try vegetable proteins such as beans, grains, and cereals.

Vitamins and Minerals

Your goal here is 100% of each for the day. Don't count on one food to do it all. Let a combination of foods add up to a winning score.

Total Fat

Aim low: *Try to limit your calories from fat.* Too much fat may contribute to heart disease and cancer. For a healthy heart, choose foods with a big difference between the total number of calories and the number of calories from fat.

Saturated Fat

A new kind of fat? No—saturated fat is part of the total fat in food. It's listed separately because it's the key player in raising blood cholesterol and your risk of heart disease. Eat less of it.

Cholesterol

Too much cholesterol—a second cousin to fat—can lead to heart disease. Challenge yourself to eat less than 200 milligrams of cholesterol each day. A single egg yolk contains 213 milligrams of cholesterol.

Sodium

You call it "salt," the label calls it "sodium." Either way, it can add up to high blood pressure in some people. So keep your sodium intake low. The AHA recommends no more than 2,400 milligrams of sodium per day for healthy adults. Your doctor may recommend an amount lower than that.

Daily Value

Feel like you're drowning in numbers? Let the Daily Value be your guide. Daily Values are listed for people who eat 2,000 or 2,500 calories each day. If you eat more, your personal daily value may be higher than what's listed on the label. If you eat less, your personal daily value may be lower.

For fat, saturated fat, cholesterol, and sodium, choose foods with a low % **Daily Value.** For total carbohydrate, dietary fiber, vitamins and minerals, your daily value goal is to reach 100% of each.

The user-friendly labels list how much fat, cholesterol, sodium, car-

Nutrition Facts

Serving Size ½ cup (114g)
Servings Per Container 4

Amount Per Serving

Calories 90   Calories from Fat 30

% Daily Value*

Total Fat 3g	**5%**
Saturated Fat 0g	**0%**
Cholesterol 0mg	**0%**
Sodium 300mg	**13%**
Total Carbohydrate 13g	**4%**
Dietary Fiber 3g	**12%**
Sugars 3g	
Protein 3g	

Vitamin A	80%	Vitamin C	60%
Calcium	4%	Iron	4%

*Percent Daily Values are based on a 2,000
calorie diet. Your daily values may be higher or
lower depending on your calorie needs:

	Calories	2,000	2,500
Total Fat	Less than	65g	80g
	Less than	20g	25g
Cholesterol	Less than	300mg	300mg
Sodium	Less than	2,400mg	2,400mg
Total Carbohydrate		300g	375g
		25g	30g

Calories per gram:
Fat 9   •   Carbohydrate 4   •   Protein 4

Nutrition labels are the new way for consumers to comparison shop.

bohydrate, or protein is contained in one serving of the product. They also show what percentage that amount represents in that category in a healthful 2,000-calorie-daily diet. These labels are a great boon to consumers. Gone are the days when health-conscious consumers had to run a quick calculation or "guesstimate" the amounts of nutrients, fat, and sodium in foods.

The law also ensures more honesty in food advertising. Advertisers can use certain words or make health claims on product labels only if the words are backed up by specific facts. The box on page 210 lists key words that you're likely to find on product labels that refer to calories, fat, cholesterol, sugar, fiber, and sodium. They tell you exactly what each claim means.

Used with the daily totals for nutrients, and limits on fat, cholesterol, and sodium, the *Nutrition Facts* labels are a smart way to keep track of what you eat. Food shoppers have long been accustomed to comparing prices; now they can compare nutritional values, too.

Reading Ingredients Lists

Be sure to read ingredients lists as well as the nutrition label on the food products you buy. Food ingredients are always listed by relative weight. The ingredient in the greatest amount is listed first. The ingredient in the least amount is listed last.

Reading for Fat

Read ingredients lists to help you avoid getting too much total fat, saturated fat, or cholesterol. Eat fewer products that list fat or oil as the first ingredient. Also choose fewer products that contain a lot of fat or oil (one of the first three ingredients on the ingredients list). The box on page 211 lists some of the more common sources of saturated fat and cholesterol in packaged foods.

Be cautious about hydrogenated vegetable oils and vegetable shortenings. They vary in degree of saturation, depending on degree of hydrogenation. Choose those that contain no more than 2 grams of saturated fat per tablespoon. Some vegetable shortenings are made from all-vegetable fats, yet contain just 10 to 30 percent polyunsatu-

What Key Words on Product Labels Mean

Key Words	What They Mean
Calorie free	Fewer than 5 calories per serving
Light (Lite)	One-third less calories or no more than half the fat of the higher-calorie, higher-fat version, or no more than half the sodium of the higher-sodium version
Fat free	Less than 0.5 gram of fat per serving
Low fat	3 grams of fat (or less) per serving
Reduced or less fat	At least 25% less fat per serving than the higher-fat version
Lean	Less than 10 grams of fat, 4 grams of saturated fat, and 95 milligrams of cholesterol per serving
Extra lean	Less than 5 grams of fat, 2 grams of saturated fat, and 95 milligrams of cholesterol per serving
Low in saturated fat	1 gram of saturated fat (or less) per serving and no more than 15% of calories from saturated fat
Cholesterol free	Less than 2 grams of cholesterol and 2 grams (or less) of saturated fat per serving
Low cholesterol	20 milligrams of cholesterol (or less) and 2 grams of saturated fat (or less) per serving
Reduced cholesterol	At least 25% less cholesterol than the higher-cholesterol version and 2 grams (or less) of saturated fat per serving
Sugar free	Less than 0.5 gram of sugar per serving
High fiber	5 grams of fiber (or more) per serving
Good source of fiber	2.5 to 4.9 grams of fiber per serving
Sodium free (no sodium)	Less than 5 milligrams of sodium per serving and no sodium chloride (NaCl) in ingredients
Very low sodium	35 milligrams of sodium (or less) per serving
Low sodium	140 milligrams of sodium (or less) per serving
Reduced or less sodium	At least 25% less sodium per serving than the higher-sodium version

rated fats. Use them infrequently, but do choose them over shortenings made from animal-vegetable fat blends.

Sources of Fat and Cholesterol

Animal fat	Pork fat	Coconut oil*
Bacon fat	Turkey fat	Hydrogenated vegetable
Beef fat	Butter	oil*
Chicken fat	Cream	Palm kernel oil*
Egg and egg yolk solids	Hardened fat or oil	Palm oil*
Ham fat	Whole-milk solids	Vegetable oil[†]
Lamb fat	Cocoa butter*	Vegetable shortening
Lard	Coconut*	(some types)*

*Sources of saturated fat but not cholesterol
[†]Could be coconut, palm, or palm kernel oil; does not contain cholesterol

Reading for Sodium

Some commercial food products advertise that they are "lite" in salt. But what does that mean? Until recently, it could mean anything the advertisers wanted you to *think* it meant. The Food and Drug Administration has established guidelines for advertising. Now the terms all mean the same thing. They're explained in the box on page 210.

If you're trying to cut down on salt, stay away from any product that lists salt or sodium as an ingredient. Be ruthlessly honest, and keep track of the sodium you do consume every day in a small notebook. Use any of the inexpensive, pocket-size sodium-counter references available in bookstores. They'll help you accurately estimate the amount of sodium found naturally in fresh foods and added to prepared food products.

Sodium content per serving of prepared foods is found on the nutrition label. Fresh fruits and vegetables are not labeled. However, your grocery store should display nutrient information for all produce offered for sale. Look for a listing of vitamins and minerals, including sodium, per serving.

Become familiar with the sodium content of the foods you eat most often. Know which foods are more or less salty than others. This will make it easier to choose wisely. Eventually, you'll develop a working knowledge of the sodium content of commonly eaten foods.

Changing Your Eating Habits

Has your doctor told you to

- reduce your intake of saturated fat and cholesterol to bring down your blood cholesterol levels—but you love rich food?
- cut back on salt to bring down high blood pressure—but you despair at giving up "flavor" at mealtimes?
- lose weight—but you've tried without luck?

You may want to change your eating habits by changing your behaviors around and expectations about food. Behavior modification involves using a logbook or diary to track *what* you eat, *when* you eat, and *how you felt* at the time. Over time (often with the help of a registered dietitian or licensed nutritionist), you may find that patterns emerge in your eating habits. Do you eat richer foods when you feel distressed? Or do you look into cupboards and taste the contents when you're in the kitchen? A behavior modification plan can help you identify those situations. Then you can devise alternative activities when those situations arise. You can also plan your diet carefully and substitute more healthful choices for what you may be tempted to eat at those times.

Progress Charts

You can keep track of your goals by keeping charts as well as diaries. Perhaps you're trying to bring down your blood cholesterol levels and blood pressure. A chart that shows your progress in these areas, along with your weight loss, can be motivating. Post it in the bathroom or wherever you'll see it often.

Plan for Success

Once you've identified the kinds of situations that cause you trouble, you can plan ways to change your responses. If you snack between meals, do something different when the urge to snack hits. Take a walk, listen to a favorite radio station for a few minutes, play with the dog, or pick up a magazine and read instead. *But plan for these troublesome situations in advance.* Some people make a deal with themselves when they find themselves reaching for a snack. They set a timer for 10 minutes and do something else in that time. Usually, they find they don't need to eat the snack. Reaching for food was just an impulse, not a response to true hunger. Or if they're still hungry, they've had time to consider what they can really *afford* to eat and still be satisfied. They're more likely to go for a rich-tasting, nutritious banana or other acceptable snack instead of an impulse food such as potato chips.

Similarly, many people find that they just don't have the energy or desire to fix a nutritious dinner every night. Unfortunately, that creates a prime opportunity for snacking on the wrong foods. To address that problem, consider making a heart-healthy casserole or roasting a chicken large enough for leftovers. After it's cooked and cooled, wrap up individual servings and pop them in the freezer. Then you can defrost and reheat them later in the week.

Special Concerns

You may be convinced that you must improve your eating habits. You may even be successful *most* of the time. Still, you may fall back into your old eating habits when special situations occur. If so, here's how you can deal with those special challenges.

Eating Out

More and more of us eat out regularly, either out of necessity or for pleasure. But eating out can pose special problems for people trying to lose weight or reduce their intake of fat, cholesterol, or sodium. If you know you have trouble staying with your diet at certain restaurants, suggest to your friends or colleagues other places that prepare lighter foods.

❦ *Rudy loved going out with friends. Dinner, dancing, sports events—whatever. He seemed to eat out at every meal. But now that he'd had a heart attack, his doctor had told him that his eating habits should change. Rudy doubted that this could work, but the heart attack had been such a terrible experience! He knew he'd have to give the doctor his best effort.*

Tonight, the gang was going out for pizza and bowling.

Rudy was worried that he'd be considered a wet blanket if he ordered something different. His friends always got a pizza with the works.

When it was time to order, everyone started to discuss what extras should go on the pizzas. Rudy was quiet. He decided he'd ask the group to leave off the meat, olives, and extra cheese on half of one of the pizzas. He'd see what would happen.

When he made his request, a couple of the guys ribbed him about it. But the waitress said it was no problem. She asked if he'd like extra veggies instead of the meat and cheese. "They're roasted and have a great Mediterranean flavor. We can still leave out the olives," she said. This hadn't occurred to Rudy. He looked at the menu again. Roasted peppers, onions, garlic, fresh tomatoes, and basil—it did sound good. "OK," he said.

When the pizzas came, Rudy made sure he took just two slices. That left some veggie-style slices for the others to try. To his surprise, there was a small scuffle at one end of the table for those remaining pieces. Rudy relaxed. Maybe adjusting what he ate wouldn't have to be as disruptive as he feared. At least, not in the way he had supposed! 💘

Even if low-fat dishes aren't on the menu, you may still be able to get a low-fat meal. Many restaurants will prepare food to order. If you're not sure about a particular restaurant, phone ahead and find out. Restaurants want your business. Most are happy to comply with requests. And if your order doesn't come to the table as you requested, send it back.

It's okay to have a plain roll (without butter). But if you're likely to feel tempted by a complimentary bowl of breads, crackers, or tortilla chips, ask that they be kept out of your reach. Or if everyone agrees, remove the bowl from the table entirely. Then order a no-calorie drink, such as flavored mineral water.

Order dishes prepared with little or no fat or oil. When you order a salad, ask for dressing on the side. Then you can control how much you use. Ask for a nonfat or low-fat dressing. If one isn't available, order an oil-based, rather than a cream-based dressing. Order soups that are broth-based instead of cream-based. In entrees, look for dishes that are steamed, broiled, stir-fried, baked, grilled, poached, or roasted. If you aren't sure how something is prepared, ask your server. Order fruit as a dessert. Or split a dessert with a friend or two if it's a special occasion.

High-fat foods include those that are fried, basted, braised, au gratin, crispy, escalloped, pan-fried, stewed, or stuffed. Cream sauces and dishes that are buttered, creamed, covered with cheese sauce or gravy, hollandaise, or marinade also tend to be high in fat. So do casseroles.

High-sodium foods may be pickled, smoked, au jus, or in broth, cocktail sauce, tomato base, soy, or teriyaki sauce.

Savor the Flavors

Whether you're the world's greatest Mexican-food enthusiast or the choosiest connoisseur of French cuisine, enjoying ethnic foods doesn't mean you're restricted to high-fat selections. Appendix A (pages 275–80) lists low-fat alternatives that are commonly available in some of the most popular restaurants. Use these tips when you eat out to help find lower-fat, healthful foods. And if you do splurge in one area of the menu occasionally, offset it by making selections in other areas that are lower in fat or sodium. Happy eating!

If You Need to Lose Weight

Obesity, or being overweight, is a contributing factor to coronary heart disease. (A desirable-weight table appears in the box on page 216.) Many scientists believe it is more significant when fat accumulates around the waist instead of the hips (the so-called "apple" body type as opposed to the "pear" body type). Obesity is often defined as being more than 20 percent above your ideal weight range. "Ideal weight" is defined as a function of your height, body build, gender, degree of muscle development, and percentage of body fat. Interestingly, if fat were removed from the equation, there would be little difference in the weights of people of the same height and build.

Best Body Weight Ranges*

Height (Without Shoes)	Weight (Without Shoes)	
(feet/inches)	Men (pounds)	Women (pounds)
4'10"	—	92–121
4'11"	—	95–124
5' 0"	—	98–127
5' 1"	105–134	101–130
5' 2"	108–137	104–134
5' 3"	111–141	107–138
5' 4"	114–145	110–142
5' 5"	117–149	114–146
5' 6"	121–154	118–150
5' 7"	125–159	122–154
5' 8"	129–163	126–159
5' 9"	133–167	130–164
5'10"	137–172	134–169
5'11"	141–177	—
6' 0"	145–182	—
6' 1"	149–187	—
6' 2"	153–192	—
6' 3"	157–197	—

*This table is adapted from the Desirable Weight Tables prepared in 1959 by the Metropolitan Life Insurance Company. It is based on weights associated with the lowest mortality. For women 18 to 25 years old, subtract one pound for each year under 25.

The 1983 revision of the Metropolitan Life Insurance Company's Height and Weight Tables allows increased weight for certain heights. However, because obesity is a contributing factor for heart disease the American Heart Association did not adopt the 1983 version.

Being even a little above your desirable weight isn't as healthful as being within the average ranges. Researchers in the Framingham Study found that the more above average a person's weight is, the greater his or her risk of developing CHD. The same study showed that men who are 20 percent above their ideal weight have fully *twice* the risk of developing CHD as their normal-weight peers. In addition, the study found that the lower your weight—the thinner you are—the lower your proportional risk of developing heart disease. This finding was also true for women.

Why is obesity a health problem? As we've seen earlier, obesity is usually the result of too many calories and not enough exercise to keep intake and expenditure in balance. Usually, the extra calories are not from low-fat, low-cholesterol foods. Obesity tends to raise blood cholesterol and triglyceride levels and lower HDL (the "good" cholesterol). Obesity also raises blood pressure. It can induce diabetes in people who are prone to developing it.

People who are overweight tend to have more episodes of angina pectoris and more heart attacks than normal-weight people do. They also have them earlier in life. In turn, these conditions are linked to the development of atherosclerosis, the major cause of heart attack. Bringing your weight into a desirable range—by eating less and getting more exercise—is a positive, highly effective way to promote personal health. It should be a major goal of anyone who has been told by a health-care professional to lose weight.

❧ *After her heart attack, Emmy knew it was time to get serious about losing weight. She had tried before, but she never really felt organized in her attempts. She was always trying to do it all by herself. She realized she might like some support. This time she was going to try something new. Her doctor recommended that she find a diet support group. She checked around and found one that met at a convenient time in the community center.*

The first visit was a revelation. It put her goals in perspective. She felt that this group understood her problem—their problems were similar. She felt at home here. The leader led an interesting discussion. It made Emmy think about how she felt about food and why she wanted to change. Here was a place she could always go if she needed support and understanding that she didn't always get from friends or family. This group would expect to see her progress. They would cheer her on and help keep up her spirits, too. And she'd do the same for them.

Emmy didn't speak during that first meeting. She saw that

*others did. Some had questions, some had successes to share.
Some had tips that Emmy knew she could use. She liked that.
She could be only as visible as she wanted to be after she'd registered and weighed in. And she was told she could always call
the leader if she needed to.*

*The best tip she got that evening was from one of the other
members of the group. She talked about a chat group on the In-
ternet for people who have quit smoking. Emmy loved to "surf
the net," but she hadn't even thought about looking there for a
support group. She couldn't wait to give it a try.* 🍒

The American Heart Association Step Two Diet is designed to provide all the daily nutrients your body requires and to help you maintain
your weight within normal ranges, according to your height and gender. But the Step Two Diet can be adapted for those who need to lose
weight (or gain it). To lose weight, choose fewer daily servings from
each of the food groups. Try to eat less food from the Fats and Oils
Group and try to avoid high-fat foods from all the categories. (To gain
weight, add servings from the fruits and vegetables and breads categories). Before starting this or any diet, however, discuss your needs
and goals with your doctor and get his or her approval.

Many people try fad, or "crash," diets to lose weight quickly. In the
short term, such diets often work. Over the long term, though, people
who go on these diets usually gain back all the weight they lost, plus a
few more pounds.

The trouble with fad diets is that they don't address the underlying
eating habits that created the weight problem in the first place. When
you stop a fad diet, you are very likely to go back to your old eating
habits because you didn't learn better ones. Some fad diets emphasize
one kind of food over others. That's a bad idea in itself. Eating moderate amounts of a wide variety of foods is the only sure way to take
weight off and keep it off. Slow and steady is a much more realistic way
to develop sound nutritional habits that will last a lifetime, seeing you
through thick *and* thin.

Secrets for Success

Of course, choosing what to eat is only one part of a successful weight-loss diet. Today we know that a number of elements need to be in place for weight loss, then weight maintenance, to be effective. The most effective programs include these elements:

- **Appropriate health-risk screening**
  Don't start any strict diet without being checked by a doctor. You may have a condition that requires restricting certain foods or eating more of others.

- **A personalized weight-loss program**
  Let your doctor or other health-care professional help you set weight-loss goals. The goal is not to look like you did at 18, but to enjoy better health and mobility. Work with your doctor to get the maximum benefit from your weight-loss plan.

- **Medical supervision**
  Check with your doctor periodically. If you feel faint or notice other changes after going on the diet, discuss them with your health-care practitioner immediately.

- **Counseling by qualified personnel**
  A registered dietitian can look at what you normally eat and work with you to modify your diet in a healthful way. Often this won't require drastic changes in the foods you like to eat. That makes it easier to stick with the diet.

- **Establishment of lifelong healthful eating habits**
  Although you may "go on a diet" to lose weight, in fact a diet is any regular eating pattern. We are all on diets, whether we're trying to lose weight or not. But some diets are more healthful than others. By following a healthful weight-loss diet, you'll begin to follow a new pattern of eating that will benefit you long after you have reached your desired weight. A healthful diet will provide you with all the nutrients your body needs every day, while you maintain a desirable weight.

- **Support from friends and family**
  Losing weight can have certain psychological as well as physical ramifications. There are many reasons that we eat.

Hunger is only one. Regular support group sessions are a good way to become more aware of why we eat the way we do and to talk about it with others in the same situation. (Support groups can be found at local hospitals or health clinics.) The support of friends and family at other times is also important.

- **Regular exercise**
  Increasing physical activity accelerates weight loss and helps keep the weight off. People who exercise expend more energy and use more calories. And they continue to burn calories at a slightly higher level for several hours after they stop exercising.

Before You Start

Be very clear before you start a weight-loss diet about why losing weight is important to you. The fact that you've been diagnosed with heart disease or have had a heart attack is one very good reason to take control of your weight now. But there may be other good reasons, too. Think about it. Write down your reasons over the course of a few days, and keep them handy. Refer to them often as the weeks go by, to remind yourself of the important job you have undertaken.

Talk with your loved ones about your new goals. Be honest with them. Ask for their help and understanding. You'll want their support to make your job easier. Most people will be happy to cheer you on in your efforts. Occasionally you may find someone who doesn't seem to value your decision or support your personal goals. That's okay. Don't expect that person's support. Stay in control by working around him or her. Imagine how to handle temptation constructively if it occurs. Avoid situations that pair that person with food, if necessary.

Set goals, and then break them into manageable pieces. Be realistic. If you have a lot of weight to lose, you may sometimes feel overwhelmed at the task before you. That's understandable. It can help to look at your goals in another way. Instead of focusing on losing 20 pounds, for example, concentrate on losing the first 5 pounds. You'll feel a well-deserved sense of accomplishment when you reach that goal. Then you can concentrate on losing the next five, and so forth, until eventually you reach your long-term goal. Celebrate a little with a nonfood reward at each goalpost, and share your achievements with the people who have supported you.

Keep your goals realistic. Working with a health-care professional can help. The purpose of losing weight should be to improve your health outlook—not to make you look like you're a teenager again.

As You Go
For some people, behavior modification is a useful dieting tool. Combined with a menu plan and the support of friends and family, behavior modification can help you learn to identify what foods and situations are problematic for you. And it can help you gain control of them. Behavior modification is discussed briefly in this book on page 212.

Dealing with Plateaus and Slips
It's typical to reach a plateau in your weight-loss efforts now and then. You may have lost weight steadily for some weeks, only to find yourself stuck at the same weight for a week or two. Or perhaps you slipped one week and indulged a craving for rich or salty foods that you've been trying hard to avoid. Setbacks like these are completely natural. They should not become an opportunity for giving up or blaming yourself for "failing." On the contrary, part of the learning curve of any diet is to adjust for the long haul—lifelong enjoyment of good eating habits. Slips happen to all of us. The best way to deal with them is to pick up where you left off and keep going. What really matters is how you compensate for them after they occur. Keep your mind on the long-term goal of good eating habits and a healthful weight. This keeps slips in perspective. It took you years to create your eating habits. Changing them won't happen overnight. But with motivation and effort, it can happen.

Plan Ahead
A good diet emphasizes foods prepared simply, without a lot of added fat or oil. On a weight-loss diet, planning for such meals is especially important. Make a menu plan for the week. Then make a shopping list and stick to it! Look for vegetables and fruits, skinless poultry, fresh or frozen fish, lean cuts of meat, bread products with low-saturated fat

content, and low-fat cereals. Avoid heavily processed food products that may contain hidden fat and sodium. Instead, buy the ingredients and make the dish yourself. Finally, don't shop on an empty stomach. You may be tempted to binge.

You Can Do It!

In this chapter, we've reviewed some of the reasons why what you eat is so closely associated with your overall health. Saturated fat and cholesterol are associated with the development of atherosclerosis, the main instigator of heart disease. We've identified some of the most commonly eaten foods that contain high amounts of these substances. We've also learned some tricks for avoiding them.

Now it's up to you. What you eat is perhaps the most fundamental contribution you can make toward your own health. Eating poorly has its consequences; eating properly has its rewards. And that's a good bargain, because you needn't sacrifice flavor or fullness in the process! You may need more help in getting right-side-up in your eating habits. Your doctor, nurse, support group, or a friend can help you get started and stay with it. Get excited about the opportunity to discover new favorites and shake up your eating routine (just a little).

There are many resources available to you in your community to provide information or support your efforts. Check out low-fat, low-cholesterol cookbooks at your bookstore or library. Take a low-fat cooking class, or subscribe to a magazine that emphasizes healthful cooking and eating. Swap heart-smart recipes with members of your club or other group. Do anything to keep your interest up until these healthful changes become second nature to you. They will, if you're willing to give them a try!

New flavor experiences are out there, waiting for you! What are *you* waiting for?

CHAPTER TEN

Exercise

Was an inactive—sedentary—lifestyle your habit before your heart attack? If so, you aren't alone. Today all too few American adults get the kind of regular exercise that conditions hearts. Physical inactivity—the lack of regular aerobic exercise—is an important risk factor for developing coronary heart disease (CHD). If you have had a heart attack or have been diagnosed with heart disease, it's likely your doctor has prescribed some kind of regular exercise program as part of your recovery plan. In this chapter we'll look at why regular exercise is so closely tied to better health. We'll also see how exercise affects the heart. We'll even show you ways to make exercise a regular and enjoyable part of your life.

Benefits and Risks

Regular physical activity may reduce your risk for heart disease. How the beneficial effect is achieved isn't precisely known. Exercise reduces the impact of some other risk factors associated with CHD, such as high blood pressure and certain abnormal lipid levels. But exercise may have an independent, direct effect on heart disease prevention, too. Regular aerobic exercise is good for everyone: adults and children alike and for both men and women.

Regular exercise confers many benefits. It conditions the heart to run more efficiently. With exercise training, the basic heart rate falls. When that happens, the heart can do the same work in fewer beats. It is able to pump more blood with each contraction. Regular exercise is to your body what regular maintenance and tuning is to your car—the best way to keep it working at its best.

There's no doubt that regular physical activity promotes better health. People who exercise realize a number of health benefits with consistent effort. Regular exercise may help:

- increase HDL levels (the "good" cholesterol)
- lower triglyceride (blood fat) levels
- improve blood sugar (glucose) tolerance in persons with diabetes
- control your weight
- reduce high blood pressure if you are susceptible to it
- improve your outlook on life and lessen feelings of anxiety or depression
- increase your awareness of your body
- inspire you to make other beneficial lifestyle changes, such as quitting cigarette smoking, losing weight, or lowering high blood pressure

Following an exercise program may or may not directly reduce your risk of a second heart attack. Doctors aren't sure yet. However, among people who do have a second heart attack, those who exercise regularly tend to have milder events than their counterparts who do not exercise.

Exercise with CHD or After Heart Attack or Bypass Surgery

Frequently, people who have been diagnosed with CHD or who have had angina symptoms, a heart attack, or bypass surgery are afraid to exercise. They worry that exercise could be bad for their heart. They fear it will trigger a fatal heart attack or severe angina. People who have heart problems should be screened by their doctor before starting any exercise program. We'll get to that in a minute. But as far as heart health is concerned, it's far riskier *not* to exercise at all than to follow an *appropriate* exercise program.

Each case of CHD, heart attack, or bypass surgery is unique. Consequently, the way each person recovers is unique, too. Some people with CHD work up to regular walks in the neighborhood within weeks or months of their heart attack. Others work up to high-intensity exercise training in time, if they want to. Very few people with CHD are prohibited from participating in any type of exercise activity. In fact, exercise is an important part of most cardiac rehabilitation programs.

So even if you rarely exercised before your heart attack, a program that gradually increases your activity level will be helpful from now on. Mild to moderate exercise, started at bedside after a heart attack, hastens recovery and a return to "normal life"—including a return to work. It is almost always an important part of cardiac rehabilitation.

Exercise Risks

Any form of regular exercise involves risks as well as benefits. The health benefits associated with most kinds of exercise outweigh the possible risk of injury, however. This is true even under vigorous training conditions, such as running. The key is to *minimize the risk and maximize the potential benefit.*

A proper medical evaluation, made before starting an exercise program, is one important way to minimize risk. Medical supervision during exercise is also important in some cases. (We'll talk more about that in a moment.) You can minimize risk of injury further by doing the following:

- Warm up and cool down before and after the activity.
- Always wear apparel that is appropriate for the activity.
- Avoid exercise on the days you do not feel at your best.
- Avoid exercising outside when it is very hot or cold.

See guidelines for exercise in the box on page 230.

Sudden Cardiac Death

Many people with cardiovascular disease fear that they could strain their heart further or even die from the extra exertion exercise requires. Overall, increased physical activity reduces risk of sudden cardiac death. Physical exercise conditions the heart and strengthens it.

There is an exception. Those with CHD should not exercise very vigorously. They are at some higher risk of sudden cardiac death *while they exercise.* Sudden cardiac death is an extremely dangerous condition in which the heart beats shallowly and ineffectively instead of strongly and steadily. The risk of sudden cardiac death even in this circumstance is very small. People with CHD, however, should discuss *any* vigorous exercise with a doctor and be screened before starting. Then they should be medically supervised until their tolerance for high-intensity exercise is established. Moderately intense activities, such as walking and swimming, are always alternatives, of course.

The Most Common Risk

By far, muscle and bone injury is the most common kind of problem associated with regular exercise. Usually the incidence of this kind of problem increases according to the intensity level of the activity and the participant's age. Some low-intensity activities are swimming, biking, and walking. These activities put little added stress on bones or joints. High-intensity activities include jogging and aerobic dancing. Such activities are much harder on the knees, ankles, and other stress-bearing joints. Wearing supportive shoes and proper clothing helps diminish this particular risk.

Some doctors recommend that persons over 40 ease away from high-intensity activities. They suggest activities that are better tolerated by the joints, such as brisk walking. A person over 40 who pursues a high-intensity activity should begin slowly and gradually work up to full steam over weeks, even months. With high-intensity exercise, it's a good idea to exercise every other day rather than every day. Skipping a day gives the body the necessary time to adjust to a higher activity level.

Injuries also tend to occur when muscles and joints haven't been warmed up or cooled down properly before and after each exercise period. Always begin each session by slowly pacing yourself as you warm up to the targeted exercise level. Be sure to end each session by cooling down and stretching.

Before You Start

Anyone who is over 40 and who hasn't exercised for a long time should see a doctor before beginning an exercise program. Anyone with CHD at any age as well as anyone who has had a heart attack, bypass surgery, or experienced angina pain must be screened by a doctor before beginning an exercise program. A medical screening helps determine which *level* of exercise will be safest. It also provides an opportunity to discuss ways to promote safety and prevent injury during the activity. Any activity that might aggravate a heart condition should be avoided for obvious reasons. In addition, patients on medication need to learn how exercise may affect their tolerance for it and vice-versa. The doctor conducts a physical examination, takes the patient's history, and considers the patient's age. Then together the doctor and patient decide which activity might be best.

The Physical Exam and History

Most people with heart disease will need to take an exercise test (sometimes called a stress test) before starting an exercise program. During an exercise test as many as 12 electronic "leads" from an electrocardiograph machine are placed on the patient's skin at different points. Rather like stethoscopes, the leads "hear" information about the patient's heart rhythm. This information is sent back to the electrocardiograph for interpretation. The patient is monitored while walking on a treadmill. The intensity of pace is gradually increased. The test is stopped after a predetermined period of time or immediately if there are signs of angina or changes in the electrocardiograph or blood pressure.

This test helps doctors identify cardiovascular problems that might not be noticeable in the patient at rest. An exercise test is a useful way to assess cardiac function and to determine what level of exercise training is likely to be appropriate. Sometimes a patient's condition makes an exercise test inappropriate. If so, that person will probably be restricted to low-intensity activities, such as stretching and flexibility exercises, until the situation improves.

Doctors also take a full medical history. They consider all health conditions that may affect an exercise program. Combined with a history of CHD or heart attack, some conditions may exclude some types of activity. They may also make medical supervision desirable, at least for the short term.

Degrees of Heart Disease

How much activity is advisable for a person with CHD depends on several factors. The degree of disease, the presence of other risk factors, the person's age, and the stability of his or her condition must all be considered.

Stable Coronary Heart Disease

A series of exercise tests can show if a patient's condition has stabilized after a mild heart attack. If the patient's blood pressure is under control and he or she can monitor his or her own exercise activities safely, the cardiovascular disease is usually stable. Such people are often allowed to pursue even vigorous exercise if they wish. First, of course, they must be checked out by a doctor over the course of a few typical exercise sessions. The risk of heart attack during vigorous exercise for someone with stable cardiovascular disease is low. However, it is still higher than that risk for someone without heart disease.

Some people who have a stable heart condition find it hard to follow the recommended activity guidelines or to identify warning signs of heart trouble. Their best bet may be to join a medically supervised exercise program. Often such programs are available in hospitals to outpatients for a small fee.

Unstable Coronary Heart Disease

People diagnosed with unstable CHD have a moderate to high risk of aggravating a heart condition with exercise. These patients shouldn't exercise until their condition stabilizes. At that time they will be monitored very closely by medical professionals until a safe level of exercise is determined. Their activity level will probably be monitored for 6 to 12 supervised sessions, or more. Until these patients stabilize, doctors generally prescribe simple daily activities, such as light housekeeping, as exercise. In time, these patients frequently "graduate" to higher activity levels.

Exercise for Health and Enjoyment

For far too many of us, physical activity isn't a regular habit. These days, few of us do the kind of work that provides the exercise we need. But there are other stumbling blocks, some of which have to do with attitudes about exercise. In our society modernization has put a great deal of emphasis on personal convenience. That tends to encourage us to prize whatever saves us time or energy. In addition, we live complicated lives in which our free time often seems severely limited. We often must carve out such time from pressing obligations to work or family. In addition, as a society, we tend to prepare ourselves rigorously for work or a career. We may not be as well prepared to use our private time healthfully and enjoyably.

Do these things affect the way Americans have come to view regular exercise? Perhaps in part. Regular exercise saves neither time nor energy—it expends both. Regular exercise can mean adding one more demand to a day that already seems crowded with activity. Regular exercise to some people means being "selfish" by taking time out for themselves. Whatever their reasons *not* to exercise, it's a fact that fewer than one in five American adults find the time to exercise moderately for at least half an hour three times a week. Our children are also learning to be sedentary, in ever-increasing numbers. That's a setup for heart disease and a host of other health problems later.

How Much Exercise Do I Need?

The amount and intensity of exercise needed for cardiovascular conditioning isn't exactly known. It is believed to vary among people. A good individualized exercise program takes into account age and health status. High-intensity activity isn't as important as getting exercise *regularly*. Even exercise programs that involve a low-intensity activity undertaken just three times a week for 30 minutes can deliver tangible health benefits.

However, the more time and energy you spend in some form of physical activity, the greater the health rewards. Those who expend 2,000 calories a week in some kind of aerobic physical activity seem to enjoy the greatest cardiovascular benefit. Such a program isn't right for everyone. A program of moderate intensity, however, such as brisk walking, is safe and desirable for most people.

Guidelines for Cardiovascular Exercise

- With guidance from your doctor, select exercises that are right for you. Aerobic exercise should be a major component of your activity. But include flexibility and strengthening exercises for a well-rounded program.
- Understand your own limitations. Check in with your doctor periodically for a reevaluation of your medical status. Ask him or her to tell you what your limitations are.
- Wear appropriate clothing and shoes. Loose-fitting clothing that "breathes" is best.
- Adjust your exercise routine to the weather. Avoid exercising outdoors in very hot or cold weather. Such extremes can be hard on your heart. Excessively hot weather is particularly dangerous. Humidity, wind, and high altitude can all affect how your heart handles extreme temperatures. Drink plenty of water. Consider exercising indoors on those very hot or cold days. Walk in an enclosed mall, pedal on a stationary bicycle, or swim in an indoor pool.
- Dress for the weather. Wear a knit cap if you're out in cold weather or a sun hat if you're out in warm weather. *Don't* dress more warmly than necessary to give yourself a more strenuous workout. Generally, for cold weather, it's best to dress as you would if you were going outside to meet a friend, plus a layer. In hot weather, wear light-colored clothing. Be sure your shoes fit properly and are right for your chosen activity. Wear thick socks to avoid blisters.
- Do not exercise vigorously soon after eating. Wait at least two hours. Exercising sooner may result in cramps, nausea, or faintness.
- Exercise only when you feel well. If you have a cold or the flu, wait two days or more after you feel better to exercise again.
- Don't overexert. Be aware of how you feel. Cut back to a lower intensity level if you begin to feel faint or show other signs of overdoing it (see box on page 241). You're more likely to injure yourself if you continue to exercise when you're exhausted.
- Slow down for hills. You should maintain the same level of exertion as in a usual workout.
- Be alert for symptoms of problems during exercise (see box on page 242). If you experience any of these symptoms, contact your doctor before continuing to exercise.

Don't expect to reach your exercise goal overnight. Just keep working slowly and increase your tolerances gradually. A sample walking program is found on page 244.

What Kind of Activity Is Best?

Physical activity can be divided into two types: aerobic (meaning "with air") and anaerobic (meaning "without air"). **Anaerobic exercise** involves short, concentrated bursts of energy by muscles acting in resistance to each other or some other object. Weight lifting or pushups are examples of anaerobic exercise. Anaerobic exercise doesn't greatly improve cardiovascular conditioning, but it does strengthen muscles. **Aerobic exercise**, which increases heart and breathing rates, is best for cardiovascular conditioning. Brisk walking, swimming, cycling, exercise dance, and jumping rope are all examples of aerobic exercise.

Why Does Aerobic Exercise Help My Heart?

During aerobic exercise, hard-working muscles need more oxygen. Breathing becomes deeper, and blood flow increases to handle the extra oxygen demands. Blood is diverted in some measure from inactive muscles to active ones but not from the brain or heart. The brain's heavy oxygen requirements remain constant. But blood flow to the heart—the most important muscle—can increase fivefold during exercise. For some people with CHD, this increase is not handled easily. For them, the increase triggers an episode of angina.

Regular exercise improves overall oxygen efficiency within the cardiovascular system. The improvement is generally less, but still important, for people who already have CHD. With regular exercise at appropriate levels, many men and women with angina report that they are able to exercise longer before symptoms interrupt their activity.

Age and Oxygen Requirements

With age, our bodies become less efficient at taking oxygen into the system and delivering it to the cells. Our heart rates also tend to drift downward. But regular aerobic exercise can reduce this effect. Studies have found that people who exercise regularly lose 5 percent of this capacity with each passing decade. This compares with 9 percent for those who are inactive. So, if you are sedentary, you will lose almost twice as much capacity as someone who exercises regularly.

Exercise! Me?

Maybe you think that you just don't have the time to exercise. It's true that our lives tend to be pretty full just the way they are. But most of us aren't as truly overscheduled as it may seem. Think for a minute about how much TV you watch each week or each day. Or how often you've driven to the corner coffee shop for a leisurely weekend breakfast instead of walking there and back. You may find that there are a number of ways to "borrow" exercise time from your schedule. After a while you'll probably begin to enjoy the activity so much that it won't seem like borrowing at all.

Many people choose not to exercise because of discomfort they think is associated with physical activity. Often people who are sedentary equate exercise with a punishing regime. They may think it involves getting out of bed at an ungodly hour, gasping for breath, or basically doing something they don't really want to do! (Just for fun, take a look at the box on page 234 for some of the more creative excuses not to exercise that some doctors hear.) But to get the results you want from an exercise program, none of that is necessary. Even moderate activity levels are beneficial if done regularly. One of the best exercise programs for the heart is simply to *walk*. Walking briskly three times a week for 30 to 60 minutes can make a substantial difference in your cardiovascular health, and the risk is minimal. It doesn't matter when you do it. It doesn't involve gulping for air (in fact, that's always the sign of a *poor* workout), and it doesn't require a special skill.

❦ *Every morning, Edgar woke up and told himself that today would be the day. But every evening, he'd go to bed without accomplishing his goal: starting that walking program the doctor had given him. He had the shoes, he had the clothing, and the weather was fine. But Edgar couldn't bring himself to leave the house and start his workout. It worried him to think he could have another heart attack at any time. What if he were a mile away from home, on a walking path, when it happened?*

His doctor asked him at one of his follow-up appointments how his exercise was going. Edgar confessed he hadn't gotten started yet, exactly. The doctor looked surprised. It had been several weeks since their last meeting. Finally, Edgar said it, straight out. "I'm afraid I'll have another heart attack if I exert myself, Doctor. I'm afraid to work out alone."

"Edgar, your heart attack was relatively mild. You've made good progress on your stress tests since then. I think you'll be fine following the program we've prepared. But if you still don't like the idea of exercising alone, I understand. Many of my patients feel the way you do, at least until they become more comfortable with their program.

"Why don't you sign up to use the stationary walking equipment in the hospital cardiac rehabilitation room? It's in the basement. For a small fee, you can use the equipment there to get started on your walking program. The people there can show you how to use the equipment and supervise your workouts. If you should have a problem, someone will always be there to help you. You can also start slowly and build up when you're ready. You can work out there as long as you like. When you feel more comfortable with your conditioning, you can take your walking program on the road. You may want to try to find someone to walk with you. You could also join a mall walkers group where you'll have lots of people around. Until you're ready to do that, you'll still get the aerobic workout you need right in the exercise room."

Edgar agreed to try it.

"I'll call you next week after you've tried it a few times to see how it's going. If it isn't working out, we'll try something else." ❦

Some people remember not liking exercise when they were kids. Often this is because they were forced to participate in competitive sports that they didn't enjoy or weren't particularly suited to play. Based on that experience, they decided that exercise was not for them. Fortunately, a good cardiovascular program doesn't have to involve competition, other people, or complicated rules if you don't want it to. For many people it is a great form of relaxation. The beauty of a customized exercise program is that it's *yours!* You might choose swimming, stationary cycling, regular walks (perhaps with your dog), tennis dates with a friend, or tending the perfect garden (yours!). Aerobic dance, golf, lawn bowling, or jogging may be your choice. Or you may want to try a combination of several different activities enjoyed over the course of the week. Just be sure you have your doctor's OK. Choose an activity that gives you a sustained cardiovascular workout and do it at least three times a week for half an hour or more. Your choices are fairly broad. You'll do your heart a lot of good—and enjoy yourself to boot.

How Do I Start?

Every good exercise program offers these three components:

- **"Warm-up" and "cool-down" periods. Start your activity slowly, letting your body warm up.** After the central activity, slow down to allow your body to cool down. Do some easy, smooth stretching activities to increase your flexibility.
- **Aerobic exercise.** The central component is designed to

What? Me Exercise?

We can all think of reasons not to exercise. But when it gets right down to it, most excuses sound pretty silly compared with the health benefits of a regular cardiovascular workout. Still, some excuses are so creative it's hard not to appreciate them—at least for the humor they can unintentionally impart! Just for fun, take a look at the following list. These are some of the most outrageous excuses for not exercising that doctors hear from their patients:

1. I'm too old.
2. I'm too fat.
3. I'm out of shape.
4. I hate to exercise.
5. I don't want to waste my time exercising.
6. My hair will get messed up.
7. I don't look good in exercise clothes.
8. My kids will laugh at me.
9. People will laugh when they see me exercising.

get the heart and blood vessels into shape and to help the
lungs exchange oxygen more efficiently.
- **Strength training.** Weight lifting is one way to promote
strength and flexibility.

A typical exercise session for heart patients or anyone who hasn't exercised for a long time might start with five to ten minutes of warm-up
activities. These may be doing your main activity at a lower level of exertion. If walking is the exercise you have chosen, you may begin by
walking slowly for 5 or 10 minutes. The aerobic segment of the exercise session is the longest, lasting 20 to 30 minutes. Then finish with 5
or 10 minutes of cool-down activity, such as stretches. (Your own program may be different, according to your doctor's directions.) More
advanced levels follow the same general outline but increase the
amount of time spent on each segment. Advanced levels also increase
the intensity of the workout.

What Intensity Level Is Right for Me?

If you have been hospitalized for heart trouble, you were probably
given an individualized exercise program that was developed just for
you by hospital staff members before you left the hospital. It may have
combined workouts to cover different parts of your body (and to keep
you interested!). Perhaps your prescription is to spend 5 or 10 minutes
on a treadmill and an equal amount of time on a stationary bicycle. As
your strength increases and your condition stabilizes, you will have
more freedom to design a program yourself, with your doctor's input.
At that point, a logical question is, "What kind of program is right for
me?"

Light

As we've noted, some people who have had major heart attacks will
need to exercise at a low-intensity level, at least for a while. Their exercise program will emphasize movements for stretching and flexibility, without an aerobic component. Those who have unstable CHD
should exercise only under medical supervision. So should anyone who
is unable for any reason to recognize symptoms of heart trouble or

other health problems during exercise. Medical supervision is also necessary for those who cannot follow a prescribed activity plan. Only very rarely are patients at this level prohibited from doing any exercise at all. They may be encouraged to join a hospital-sponsored, supervised program, however.

Moderate

Most people who survive a heart attack, have bypass surgery, or suffer bouts of angina can eventually follow a moderately intense exercise program. People in a moderate physical activity program should expend approximately 700 calories a week, over at least three nonconsecutive days. (The chart on page 237 indicates how many calories common activities burn per hour.)

Intense

An intense conditioning program burns 2,000 calories a week and provides maximum cardiovascular benefit. Rowing machines, cross-country skiing, or a very vigorous game of singles tennis are all examples of very intense athletic activity. Such a program may not be appropriate for you, however. Nor is such a vigorous program necessary to improve cardiovascular conditioning. Be especially cautious about attempting such a program if you have evidence of heart disease, and start slowly.

Note: No one with heart disease who is new to exercise training should expect to start at even a moderate intensity level. Take it slow and start low! People who take on too much at first are more likely to find the activity unpleasant and injure themselves. They are also more likely to "burn out" and finally drop exercise altogether. The key is to find an activity you really like to spend time doing. Then work up to the intensity level that is right for you. It may take weeks or even months. Take all the time you need to get there, but *keep at it.* Research shows that consistent effort at a lower intensity level is better for the heart than sporadic effort at a higher intensity level. Don't try a higher level until you find it easy to exercise at your current level and you aren't tired after a workout. That generally takes at least two weeks and frequently takes longer. Slow and steady really does win the cardiovascular conditioning "race."

Exercising at the right intensity strengthens your heart muscle. If

How Many Calories Will You Burn?

The figures below show the approximate calories spent per hour by a 100-, 150-, or 200-lb person doing a particular activity.

Activity	100 lb	150 lb	200 lb
Bicycling, 6 mph	160	240	312
Bicycling, 12 mph	270	410	534
Jogging, 7 mph	610	920	1,230
Jumping rope	500	750	1,000
Running, 5½ mph	440	660	962
Running, 10 mph	850	1,280	1,664
Swimming, 25 yd/min	185	275	358
Swimming, 50 yd/min	325	500	650
Tennis, singles	265	400	535
Walking, 2 mph	160	240	312
Walking, 3 mph	210	320	416
Walking, 4½ mph	295	440	572

your workout is too easy, you aren't getting the cardiovascular punch out of your exercise session that you should be. Working too hard doesn't do your heart any special favor, either. In fact, the heart's efficiency begins to drop again when you exercise too hard. You will find yourself gasping for breath and feeling uncomfortable as well. In short, stay within the range of intensity that is right for you.

Rating Your Workout

Once you've figured out what intensity level is right for you, you need to do your chosen activity at that level. There are three ways to find out if you are working out at the right intensity level. One is the talk test. Another is the rating of perceived exertion. The most complex is the target heart rate.

The Talk Test

The easiest way to determine your level of intensity is to take the talk test. You should be able to talk while you are exercising. If you are not able to talk, you are working too hard. Slow down a little. If you can sing while exercising, you need to work a bit harder.

The Rating of Perceived Exertion

There is another easy way to find out if you are working out at the right level. It's the rating of perceived exertion. How hard does the workout feel to you? If you feel as if your heart rate has increased only slightly, you would rate the effort as easy. If you are tired and gasping for breath, you would rate it as hard. You need to aim for a perceived rating of medium. Maybe you are looking for a more precise way to measure your intensity level. If so, try the target heart rate method.

❦ *"Hey, guys," Vincent said between gasps for air, "this heat is really getting to me." Vincent walked over to the side of the court.*

"I'm out of breath," he said. "I think I'm working a little too hard." Ever since his heart attack two years ago, Vincent had been careful to exercise regularly—at the right pace. He knew he had a tendency to overdo it sometimes, so he knew if he couldn't talk easily, he needed to slow down. He was also getting pretty good at rating his exertion level. Today, it felt like it was a hard workout. He told the other guys to go on without him. He took a walk around the park to cool down. After that he thought he'd go inside and get a glass of lemonade. Next time he wouldn't push himself quite so hard. ❦

Your Target Heart Rate

The target heart rate is the level at which the heart works most efficiently—with the least effort—to pump the most blood through the cardiovascular system. The average rate varies among individuals according to age. Refer to the box on page 239 for a list of average target heart rates.

The target heart rate is usually 50 to 75 percent of the heart's **peak heart rate,** or what the heart can pump at its uppermost limit. Some heart medications lower this range, however. Beta-blockers and calcium channel blockers are two examples. Your doctor will help you determine what your own target heart rate should be during the aerobic portion of your workout. Usually the target heart rate for heart patients is determined by the results of an exercise test.

After you've warmed up and started the aerobic portion of your exercise session, you'll need to check your heart rate periodically. That way you can see whether you're working within the target range. You also need to check your heart rate immediately after you stop exercising.

Here's how to check your own heart rate:

1. Keep moving as you press gently to quickly find your pulse at the wrist, temple, or neck (see figure, page 240).
2. Count your pulse for ten seconds.
3. Multiply the number you get by 6. This number equals your present heart rate. It should fall within the target range for your age (or whatever range your doctor recommended for you).

If you are under the target range, work a little harder and then check the rate again. If you're working too hard, ease back just a little, and then recheck your rate.

Finding Your Target Heart Rate

Age (yr.)	Target Heart Rate Zone in Beats per Minute (50–75% of Maximum)	Average Maximum Heart Rate in Beats per Minute (100%)
20	100–150	200
25	98–146	195
30	95–142	190
35	93–138	185
40	90–135	180
45	88–131	175
50	85–127	170
55	83–123	165
60	80–120	160
65	78–116	155
70	75–113	150

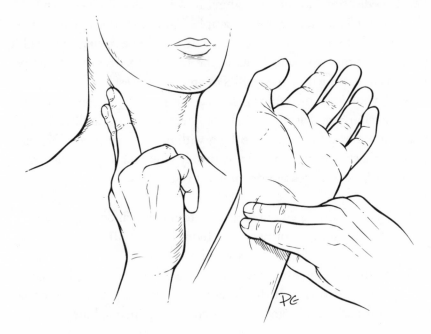

Check your heart rate by counting your pulse at the neck or wrist.

Exercise is great, but pay attention to your body. Be careful not to overdo it (see the box on page 241 for how to tell if you are overexercising). Also, be alert to symptoms of problems (see the box on page 242).

Exercise becomes easier the more you do it. Even very active people feel like exercising more on some days than on others. On the days when you aren't feeling top notch, you may need to take it a little easier. Here are some suggestions for staying with the exercise program you and your doctor have decided is best for you.

- Follow the suggestions made in "Guidelines for Cardiovascular Exercise" in the box on page 230.
- Don't rush—take your time.
- Alternate harder workouts with easier ones.
- Breathe deeply and regularly as you exercise. Remember: You should be able to carry on a conversation during your activity.

How to Tell if You Are Overexercising

- You can't finish your workout.
- You can't talk while exercising. Breathing shouldn't be uncomfortable.
- You feel faint or nauseated after you exercise. Avoid this by cooling down properly.
- You are very tired and remain that way long after your workout has ended. A proper workout should leave you feeling rejuvenated, not tired.
- You can't sleep at night.
- You have aches or pains in your joints. You might normally have some minor discomfort after a workout, but you should never feel a sharp pain or stiffness. You may need to reevaluate your warm-up exercises. You may not be allowing your body to warm up enough before moving into the aerobic portion of your workout, or you may not be stretching in the right way at the end of your workout.
- Check with your doctor if any of these symptoms persist.

- Get plenty of sleep every night—seven to eight hours.
- Rest 20 or 30 minutes twice a day in an easy chair or on the couch. Put your feet up and close your eyes—you don't need to fall asleep.
- Don't overexercise.
- Be alert for symptoms of problems.
- **Stop the activity if signs of heart attack appear.** (See page 269.)

Warming Up and Cooling Down

Warming up and cooling down are important parts of every workout session. Plan to spend 5 to 15 minutes at the beginning of each workout warming up and an equal amount of time at the end cooling down. The more time you intend to spend working out aerobically, the more time you need to allow for warming up and cooling off before and after.

Warming up prepares the muscles and joints in your body for more strenuous activity. Muscles and joints that are not properly prepared before an aerobic workout are more prone to injuries such as muscle pulls, twisted ankles, and so forth. Nurses or physical therapists at the hospital can teach you how to do the right warm-ups for your chosen

Symptoms of Problems

Be alert for any of these symptoms while you are exercising. They should always be taken seriously.

- Discomfort in the upper body (chest, arm, neck, jaw) during exercise. This might be a feeling of tightness, fullness, aching, or burning sensations. Seek emergency medical care immediately.
- Faintness during exercise. Stop exercising and see your doctor. This is different than feeling faint after you exercise, which is a sign that you haven't taken enough time to cool down properly from your aerobic workout.
- Shortness of breath during exercise. It shouldn't take you more than five minutes to catch your breath after you stop exercising.
- Bone or joint discomfort during or after exercise. Have problems in your bones or joints checked out by a doctor.

activity. Stretching exercises should be done as part of your cool-down, when your muscles are warm. Many people learn stretching exercises by participating in a supervised exercise class in which stretching is part of the program. Books and videotapes can also be instructive. Look for classes at your local hospital, recreation centers, YMCA, or health club. Look for books and videotapes from the library or your local bookstore.

A Typical Aerobic Exercise Program

Many people choose walking as an important part of their cardiac rehabilitation program. Walking is an easy way to get regular exercise, as we have enthusiastically noted already. You don't need special equipment other than sturdy, supportive shoes and clothing appropriate for the weather. Nor do you need a special facility in which to walk—your own neighborhood is fine. Many people find that walking in a nearby indoor shopping mall is a great way to walk. The weather is always fine, and the people-watching can be great! In many areas men and women meet informally at malls before the stores open to walk together while the concourse is clear.

The following sample walking program can help you start a sensible exercise program of your own after your doctor has okayed it. If walking doesn't satisfy you, ask your doctor or another member of your cardiac rehab team for ideas. There are also many pamphlets and books on aerobic exercise programs.

The walking program outlined here shows how to build aerobic endurance slowly, over 12 weeks. You may need more time to build up your endurance to that level. That's OK. There's no hurry! Move up to the next level of intensity only when you or your doctor feels you can do so. If you aren't quite ready, repeat that week's program until you are comfortable with it. Be sure that your pulse is within your target heart rate during your walk and at the end of each session.

Sticking with the Program

Finding an activity you enjoy may be the most important part of a successful long-term exercise program. But there are other considerations, too. Changing habits is hard. After following your new routine for a while, your initial enthusiasm may decrease a bit. You may not see the results you want as quickly as you thought you would. You may not be getting the kind of support you expected from family members. Or you may have had a medical setback that slowed or stopped your exercise program for a while. If so, you may not feel too excited about the prospect of going back to a lower intensity workout.

These are common roadblocks and they can be overcome. Here are some tips that can help you stay with your training goals.

- **Make short-term as well as long-term goals.** This can apply to any number of goals as well as exercise goals. Maybe your long-term exercise goal is to swim 20 laps. Then your short-term goal might be to swim two laps comfortably. After that, you might aim for five laps, and so forth. Gradually increase your target number until you reach 20. Don't rush. There's no need to tell yourself, "I have to do

A Sample Walking Program*

	Warm-up	Target zone exercising	Cool-down	Total time
Week 1				
Session 1	Walk slowly 5 min.	Then walk briskly 5 min.	Then walk slowly 5 min.	15 min.
Session 2	Repeat above pattern.			
Session 3	Repeat above pattern.			

Continue with at least three exercise sessions during each week of the program.

	Warm-up	Target zone exercising	Cool-down	Total time
Week 2	Walk slowly 5 min.	Walk briskly 7 min.	Walk slowly 5 min.	17 min.
Week 3	Walk slowly 5 min.	Walk briskly 9 min.	Walk slowly 5 min.	19 min.
Week 4	Walk slowly 5 min.	Walk briskly 11 min.	Walk slowly 5 min.	21 min.
Week 5	Walk slowly 5 min.	Walk briskly 13 min.	Walk slowly 5 min.	23 min.
Week 6	Walk slowly 5 min.	Walk briskly 15 min.	Walk slowly 5 min.	25 min.
Week 7	Walk slowly 5 min.	Walk briskly 18 min.	Walk slowly 5 min.	28 min.
Week 8	Walk slowly 5 min.	Walk briskly 20 min.	Walk slowly 5 min.	30 min.
Week 9	Walk slowly 5 min.	Walk briskly 23 min.	Walk slowly 5 min.	33 min.
Week 10	Walk slowly 5 min.	Walk briskly 26 min.	Walk slowly 5 min.	36 min.
Week 11	Walk slowly 5 min.	Walk briskly 28 min.	Walk slowly 5 min.	38 min.
Week 12	Walk slowly 5 min.	Walk briskly 30 min.	Walk slowly 5 min.	40 min.

Week 13 on:

Check your pulse periodically to see if you are exercising within your target zone. As you get more into shape, try exercising within the upper range of your target zone. Gradually increase your brisk walking time from 30 to 60 minutes, three or four times a week. Remember that your goal is to continue getting the benefits you are seeking and enjoying your activity.

*This program was designed for healthy people. The times given here are the average suggested for healthy people. If you have heart problems, be sure to check with your doctor before starting this or any exercise program.

five laps by next Tuesday." Work up to your goals at a pace that is naturally comfortable for you.

- **Get support from your family and friends.** You can succeed without it, of course. But the encouragement of friends and family can help you stay on track. Talk with the people who are closest to you about your exercise goals. Ask them to support you by giving you encouragement when you need it. You might find that they'd like to join you.

- **Reevaluate your activity periodically.** Just because you started with one activity doesn't mean you have to stay with it forever. Think about why you chose the activity originally. Are you still satisfied with it? If not, why not? Perhaps you chose a solitary activity originally because you weren't comfortable exercising. Are you more confident now? Maybe you're ready for some companionship. Needs change, and your exercise routine can change, too. You can modify your activity or choose another one. Just be sure to choose an activity that satisfies your cardiovascular requirements. That way you can make an even trade between your old aerobic exercise and a new one. The new one may be better suited to your personality and present fitness level.

- **Make it fun.** Physical activity should be fun. Express yourself through your chosen activity. If you walk for exercise, vary your route occasionally, invite a friend along, or walk the dog. Try listening to your favorite music on a cassette or compact disk player with earphones. If you bicycle, hike, swim, or jog, join an interest group. Like-minded enthusiasts participate in organized activities, such as noncompetitive fun runs or bicycle tours. Read a magazine that specializes in your favorite activity to learn more about it. Give yourself a boost the next time you need to replace some part of your exercise clothing: Choose an outrageous color that amuses you, or your favorite color, or the colors of your favorite sports team. Take a creative approach to exercise.

- **Keep a log.** It doesn't have to be fancy—a small spiral notebook will do nicely. In it, jot down particulars about your workouts. Record what you did and how it felt. Also write down how long you exercised and whether you worked at, below, or above your target heart rate. When you have doubts about the progress you've made, look back at where you started. Then congratulate yourself for your achievement.

❦ *Lately, Karen had been avoiding the mall. It wasn't that she didn't like shopping any more; she did. She only avoided it in the mornings. That was when she usually joined other "mall walkers" and briskly strode laps around the indoor concourse before the stores opened.*

She had walked at the mall for almost a year now. She walked at a good pace, waved to familiar faces, and sometimes brought her husband along. They'd catch a cup of coffee together before heading home. But at this point, it felt a little too . . . predictable, and Karen wasn't really a predictable sort.

She knew she needed and wanted to keep exercising. She felt so much better when she was active. She hadn't found anything else she particularly wanted to do three or four times a week. Sometimes she'd go to an aerobic dance class. If the weather was good, she rode a bike around her neighborhood. But these activities seemed good once in a while. She didn't want to do them several times a week.

Karen hit on an idea. She decided she'd amuse herself through this restless period by walking twice a week. She'd choose another activity the other days. She would still keep her commitment to moving aerobically for at least 30 minutes, three times a week. She also decided to look for other things to do to stay active.❦

Physical Activity: A State of Mind

Don't limit your physical activity to your three or four regular exercise sessions each week. Try to develop a more active approach to your daily activities as well. Anything that gets you moving is good. Here are some tips that can provide some opportunities:

- Use the stairs instead of the elevator. You can do this at your office, department stores, parking garages, and so forth. Start with one floor and gradually work up to more.
- Walk to work. If that's too far, try to at least walk from the far end of the office parking lot to the main entrance. Park on the far side of the mall from where you intend to shop. Get off the bus at the stop *before* your regular stop. Walk the rest of the way. Take your children on a bike ride instead of to a matinee. Walk the dog instead of just letting him out.
- If you work at a desk, take a break to stretch and clear your head. Walk to a colleague's office to deliver a message instead of using the phone. Use part of your lunch time to take a walk around the block.
- Consider yourself a role model. Do you have young children or grandchildren? Are there small children in your neighborhood? If so, remember that you have a certain power simply by being an adult. You can set an example through your behavior. You can show that physical activity is important and can be fun. It's a fact that children are more likely to be physically active and to remain that way as adults if their parents (and other adults around them) are physically active, too. Smile—and show off a little!

Discover how good regular exercise can make you feel. Now you'll know why.

CHAPTER ELEVEN

The Role of Stress

"Don't give yourself a heart attack!"
"He's been working so hard, I'm afraid he'll have a heart attack."
"She was laughing so hard, she almost had a heart attack."

Have you ever warned an excitable friend, jokingly or otherwise, "not to have a heart attack" during certain situations? Did you think emotions were about to get out of control? Or have friends tried to calm you down this way? For years—centuries, even—people have made a casual association between certain behaviors and heart attack. But do strong emotional states truly have a bearing on ill health? Do personality traits such as a driving ambition and feelings of anger and hostility really make you more prone to heart attack? In this chapter we'll consider what is known thus far about the subtle links between behavior, personality, and heart disease.

The Missing Link?

Medical researchers know that an individual's health profile is important. Certain risk factors and contributing factors (see pages 124–25) can predispose a person to heart disease. Chronic high blood pressure, high blood cholesterol levels, smoking, and a lack of exercise, among other factors, are all associated with a higher-than-normal risk of developing heart disease. We've seen that in most cases, the more pronounced these risk factors are in someone, the more likely it is that he or she will become ill.

However, despite these findings, doctors remain somewhat puzzled by another fact. Many people who have heart attacks do not have traditional risk factors for the disease. Others have them only to a mild degree. Their cholesterol levels or blood pressure may be only moderately higher than normal, for example. In some people, then, even seemingly minor variations from the norm make a difference as to whether or not they develop illness. But why?

According to a number of doctors and researchers, the answer may lie in the way some people respond to stress in their lives. (In others it may be due to a genetic predisposition.) Some people respond to stress with anger and hostility. They may follow behavior patterns that predispose them to coronary heart disease (CHD). Their behaviors have certain physical consequences that are associated with other risk factors for CHD and with the development of atherosclerosis. Interestingly, while researchers have identified a number of risk factors for heart disease, they haven't always been able to say exactly how every risk factor exerts its effect.

It's possible that a person's personality type may influence the severity of some risk factors. Or personality may influence whether some people pursue risky habits, such as cigarette smoking or excessive consumption of alcohol. More research is needed to establish the exact relationship between personality and heart disease. Meanwhile, some scientists think there is a certain correlation between personality traits and some physical responses to stress.

Almost all of us now and then face stressful instances over which we have no control. We tend to respond in different ways. Both the amount of uncontrollable stress we face regularly and our response to that stress may be associated with the development of heart disease. This fact becomes important when intervention is considered. Stress management, however, is no substitute for solid intervention on other risk factors, such as smoking, high blood cholesterol, high blood pressure, and physical inactivity. In fact, mastering the other risk factors may give you a feeling of control over your fate. That itself may reduce the anxiety you feel as stress.

What Is Stress?

Stress is tension felt in the body (a physical reaction) or the mind (a mental reaction). Although it is almost impossible to define and measure someone's level of emotional stress, it seems to be a common reaction to problems in our lives. Measuring high levels of stress accurately is hard. That's because people react to stress in different ways. We may feel stress as a tenseness in the body accompanied by feelings of distress or irritation. Our bodies may respond to stress sometimes without our being entirely conscious of these reactions, however. When we are stressed, our heart rate increases, our blood pressure goes up, and changes occur in the chemical makeup of our blood. Stress can also affect other risk factor behaviors. Some people start smoking or smoke more than usual to alleviate feelings of stress. Others may drink excessive amounts of alcohol.

Feelings of stress are aroused in response to some kind of stimulus overload. Too much to do in too short a time is a good example. Another is inability to complete a task because of factors out of one's control. Stress is also a typical reaction to major life changes. These can range from marriage or divorce to the death of a loved one or the loss of a job. Curiously, not having enough stimulation can also produce a stressful response. Feelings of stress can be a reaction to boredom and monotony.

No one is completely free at all times from stressful feelings. Feeling stressed is as much a part of life as laughing or crying. Indeed, stress is often beneficial. It temporarily increases alertness and prompts action. The "fight or flight" response is an appropriate reaction to stressful situations. It helped our ancestors adapt to an unpredictable, hostile wilderness environment.

In our urban society, however, a physical response to stress is likely to be muted or suppressed entirely. Think about it: You can't always jump up and down or pound the wall when someone makes you mad at work! Instead, while you remain quiet outwardly, your body itself is likely to bear the brunt of an "activity surge" made in response to a stressful situation. Over time that may have a negative effect on health.

Physical Indications That Link Stress Responses to Heart Disease

Many studies have investigated who develops coronary heart disease and who doesn't according to risk factors. But not all heart attacks are explained by individual risk factor profiles. That fact has led researchers to consider other possible influences, including stress.

Studies over the last 30 years reveal some interesting facts. An unrelieved sense of stress—and the physical responses that stress triggers—can have an adverse effect on cardiovascular activity (heart, blood, and vessels). During a stressful situation heart rate increases and blood pressure rises. Blood is redirected from the skin and organs to the muscles. Certain chemicals can be released into the bloodstream, blood vessels can be narrowed, and cholesterol levels may rise as well. These preparations are automatic and temporary. They are part of the ancient "fight or flight" response. The body mobilizes a lot of energy quickly to act against or run away from perceived danger.

Currently there is no solid evidence that how much stress we have and how we respond to it—in particular, the hostility component—contributes to the *initial* development of atherosclerosis. However, some studies suggest that it contributes to the acceleration and complications of established CHD.

Even some people who often respond to stress with hostility never develop CHD, of course. These folks may be otherwise genetically protected from developing it. Or they may have effective ways of working through their hostility. The alternatives may be healthful or unhealthful. Some people, for example, may not exhibit hostility as a response to stress. However, they may develop other damaging behaviors in an effort to cope with those feelings temporarily. These behaviors may include smoking, overeating, or drinking excessively.

For that reason, it's worth attention as part of an *overall* recovery program. Remember, learning to deal with stress is only a small part of the program. Your recovery program should focus on the major risk factors for heart attack: smoking, high blood cholesterol, high blood pressure, and physical inactivity.

Are You Stressed Out?

Remember, the focus is on an individual's hostile, angry *response* to stress. To some extent, anyone can learn to control the response pattern and avoid its negative consequences. Many people don't have a realistic perspective on their own habitual behaviors, however. It may be a good idea to ask your spouse or close friends to describe how they think you typically react to stressful situations. If you suspect that you fit the hostile, angry behavior pattern, talk to your doctor about it. He or she may ask you to take a short written quiz that is designed to identify these tendencies.

What Bothers You?

Where does stress come from? Too often it seems to be all around! To complicate matters, what is stressful for one person may be exhilarating to another. The *perception* of stress is a matter of perspective—your perspective. The important thing, then, is to learn what is stressful to *you*.

Having a heart attack or being diagnosed with heart disease certainly qualifies as a stressful event. But day-to-day, less dramatic events can be stressful for you as well. Being angry on most days because you are stuck in rush-hour traffic, for example, may be more stressful for you than seeing someone run a red light in front of your car.

Stressful occasions don't always feel "bad." Major life changes such as marriage or the birth of a baby can prompt feelings of anxiety that last a while on some level. They are examples of stressful but happy occasions.

❦ *Melvin was getting more and more tense as the deadline for his report drew near. As a consultant, he worked at home and faxed his work to his clients. But on deadline days, he hated the quiet and lack of distractions. He paced through the house repeatedly. Usually he stopped in the kitchen and wolfed down whatever was in the refrigerator. This didn't help get the report written. Melvin was feeling the pressure, just as he always did.*

It happened every time he had to produce for a client, which was several times a week.

Melvin took a deep breath and checked his watch. He had five hours to finish the report and fax it to his client. He knew he could do it. He had all the information he needed. He just needed to get started and forget the pressure he was adding to the job.

To break the pattern, Melvin decided to do something different. He sat down and wrote an outline for the report. Then he estimated how much time he should spend writing each section. He left some time to review everything and write a short cover letter. By his calculations, he could write the report and send it in three and a half hours. Good. So he had enough time after all. Still, he felt jumpy. So he took a 15-minute walk around the block to clear his head. He didn't let himself think about the report as he walked. Instead, he made a point of noticing landscaping and birds in the neighborhood.

When he finished his walk, he was ready to sit down and begin the report. He felt wide awake, calm, and confident about his writing strategy. And because he wasn't eating every 20 minutes, he worked more efficiently and felt more alert.

Stop Stress in Its Tracks!

Were you ever told, "That person can't bother you unless you *let* him"? It's good advice where stress is concerned, too. At times it may be easier said than done. Changing a behavior pattern takes conscious effort. The next time a stressful situation is about to get your goat, try one of the following tricks to help you stay cool.

Take a break. Stop whatever you were doing that made you feel tense (a conversation or an activity). Go back to it when you feel calmer.

Count to 10 before you speak. Sometimes the response you want to make in anger or out of frustration will only escalate the level of tension you feel. Counting to 10 slowly will give you time to think about another way to handle the situation *and* keep your cool.

Change your environment. Leave the place where you became upset, even if you only go into another room.

Engage in physical activity. Many people find that physical activity serves as a great outlet when they feel "stressed out." Be sure to check with your doctor to find out which forms of physical activity are best for you. You may want to try a quick, brisk walk around the block, or even around the office, to help you clear your mind and calm you down.

Take a penalty! If you find yourself getting consciously angry at someone or something, or hurrying unnecessarily, or following some other "Type A" behavior, acknowledge it. Then extract a small, private "penalty" that reinforces the behavior you want to cultivate instead. For example, you may find yourself rushing impatiently through a museum instead of enjoying what it has to offer. Make yourself stop and read the explanatory labels of at least five objects in the exhibit.

Don't "catastrophize." Don't let a small problem become a bigger one by letting negative thoughts get the best of you. Tell yourself, "Stop!" when you begin to turn a "molehill" problem into a mountainous one. That breaks the pattern. Then use one of the other tricks listed here to keep negative thoughts away.

Sit quietly and breathe deeply. If you find your emotions getting a little out of control, sit down, close your eyes, and concentrate on slow, regular breathing for several minutes. Put your hands across your stomach and feel the breath go in and out of your body.

Know who "owns" the stress. If other people's problems tend to put your stomach in knots, remember that you can listen sympathetically without having to solve them.

Talk with someone about what bothers you. It helps to tell another person how you feel. Tell your spouse, a friend, someone in the clergy, or a doctor what is worrying you. Often that's enough to put the problem in perspective, and you may even find a way to resolve it.

Do some work you've been putting off. You'll love the sense of accomplishment you'll feel.

Break up a big chore into manageable pieces. Perhaps your house is a mess, but you can't seem to find the time to put it back in order. Living with the mess upsets you. Instead of waiting until you can clean the entire house, clean whatever you have time to do. Clean one bedroom, wash one stack of dirty dishes, or wipe one windowpane. Bit by bit, you'll get the job done.

Exercise regularly. Keeping your body in shape and giving it regular opportunities to bend, stretch, and "get the kinks out" helps protect against stress as well as protect the heart. A regular exercise program is discussed in Chapter Ten.

Reduce chemical stressors. Alcohol, nicotine, and caffeine are all chemicals. Many people turn to these drugs to help them relax. The truth is, however, that each one can amplify your reactions to stress. People who smoke should quit for a number of compelling health reasons. One is the effect smoking has on feelings of stress (for information about quitting, see pages 162–68). As for alcohol, drink no more than one or two beers or two glasses of wine a day. Keep your caffeine consumption low. Try to drink no more than three cups of coffee, tea, or cola a day. (People who cut back on caffeine, a stimulant, may have headaches or feel drowsy for a week or two, but after that it will pass. You'll feel more awake *and* less stressed.)

Smile! Even if you aren't in the mood and feel a little foolish at first, try smiling at a tense moment. It actually relaxes facial muscles and will make you feel better. Smile whether you're alone or with other people. Smiling is contagious. You'll be amazed at the positive reaction it has on those around you.

Some of these suggestions may work better for you than others. Some may be more effective in certain situations than others. Experiment! These remedies may help you stop stress in a pinch.

❦ *"Hey, John! The boss wants to see you right away!"*

John knew that when the boss wanted to see someone, it was usually about some "urgent" problem that wasn't really urgent and wasn't a big problem. It drove him crazy. He'd had bitter arguments with his boss time and time again. This time he was pretty sure he knew what the problem would be. The engineering project he headed—designing brakes for a new commercial aircraft model—was extremely complicated. Many lives depended on engineering the brakes properly. His boss always wanted to see results—preferably yesterday. Feeling tense, John entered the boss's office.

"John, what have you got that I can show my boss at our meeting tomorrow? Have you figured out a way to increase the

load capability on those brakes yet? What's the problem? Why is this taking so long? Should I put someone else on the job?"

John didn't appreciate his boss's tone. It implied that someone else could engineer the project better and faster. That wasn't true! John mentally counted to 10. Saying what he really wanted to say would only precipitate another argument. John didn't have time to indulge himself. Instead, he took another long breath. He even managed to smile.

"No, Mike. This project is taking as long as we expected it to—because we're doing it right. I've kept you apprised of our progress and problems. As you know, we learned only last week that the load capacity of the brakes was actually going to be 8 percent above the figures we were given to work with origi-nally. So we've had to go back to the drawing board." John kept the conversation focused on the project, not his boss's irritating personality. "If you need some information to take to the meet-ing, my assistant can provide you with a summary of every-thing we've done so far. But I'm afraid I can't give you a deadline yet. We just don't know all the variables that this new information will create."

"All right. That will be fine. Thank you, John." John left and shook his head gently as he walked down the hall. By stick-ing to the facts, he'd caused his boss to do the same. That wasn't such a bad interaction, compared with the old days, he thought. No, not bad at all! ❦

Putting It All Together

Chronic stress as a risk factor for heart disease is beginning to receive attention from some researchers. Although it hasn't been proven that stress can cause heart disease, there is limited evidence that chronic stress may worsen existing heart disease. A heightened sense of anger and hostility, among other emotions, may have a negative effect on health.

How much stress is too much? It's almost impossible to define and measure someone's level of emotional stress. There's no way to mea-sure the psychological impact of different experiences. All people feel stress, but they feel it in different amounts and react in different ways. Both the amount of uncontrollable stress and one's response to it may be important.

People who exhibit angry, hostile behavior may need to evaluate the stress they feel and their response to it. Learning to let go of old response patterns may be hard. The hints in this chapter may help you find ways to do it.

If you've tried to "stay cool" since your heart attack and feel satisfied with your progress, congratulations! (If you aren't sure if your behavior has really changed for the better, ask your spouse or a close friend to tell you honestly if you seem calmer now than you were before.)

The suggestions in this chapter cannot effectively reduce all feelings of stress and anxiety. They are just a starting point. If you still find it difficult to maintain a calm outlook, talk to your doctor. He or she may be able to suggest some other ways to deal with stress or refer you to a counselor or other professional who can help you learn how to relax.

Remember, family and friends can be an important source of support. They can help by being good listeners. They may also show their support by joining you in your efforts to relax—or by being good models of the behaviors you wish to develop.

Be assured that changing your response to stress from an angry, hostile pattern to a more relaxed one need not make you a less productive person. In fact, you can be just as productive as ever, *but you can learn to accomplish what you want in a more health-affirming way.*

CHAPTER TWELVE

Coping with Emotional Aspects of Heart Attack

Did you know that up to half of all people who survive a heart attack go through a period of depression afterward? Feelings of depression and anxiety are understandable. After all, a heart attack is a traumatic experience. Feelings of anger and guilt are common, too. Fortunately, the symptoms of depression subside fairly quickly. For most patients this happens as they begin to recover their strength and feel more like themselves.

A small percentage of survivors react more profoundly to the heart attack, however. It doesn't matter whether the attack was severe or mild. For them, feelings of vulnerability—or anger or even guilt—persist. They may express these feelings as anxiety, depression, or denial of their illness. Carrying the added burden of these feelings over time can seriously interfere with a good recovery. This is true for a couple of reasons.

First, chronic depression appears to take a toll on the heart. People who remain depressed after a heart attack are more likely to suffer another, with a possibly poorer outcome. Second, people who are depressed, anxious, or in denial after a heart attack have another problem. They don't make the effort to modify their risk factors or participate in rehabilitation as well as others. Therefore, they don't reap the health benefits of changing their habits. Instead, they set themselves up for further problems.

A heart attack patient can develop long-term feelings of denial, anxiety, or depression at any time. These emotions can appear at the time of the heart attack or during the hospital stay. They can also occur after the patient is discharged.

In this chapter we'll look at the emotions that can interfere with heart attack recovery. We'll show you how to recognize some of the signs of emotional problems. We'll also consider treatments to help you feel stronger again emotionally.

Reacting to the Unexpected

No one, of course, expects to have a heart attack. It usually comes as a terrifying surprise. Fear or denial can be the first emotional response to heart attack. Later, in the emergency room, there are feelings of discomfort and disorientation. Activity swirls rapidly around you. There are unfamiliar machines all around. You'll undergo a number of medical procedures as a diagnosis is made and treatment is begun. Often there is little time for reassurance in the ER. Medical personnel are focused on stabilizing you physically. This may leave you feeling strangely, even fearfully, isolated.

Anxiety can remain high even after you leave the ER. Immediately after a heart attack, you're likely to feel small aches and pains in the chest. To someone who has just had a heart attack, any chest pain is highly alarming. It may even promote further anxiety. Fear of limitations or death combines with a sense of dread or foreboding. Often you'll be restless, unable to sleep, or feel very unsure of yourself.

Time for Reassurance

Calming the patient becomes a priority only after emergency care has been given. A patient who is concerned for his or her welfare needs reassuring. Helping you work through feelings of anxiety has physical as well as emotional benefits. Anxiety can have a negative effect on your heart. It can promote rapid heartbeat and high blood pressure. It can also increase the heart's demand for oxygen at a vulnerable time.

Often medical staff can calm you simply by taking time to talk with you about what happened. They can explain why the emergency procedures are important. Family members can help, too. They can listen to your fears and provide reassurance. Some patients find it difficult to talk about what worries them. In that case, family members' gentle questions can be a great help. Many times, the worries are unrealistic and are easily resolved. Sometimes anxiety isn't relieved with these methods. Then the doctor may decide that medications can help. Medications are discussed at the end of this chapter, on pages 264–66.

Almost every heart attack patient goes through a brief period of depression a day or two after the heart attack. Typically, feelings peak on the third and fourth days after the event. They subside as the pain lessens and you feel more confident about recovering. However, a small percentage of patients continue to experience emotional problems for a long time after the heart attack. For many, the problems emerge in the cardiac care unit (CCU).

Settled into the quieter atmosphere of the CCU, you face a slightly different set of concerns. Anxiety often lessens as your condition stabilizes medically. However, now there is time to dwell on long-range issues associated with the heart attack. Over the course of several days, you've had time to adjust to the diagnosis and the immediate limitations it implies. You may have concerns about going back to work or paying the hospital bill, and about resuming previous physical and sexual activity. You may begin to feel some pressure to make lifestyle changes to reduce your risk of another heart attack. Even if you understand that such changes are beneficial and offer their own rewards, at first these changes may feel more like they crimp your lifestyle. This comes at a time when all you want to do is return to "normal."

In the CCU you'll still feel weak and tired. Fatigue following a heart attack is a natural, temporary condition. But many patients think it is permanent. They are afraid that because they had a heart attack, they will be tired, weak, and dependent on others from now on. They may feel they cannot "trust" their own bodies. Feelings like this can give depression a foothold.

The solution is to be sure you know what to expect. Be reassured that this fatigue is normal and will pass. Medical staff and family members who have discussed the situation with a doctor can all help convey this information. In addition, you should begin easy, supervised exercise activities as soon as possible. These may include taking short walks around the hospital room. Activity helps prevent muscles from weakening further. It's also a tangible sign that your recovery has already begun.

❦ *Jose was drowsy. He wasn't sure exactly what time it was. In the CCU it was hard to tell. All he knew was that he felt tired. His wife sat next to his bed. He told her he didn't want to be dependent on her. Alicia chided him gently for such a thought. "You will be fine, Jose! The doctor told me so. You will be up walking around in no time," she said. Still, Jose felt anxious. His body had betrayed him once, hadn't it?* ❦

The Effects of Denial

Occasionally, heart attack patients will deny their symptoms. They may even deny that they had a heart attack at all. Denial of symptoms is common when a heart attack takes place. Denial is a way of reacting to a life-threatening situation. When someone is in denial, emotions that could get in the way of taking action and getting help are suppressed. When denial appears early after a heart attack, it appears to have a protective effect. People who are in denial of their heart attack initially have less anxiety and evidence of depression than those who are not.

However, long-term denial of heart attack is a different story. Some patients continue to deny that they had a heart attack. This may happen even while they are lying in the CCU. Patients who deny they are ill will not change their risky behaviors to prevent other heart attacks. They will not change their eating habits or quit smoking.

Long-term denial of CHD is a serious problem. Family members can help the patient accept the diagnosis. They can gently assure the patient that he or she is indeed ill and that treatment is necessary for him or her to feel better. Family members need to be particularly supportive of lifestyle changes that their loved one needs to make. However, they should resist the temptation to argue with him or her about whether or not he or she is sick. That tends to make the problem worse.

❦ *"I'd like that with fries, please." Jill was out at a restaurant for the first time since her heart attack. Her husband sighed. He'd heard this before. It was as if Jill didn't want to admit she had had a heart attack. Jill's friend Kelly giggled nervously.*

"I thought people who've had heart attacks shouldn't eat that high-fat stuff," Kelly said.

Jill frowned. "Look, it wasn't like that. I'm fine. Don't worry about it!"

Now her husband spoke and took Jill's hand. "Honey, you did have a heart attack, but you're doing fine. I wish you could look at it as a warning and work with your doctor and me to make sure it doesn't happen again. The fact is, your cholesterol level is still high. We're eating better at home, and you're taking your medication. We just need to keep it up when we eat out too. How about it?"

"Oh, all right, scratch the fries," Jill said. "I guess if my husband is willing to be a health nut, I can, too. Now can we talk about the movie we're going to see after dinner?" ❦

The Role of the Family

Leaving the hospital after a heart attack is a happy occasion. It can also be a stressful time for the heart attack survivor and his or her family. Anxiety and depression can appear or worsen upon going home.

Family members should be aware of signs of depression that may appear at home (see list on page 265).

In addition, the lack of physical activity that goes along with depression can make medical conditions worse. Depressed people tend to worry more about minor aches, pains, and tiredness. They are more likely to suffer anxiety attacks, which mimic angina symptoms (see page 8).

At home, the heart attack survivor may be told to take it easy for a while. Restrictions on activity may lead to boredom. Boredom gives susceptible people time to worry. During this period it's a good idea to plan a number of quiet activities. Try to encourage the heart attack survivor to read or pursue other hobbies every day.

❦ *The doctor picked up the phone. The caller identified herself as the wife of one of his patients.*

"I'm a little concerned about Paul, Doctor. Since he's come home from the hospital, it's all I can do to get him to get dressed in the morning. It's almost impossible to get him to go outside for a walk, or to the grocery store, or anything. It's as though he's afraid of leaving the house. This isn't like him. Should I be worried?" ❦

Some patients have a certain amount of separation anxiety when they leave the hospital to go home. At the hospital their needs were addressed promptly. Their health was monitored 24 hours a day. They probably felt very safe there. At home they may feel more vulnerable to heart problems again. Families should be aware of this natural nervousness. It will usually diminish as the patient's physical condition continues to improve.

❦ *"Lin, come with me. I want to show you something."*

Lin didn't want to follow her husband outside. She knew he was trying to help her, but she just didn't feel like moving. Maybe he could bring whatever it was inside for her to see, if he wanted to. It really didn't matter to her. Since her heart attack, she didn't feel much good for anything.

"No, you've got to come! You'll be OK, I promise. Our apple tree is blooming. It's spectacular! It smells so good." Despite Lin's indifference, her husband, Walter, managed to put a sweater around her shoulders. He steered her outside and down the walk to the tree. It was pretty. It did smell good . . . Lin smiled a little. Although she was anxious about being outside, she supposed that if she did have another heart attack right

then, Walter would know what to do. She relaxed a little more and looked around. "It is nice out here today," she offered. Now Walter smiled. ❧

The family needs to be aware of the heart attack survivor's emotional state. You can help your loved one in a number of ways. Remain positive and support efforts to change risk factors. Listen to your loved one's fears and provide reassurance. Look for signs of deep anxiety, denial, or depression. If these don't seem to be going away, alert the doctor. At this point, the patient may need medication or counseling.

Family members can sometimes be too protective. That may contribute to depression by lowering the heart attack survivor's self-esteem. Remember, when heart attack survivors are released from the hospital, they are somewhat weakened. But they aren't completely fragile, either. There is a lot they can do for themselves. Be sure to give your loved one some breathing room. Spouses may wish to take the same treadmill test that the heart attack survivor takes before being discharged from the hospital. Many spouses are reassured when they experience for themselves the degree of activity that is possible.

Recognizing Depression

Many depressed people deny their depression or don't complain about it. For that reason, it's a good idea for family members to be able to recognize some accepted symptoms of depression (see box on page 265). Depressed persons will exhibit four or more of the symptoms for at least two weeks. For a person to be classified as depressed, at least one of the four symptoms must be "depressed mood" or "marked loss of interest or pleasure."

Medication or Counseling May Be the Answer

Sometimes, feelings of anxiety or depression are very serious. When that occurs, the doctor may decide to prescribe medications for a certain period of time. Drug therapy may take days or weeks to show effects. Generally, the medicines are given for about six months after they take effect. That minimizes the chances of a relapse.

Many people are afraid to take medicines for depression or anxiety. But, used in a very limited way, they can help people break out of severe depression. Doctors monitor patients on medication and watch for any side effects. These drugs are not habit-forming when taken as prescribed.

Antidepressant drugs treat more than symptoms of depression. They are often used to treat other problems, too, such as panic disorders and chronic pain. It isn't clearly understood how antidepressants work. They do have some side effects. These may include rapid heartbeat and feelings of dizziness when standing up quickly. They may also include electrical conduction problems across the heart and heart rhythm abnormalities. Generally, dosages are low at first. That way side effects can be identified early and managed appropriately.

Antidepressant drugs include tricyclics, trazodone, maprotiline, amoxapine, bupropion, and fluoxetine. Monoamine oxidase inhibitors (MAOIs) are a newer class of antidepressant medication. These in-

Signs of Depression

- Depressed mood (despondent, pessimistic about the future, hopeless, withdrawn)
- Marked loss of interest or pleasure
- Feelings of worthlessness or guilt
- Change in appetite or weight
- Loss of energy
- Fearfulness of activity
- Sleeplessness
- Lack of interest in personal hygiene
- Lack of interest in sex
- Anxiety
- Tearfulness
- Easily distressed
- Agitation or restlessness
- Inability to concentrate, make decisions, remember, or comprehend instructions
- Thoughts of death or suicide
- Failure to return to work

clude phenelzine, tranylcypromine, isocarboxazid, and pargyline. Some foods may be off-limits to persons taking MAOIs.

Medications to treat anxiety are often prescribed for heart attack and CHD patients. Such drugs are effective and relatively safe. They include diazepam (Valium), lorazepam (Ativan), and chlordiazepoxide hydrochloride (Librium). These drugs can do more than calm the patient. They also have beneficial effects on heart function. They reduce the heart muscle's oxygen demand without altering coronary blood flow. Possible side effects include drowsiness and dizziness.

If you are under the care of more than one doctor, remember that all your doctors need to know what medications you are taking. You may want to make a list of all the prescription and over-the-counter drugs you take. Give that list to each of your doctors at your next appointment. That way they can help plan your entire drug therapy regime. They can also be on the lookout for drug interactions.

Some cases of depression, anxiety, or denial become very serious. When that happens, you may need professional psychological counseling. A doctor can help you decide whether you'll benefit from a specialist. A cardiologist may just as effectively counsel and reassure someone who is very fearful following a heart attack.

Counseling can also be helpful in other situations. It may help family members adjust to new circumstances in the wake of family illness. Some heart attack survivors are not depressed but have difficulty modifying some of their behaviors. Counseling may help the survivor deal with hostility or excessively competitive impulses.

Help Is Available

Long-term depression is not common among heart attack survivors. However, it can be devastating to those who are susceptible to it. Having a severe heart attack does not make you more susceptible to depression afterward. A person who has had a mild heart attack is as likely to become depressed later as someone whose heart attack was more serious.

Depression and long-term denial can obstruct your recovery efforts.

Fortunately, these problems are relatively easy to treat. Family members can help a lot by urging their loved one to discuss his or her concerns. Your doctor can help you decide whether professional counseling or medication is a good option. Help is available. Don't hesitate to ask for it.

CHAPTER THIRTEEN

Being Prepared

Hopefully you'll never have another heart attack. But if you do, you should be prepared to act quickly, and so should family members. Be sure you know all the warning signs of a heart attack. Be ready to act if they should appear. Minutes count! The sooner you get to an emergency room, the sooner physicians can begin treatment that may save heart tissue—or your life.

Make a copy of this information and post it where you can see it readily.

Bear in mind that each heart attack experience is unique. You may not experience *all* the possible warning signs. The sensations may come and go. You may not feel a lot of pain. Sometimes you'll feel only a strange pressure or fullness in the chest. However, *you may still be having a heart attack* and should be checked out at a hospital as soon as possible. Don't worry that you may "bother" the medical staff unnecessarily. Catching a heart attack in progress is much more important than the "inconvenience" of checking out a false alarm.

Make a checklist of the warning signs and post them in several places around your home where you can see them easily. (Photocopy the box on page 269 for this purpose. Tape one copy to a kitchen cabinet and another to the bathroom mirror.) Family members should also learn the warning signs.

In addition to knowing these important signs, of course, your family

The Warning Signs of Heart Attack

Not all of these signs appear with every heart attack. Sometimes they go away and then return. If you experience any of these sensations, *don't delay: get help immediately.* Call the emergency rescue service, or if you can get to the hospital faster by car, have someone drive you to the nearest facility with a 24-hour emergency cardiac care unit (select this in advance if you have had a heart attack previously or are at risk for one).

Unless it is massive, a heart attack is usually preceded by certain warning signs:

- Uncomfortable pressure, fullness, squeezing, or pain in the center of the chest that lasts more than a few minutes, or goes away and comes back
- Pain that spreads to the shoulders, neck, or arms
- Chest discomfort with lightheadedness, fainting, sweating, nausea, or shortness of breath

(or anyone else present) needs to know what to do with that information. The person having the heart attack may deny the symptoms, so it's especially important for others to be prepared to act.

Have a Plan Ready

You must be prepared to act immediately to get to a hospital. Get the family together now and talk about what they will do if you have another heart attack. Having a plan ready will save you time when you need it most.

1. **Act quickly to get help.** This is perhaps the single most important step you can take to save your own life or the life of someone you love. The technologies and medicines available in hospitals today can do much to stop a heart attack that is in progress. Stopping a heart attack in its tracks saves heart tissue. But there is little time in which to administer these lifesaving medicines. Most are useless as soon as two hours after the initial symptoms appear.

2. **Identify the hospitals in your area** that provide 24-hour emergency cardiac care. Know which of these are closest to your home and

workplace. Share the information with your family, coworkers, and friends. They should learn the fastest way to the hospital in case of an emergency.

3. **Keep the name and number of the hospitals near the phone** at home and at work. If your telephone has a quick-dial feature, you might even preset the numbers so that the call can be made as quickly as possible in an emergency. However, be sure to keep the number clearly posted by the phone anyway, in case you aren't the one who makes the call.

4. You should not try to drive to the hospital. Take a car if the hospital is nearby and someone is immediately available to drive you there. Otherwise, **dial 911** for emergency rescue. A friend can still help by going to the street and directing the emergency crew to your side. This is especially useful if the heart attack occurs in an apartment building or a large office.

5. **Keep a list of the medications you or your loved ones take in a handy place,** such as a medicine cabinet or a wallet or pocketbook. Be prepared to take it along to the hospital.

6. **Have a family member or friend prepared to administer CPR** (see below).

Cardiopulmonary resuscitation (CPR) can help restore heart function and breathing to collapsed or unconscious persons. Every year this emergency technique saves thousands of lives in the United States. If you have had a heart attack or are at risk for one, ask family members to consider taking a CPR class. They will learn a skill that may save someone's life. Knowing CPR can contribute to their peace of mind.

CPR classes are offered regularly by community centers, fire stations, and organizations such as the American Heart Association and the American Red Cross. Contact your local chapters to find courses in your area.

🍃 *Janet was a little nervous. She had been doing fine since a mild heart attack several weeks ago. Still, she felt panicky every time she remembered that trip to the emergency room. Thank goodness she'd been at home with Chip! If there were a next time, she wanted to be prepared. She wanted Chip to be prepared if it happened to him, too.*

Janet pulled out a small stack of notecards and began writing on them. She posted two around the house, one next to the kitchen phone and one next to the bedroom phone. She outlined the two cards in red ink so that they would be easy to find even if they got mixed up with other papers. On the cards, Janet listed important telephone numbers: the number for an ambulance service, their primary-care physicians' numbers, their next-door neighbor's number, and at the top, 911, the emergency number. She also wrote down the name of the nearest hospital with emergency cardiac care services, the address, and phone number. On a third card, Janet listed the signs of heart attack and simple steps to follow if they were to appear. She taped this one on the inside of the kitchen cabinet door.

Finally, she listed the names and numbers of the hospitals closest to her and her husband's workplaces. Again, she wrote down simple instructions for what to do if she experienced any of the signs of having a heart attack. She gave one to Chip to keep handy in his office. She took one to her office, posting it on a bulletin board behind her desk and telling coworkers where to find it.

Janet felt more in control of her situation after she had taken these precautionary steps. Now, even if she were very frightened in the event of another heart attack, she was confident that the cards would help her or another person nearby to take action without losing valuable time. ❧

Small Changes, Big Payoff

No one likes to think that he or she might have a heart attack at any time, but it pays to be prepared. We've just reviewed the steps to take in such an emergency. We've tried to show you many of these steps in this book. But there are many ways to take care of yourself that can help you avoid a heart attack—or another heart attack—in the future.

You can identify your personal risk factors for heart attack and take steps to help eliminate or reduce their effects. That way you can fight back against heart disease and improve your health. High blood cholesterol levels, uncontrolled high blood pressure, cigarette/tobacco smoke, and a lack of exercise are all risk factors for heart attack that you can change. Your doctor will be involved with your efforts and will help you establish your priorities. You'll want your family's and friends' support, too.

The notion of making wholesale changes to your lifestyle may be a little scary. You might think, "That's a lot to ask. I'm not Superman (or Superwoman). I can't change all those things and suddenly become Mr. (or Ms.) Perfect." In fact, you don't have to be Mr. or Ms. Perfect to benefit from the lifestyle modifications suggested in this book. The scientific evidence overwhelmingly proves that even *small* changes in your overall diet, blood pressure, and exercise habits can reap *big* health benefits. The one exception among the modifiable risk factors described in this book is cigarette smoking. Cigarette smoking is so bad for your health that you really must break the habit altogether. Trying to smoke fewer cigarettes per day still puts you at an unacceptable level of risk for another heart attack.

If you feel overwhelmed by the prospect of making a lot of changes, talk over your fears with your doctor or another health-care professional. You don't have to do everything at once. Any healthful changes you make to your lifestyle will help you in the long run. Concentrate on a few important areas first, and then add others later. Give yourself time to become comfortable with your new habits. And always keep in mind that *whatever* effort you make helps and puts you in better control of your own health. For example, by lowering your total blood cholesterol levels by 1 percent, you reduce your risk of heart attack by 2 percent. Two-for-one offers like that don't come along every day. Following a low-fat, low-cholesterol diet for a lower heart attack risk is a very good return on your "investment," don't you think?

Exercise is another area in which small adjustments can make a big difference. Contrary to popular opinion, you don't have to be an athlete or play a sport to enjoy better health. You don't have to make an unrealistic time commitment either. Just 20 minutes of exercise at your target level each day may help raise your good cholesterol levels. It may also help keep your blood pressure and weight under control. It can also help keep diabetes under control, too. You don't even have to "spend" those 20 minutes at one time. Two 10-minute sessions count (if you meet your target exercise levels each time). Even better, you can count all kinds of typical daily activities as "exercise," as long as you work at your target energy level while you do them. Gardening, playing with the kids in the park, hand-polishing the car, carrying groceries into the house—any of these might be considered exercise activities. The point is to *get moving* and give your heart a bit of a workout while you're at it.

❧ *"Sometimes it really is the little things that mean the most," Don told himself as he walked the dog. A year ago to that day he had had a heart attack. At the time he thought he would never live so well again. And yet, just by making several moderate adjustments and one bigger one, he felt better today, after his heart attack, than he had ever felt in his life!*

Walking the dog, for example. He never used to walk the dog. No one did. But walking the dog every morning became his exercise ritual after his doctor told Don to "get moving." Now he hated to miss it—go figure! It set him up for the day, somehow. And of course his dog, Sammy, worshipped him now. Don smiled.

The biggest change, of course, was that he was an ex-smoker. Quitting that habit had triggered a lot of the other changes naturally, Don mused. Like where he ate. After he quit smoking, Don sought out restaurants that prohibited smoking. Ordering from a brand-new menu made it easier for Don to resist the heavy meals that had been old favorites and to try new, lighter dishes. His sense of taste was more acute now. He enjoyed the fresh flavors of simply prepared foods, and he found that he didn't need to salt his plate the way he used to. These and other dietary changes Don made, along with exercise and quitting smoking, had all worked together to lower his cholesterol levels, his blood pressure, and even his weight.

These days, people told Don he looked healthy and happy. More important, his doctor told him yesterday that the changes he had made were working. That felt best of all. ❧

One More Thing

You've been through a difficult experience—but you're getting better. You have been given a second chance to live a more healthful life. You can't change all of your risk factors for coronary heart disease, but you can change some. Concentrate on changing the ones you can, and you will improve your health. It won't always be easy to make the changes you need to make, but you'll be ahead of the game if you know the answers to these three questions:

- Which risk factors can I change?
- How do they affect my overall health?
- What can I do to eliminate or modify their effect on my health?

Use your illness as a motivational tool to implement the changes you need to make. Then be sure to check on your progress as you go, so you stay motivated. Don't try to do it alone. Get your spouse, other family members, and friends involved—and talk with your doctor when you need to. Reading this book demonstrates that you have plenty of motivation to improve your health. We hope this book helps you get started. But don't stop there. Talk with people, read other books and magazines that might be useful, and change your strategies now and then, just to keep things interesting.

Most important of all, take the time often as you go along to remind yourself of how far you've really come. You've taken control of your life—and it feels great!

APPENDIX A

Eating Out

You can find low-fat foods at almost any restaurant. Here's some ideas to help you.

The Breakfast Menu

While lunch and dinner menus often have lots of low-fat choices, breakfast menus can be loaded with high-fat items. Here are some low-fat alternatives:

Tip: Order fresh fruit, fruit juice, or nonfat or low-fat yogurt to begin your meal.

Instead of	*Try*
Whole milk	Skim milk
Cream in your coffee	Skim milk
Whole eggs	Omelet or scrambled eggs made with egg substitute
Waffle with butter and syrup	Waffle with fresh fruit
Breakfast pastries	English muffin or bagel with jelly or jam
Cream cheese	Nonfat or low-fat cream cheese
Sausage or bacon	Lean ham or Canadian bacon
High-fat granola cereal	Hot cereal or whole-grain low-fat cereal

Chinese

Chinese food is one of America's most popular ethnic cuisines. It can also be one of the most healthful—if you know what to order. Ask the cook to use less oil when preparing stir-fry and other dishes. If you have high blood pressure, ask the cook to leave out the soy sauce, monosodium glutamate (MSG), and salt. Main-dish portions are often quite large, so try ordering fewer entrees than you have dinner companions. Then divide and devour!

Tips: Choose entrees with lots of vegetables—chop suey with steamed rice for example. Substitute chicken for duck (remember to remove the skin before eating the chicken). Skip the crispy fried noodles.

Instead of	*Try*
Egg drop soup	Wonton or hot-and-sour soup
Egg rolls or fried wontons	Steamed dumplings
Fried entrees	Boiled, broiled, steamed, or lightly stir-fried entrees
Dishes with fried meats	Dishes with lots of vegetables
Dishes with cashews	Dishes with water chestnuts
Fried rice	Steamed rice
Lobster sauce (egg yolks); oyster, bean, and soy sauce (high sodium)	Sweet and sour sauce; plum or duck sauce

Family-Style

No need to avoid popular, mid-priced family-style restaurants when you're too tired to cook. Just keep the following tips in mind.

Tips: Avoid dishes with lots of cheese, sour cream, and mayonnaise. Instead of fried oysters, fish, or chicken, choose boiled or baked shrimp or broiled or grilled fish or chicken. Choose bread or pita pockets over croissants. Salads make great meals, but be careful of the dressing and high-fat toppings such as croutons, bacon bits, and whole-milk cheeses. If you must have a high-fat entree, split it with another family member. You'll save dollars and fat!

Instead of	*Try*
Cream soups	Broth-based soups with lots of vegetables
Quiche and salad	Soup and salad
Buffalo chicken wings	Peel-and-eat shrimp
Chicken-fried steak	Veggie burger
French fries or potatoes and gravy	Baked potato; potatoes without gravy; rice without gravy; cooked greens made without salt pork or lard
Creamy coleslaw	Sautéed vegetables or tossed salad
Hot fudge sundae or ice cream	Nonfat yogurt, sherbet, or fruit ice

Fast Food

It used to mean "fried food," but today more and more franchises offer low-fat alternatives.

Tips: Avoid topping burgers with sauces, cheese, or bacon, which add fat and calories. Condiments such as pickles, fresh onion, lettuce, tomato, and mustard add flavor without fat. Stay away from fried fish sandwiches. Baked potatoes can be healthful, but don't add butter, sour cream, or other high-fat toppings. Have it plain, or with yogurt.

Instead of	*Try*
Jumbo cheeseburger	Grilled chicken, sliced meats, or even a regular 2-ounce hamburger on a bun with lettuce, tomato, and onion
Fried chicken or tacos	Grilled chicken or salad bar (but watch out for high-fat dressings and ingredients)
Fried chicken pieces	Chicken fajita pitas
French fries	Baked potato with vegetable or yogurt topping
Potato chips	Pretzels
Milkshake	Juice, low-fat or skim milk

French

Look for "nouvelle cuisine," which promotes a lighter style of cooking.

Tips: Skip the rich entrees, desserts, and sauces. Look for simple dishes. Ask for sauces on the side, so you can monitor how much you eat. Nouvelle cuisine or Provençal (tomato-and-herb-based) entrees are good choices. Ask that margarine rather than butter be used in making your dishes.

Instead of	*Try*
Appetizers with olives, capers, or anchovies	Steamed mussels or salad
Pâté	Steamed mussels
Croissants	French bread
Rich, heavy entrees	Lighter nouvelle cuisine
Hollandaise, Mornay, Bechamel, or Bearnaise sauce	Bordelaise or other wine-based sauce
Creamy au gratin potato dishes	Lightly sautéed, crisp vegetables
Crème caramel	Peaches in wine or flambeéd cherries

Health Food and Vegetarian

Health food and vegetarian foods are usually fresh and wholesome. But watch out for fats and oils. Sometimes vegetarian dishes have added fat to compensate for meatless entrees.

Tips: Avoid dishes with lots of cheese or avocado.

Instead of	*Try*
Granola made with oil	Fat-free or low-fat granola
Salads with oil-based dressing	Salads with fat-free dressing
Sandwich fillings with mayonnaise	Sandwich fillings with mustard, nonfat or low-fat mayonnaise, or yogurt sauce
Whole-egg dishes	Yogurt-based dishes made with skim milk

Italian

Pasta is the great heart-healthy Italian food. By itself, pasta is low in fat. Some toppings, however, are high in fat: pesto and cream sauces, for example.

Tips: Treat pasta as a main dish instead of an appetizer. Hold the Parmesan (grated) cheese—and bacon, pine nuts, and olives. If you order pizza, choose ingredients such as mushrooms, broccoli, and roasted peppers.

Instead of	*Try*
Cheese or meat-filled pastas or casserole-type dishes	Pasta primavera (with sautéed garden vegetables) or pasta with white or red clam sauce
Pasta with butter or cream sauces (such as Alfredo sauce)	Pasta with marsala or marinara sauce
Any scallopini or parmigiana (floured, fried, and baked with cheese) dish	Marsala and piccata dishes
Italian pastries, such as cream cake	Italian ices

Mexican

A lot of Mexican food is fried with lard and topped with cheese, so it's loaded with fat. But if you know what to choose, Mexican food can be fresh, tasty, and low in fat.

Tips: Tell your server not to bring fried tortilla chips to your table. Avoid sour cream and guacamole. Use salsa for flavor. Vera cruz or other tomato-based sauces are better than creamy or cheesy sauces. If you order a taco salad, don't eat the fried shell.

Instead of	*Try*
Flour tortillas (made with lard)	Corn tortillas (made with almost no fat)
Nachos	Ceviche (raw fish soaked or "cooked" in lime or lemon juice for many hours)

Carnitas (fried beef or pork) or chorizo (sausage)

Grilled fish or chicken breast

Refried beans

Frijoles a la charra or borracho beans and Spanish rice

Sour cream, cheese, or guacamole

Salsa, pico de gallo, cilantro, jalapeño peppers

Quesadillas (tortillas filled with meat and cheese)

Chicken fajitas (marinated chicken grilled with vegetables and served with tortillas)

Chalupas and tacos

Taco salad or fajita salad (Skip the tortilla shell)

Burritos (flour tortillas filled with beans or meat and topped with cheese) or chimichangas (flour tortillas filled with meat and cheese, fried, and topped with tomato sauce)

Chicken or beef enchiladas with red sauce or salsa

Steakhouses

Beef is okay, as long as it's lean and portions are reasonable.

Tips: Don't order huge cuts. About 3 ounces of a thinly sliced cut is good, or choose a 5-ounce steak and enjoy meatless entrees the rest of the day. Ask your server to trim all visible fat from your order before cooking.

Instead of

Try

Fatty cuts of meat, such as rib eye, porterhouse, or T-bone

Leaner cuts, such as London broil, filet mignon, round or flank steak, sirloin tip, tenderloin

French fried, au gratin, or scalloped potatoes

Baked potato or rice

Caesar or marinated salad

Green salad with dressing on the side

Pie and ice cream

Angel food cake or sherbet

American Heart Association Affiliates

For more information about American Heart Association programs and services, call 1-800-AHA-USA1 or contact us online at http://www.amhrt.org.

American Heart Association
National Center
7272 Greenville Avenue
Dallas, TX 75231-4596

AHA, Alabama Affiliate, Inc.
Birmingham, AL

AHA, Alaska Affiliate, Inc.
Anchorage, AK

AHA, Arizona Affiliate, Inc.
Tempe, AZ

AHA, Arkansas Affiliate, Inc.
Little Rock, AR

AHA, California Affiliate, Inc.
Burlingame, CA

AHA of Metropolitan Chicago, Inc.
Chicago, IL

AHA of Colorado/Wyoming, Inc.
Denver, CO

AHA, Connecticut Affiliate, Inc.
Wallingford, CT

AHA, Dakota Affiliate, Inc.
Jamestown, ND

AHA, Delaware Affiliate, Inc.
Newark, DE

AHA, Florida Affiliate, Inc.
St. Petersburg, FL

AHA, Georgia Affiliate, Inc.
Marietta, GA

AHA, Hawaii Affiliate, Inc.
Honolulu, HI

AHA of Idaho/Montana
Boise, ID

AHA, Illinois Affiliate, Inc.
Springfield, IL

AHA, Indiana Affiliate, Inc.
Indianapolis, IN

AHA, Iowa Affiliate, Inc.
Des Moines, IA

AHA, Kansas Affiliate, Inc.
Topeka, KS

AHA, Kentucky Affiliate, Inc.
Louisville, KY

AHA, Greater Los Angeles Affiliate, Inc.
Los Angeles, CA

AHA, Louisiana Affiliate, Inc.
Destrehan, LA

AHA, Maine Affiliate, Inc.
Augusta, ME

AHA, Maryland Affiliate, Inc.
Baltimore, MD

AHA, Massachusetts Affiliate, Inc.
Framingham, MA

AHA of Michigan, Inc.
Lathrup Village, MI

AHA, Minnesota Affiliate, Inc.
Minneapolis, MN

AHA, Mississippi Affiliate, Inc.
Jackson, MS

AHA, Missouri Affiliate, Inc.
St. Louis, MO

AHA, Nation's Capital Affiliate, Inc.
Washington, D.C.

AHA, Nebraska Affiliate, Inc.
Omaha, NE

AHA, Nevada Affiliate, Inc.
Las Vegas, NV

AHA, New Hampshire/Vermont Affiliate, Inc.
Williston, VT

AHA, New Jersey Affiliate, Inc.
North Brunswick, NJ

AHA, New Mexico Affiliate, Inc.
Albuquerque, NM

AHA, New York City Affiliate, Inc.
New York, NY

AHA, New York State Affiliate, Inc.
North Syracuse, NY

AHA, North Carolina Affiliate, Inc.
Chapel Hill, NC

AHA, Northeast Ohio Affiliate, Inc.
Cleveland, OH

AHA, Ohio/West Virginia Affiliate, Inc.
Columbus, OH

AHA, Oklahoma Affiliate, Inc.
Oklahoma City, OK

AHA, Oregon Affiliate, Inc.
Portland, OR

AHA, Pennsylvania Affiliate, Inc.
Camp Hill, PA

Puerto Rico Heart Association, Inc.
Hato Rey, Puerto Rico

AHA, Rhode Island Affiliate, Inc.
Pawtucket, RI

AHA, South Carolina Affiliate, Inc.
Columbia, SC

AHA, Southeastern Pennsylvania Affiliate, Inc.
Conshohocken, PA

AHA, Tennessee Affiliate, Inc.
Nashville, TN

AHA, Texas Affiliate, Inc.
Austin, TX

AHA, Utah Affiliate, Inc.
Salt Lake City, UT

AHA, Virginia Affiliate, Inc.
Glen Allen, VA

AHA, Washington Affiliate, Inc.
Seattle, WA

AHA, Wisconsin Affiliate, Inc.
Milwaukee, WI

INDEX

acquired heart disease, 14
acupuncture, 177–178
acute care, 36
African-Americans, high blood pressure and heart
    attacks among, 128
age, 13–14, 47
    in blood pressure measurement, 27
    exercise and, 145, 226–29, 231, 234
    medications and, 65, 82
    nutrition and, 181
    oxygen requirements and, 231
    personal health profile and, 49
    risk factors and, 32–33, 123, 125–31, 135, 139,
        141, 145–50, 152
    smoking and, 154, 158–62, 168–69
    surgery and, 92–93, 98
alcohol, 86
    medications and, 69, 71–72, 78
    nutrition and, 204
    recovery and, 106
    risk factors and, 141, 149
    smoking and, 160
    stress and, 149, 249–51, 255
alveoli, 18
American Cancer Society, 165, 171, 173
American Heart Association (AHA), 73, 171, 173,
    270
    affiliates of, 281–85
    on nutrition, xvi–xvii, 184, 186–91, 194,
        198–99, 201, 207, 218, 216
    Step One Diet of, 188
    Step Two Diet of, 184, 188–91, 198, 201, 219
American Lung Association, 171, 173
American Red Cross, 270
anaphylaxis, 65
anemia, 63–64
anger, 256–58, 266
    coping with, 56–58
    progress assessments and, 122
    stress and, 248–49, 251–52, 254, 256–57
angina pectoris, 13, 28–30
    in CCUs, 49
    emotions and, 262
    exercise and, xvii–xviii, 224, 227, 231, 236
    exercise tests and, 55

heart attack warning signs and, 7
high blood pressure and, 46
incision pain compared to, 106
medications and, 63, 71, 73, 77–78
nutrition and, 217
prevalence of, 5
progress assessments and, 113–14
recovery and, 106, 110
risk factors and, 5, 125, 128, 132, 142, 145
smoking and, 132, 154, 171–72, 175, 177
surgery and, 86, 90–91, 94, 97–99
vasospasm vs., 30
see also chest pain
angiograms and angiography, see cardiac
    catheterization
angioplasty, see percutaneous transluminal
    angioplasty
angiotensin-converting enzyme (ACE) inhibitors,
    68, 73, 79, 114
antacids, 79–80, 186
antianginals, 77–78
antibiotics, 78, 102
anticoagulant drugs, 51, 65–66, 76, 78
    surgery and, 90, 93, 97, 102
antidepressant drugs, 265–66
antihypertensive drugs, 72, 178
antioxidants, 77
antiplatelet agents, 51, 71–72
anxiety, 258–66
    in CCUs, 42
    coping with, 56, 58–59
    and events during heart attacks, 3
    exercise and, 224
    medications and, 70, 264–66
    smoking and, 160, 168–69, 171
    stress and, 252, 257
aorta, 20–21, 151, 157
    surgery and, 94, 96–97
aortic valve, 19–20
appetite, 69, 80, 265
apple body types, 147, 215
arm pain, xiii, 6, 8, 269
arrhythmias:
    CCUs and, 38, 49–50
    cocaine use and, 150–51

287